Speaking Your Truth
Courageous Stories from Inspiring Women

www.speakingyourtruthbook.com

Illustrator: Janice Earhart, iZoar
Book Cover: Nick Zelinger, NZ Graphics
Editing by Pamela Hertzog & Rhonda Barry
Layout/Design: Melissa Levad
Author Photograph by David Weihnacht, David Marc Photography, www.davidmarcphoto.com.

Printed in the United States of America

First Edition
ISBN 978-0-615-37738-4

A special thanks to Rhonda Barry for many hours of dedicated polishing and perfecting before going to print and all of the contributing authors and those who offered their unconditional advice, support, and suggestions for this book.

"*Speaking Your Truth* sizzles with brave energy. These amazing stories are a powerful testimony to the strength of human spirit, and a source of hope to all."
~ Sharon Lippincott, Life Writing Coach and author of *The Heart and Craft of Lifestory Writing*

"Read one of these stories and you'll keep turning the pages for more. *Speaking Your Truth* taps into a range of life experiences as women share their deepest hurts, triumphs and growth that once seemed unlikely or impossible."
~Susan K. Elliott, entrepreneur and author of *Start Your Own Home-Based Summer Camp*, HomeSummerCamp.com

"The courageous stories of these women proves that there can be triumph over tragedy. What an inspiration to read their remarkable stories of resiliency in overcoming difficulty."
~ Danielle Waagmeester – Narrative Therapist

"*Speaking Your Truth* is like a bowl of grandma's soup on a cold day. These wonderful, inspiring stories feel like a long-lost friend who cares about your success and well-being. The voices of these women will be with me every twist and turn and sometimes every dead-end of my journey."
~ Sara Ortiz, Authentic Coach and CEO of Sara Ortiz Workshops

"*Speaking Your Truth* is full of hope. Inside these pages are inspiring stories from courageous women who have overcome life's obstacles. No matter what life throws at you, when you are surrounded by your girlfriends, you find the strength and the love you need make it through, often discovering that the pain was part of your beautiful journey. As girls grow up to become women, you never outgrow your need for girlfriends. *Speaking Your Truth* is full of all your girlfriend's stories all wrapped up in one beautifully written book."
~ Angel Tuccy, Author of *Lists That Saved My Life*

"This inspirational book reveals the sisterhood that women share on journeys to healing, choice, change, and self realization. The stories will touch your soul."
~ Shelly Moorman, Parent Educator, Coach, and Speaker, Head & Heart Parent

"A treasure chest of rich and inspiring words of wisdom from women who have delved deeply into their psyche and souls. Minds are expanded and hearts opened by readers wandering through each grace-filled chapter. A most precious gift to your best friend, mother, daughter or yourself. Dive in and enjoy the warmth of women speaking their truth. I have, and have been touched and divinely blessed."
~ Carolyn Craft, www.carolyncraft.com

"If you are a woman who's on the path to self discovery and want to live an authentic, rich, joyful life, then you are in for a treat with this wonderful book. You will laugh, cry and be inspired by true stories by true woman who share with us their most profound life lessons that lead to soul-satisfying new beginnings."
~ Diana Long, Life & Business Success Coach, Author, Speaker

"The inner strength of women, the power of intuition, the voice of truth and practical wisdom fill this gem of a read. It will stir your soul, touch your heart and inspire you to keep the faith to move through whatever comes your way. If you feel like you just can't take another step, doubt what's possible, and find yourself afraid to be seen and heard, it's no coincidence that you stumbled upon this book."
~ Michelle Conboy, MA, Founder of Relationship Cafe and Men, Money and Meaning Mentor Program www.relationshipcafe.net

"Intuitively choosing a story to read and then another and another, I discovered an impressive consistency with the women in *Speaking Your Truth.*" Amazing courage, inner strength and vulnerability, coupled with an inner drive to love and be true to themselves is evident throughout. Whether read from cover to cover, or a random opening to receive what the universe presents, this book offers inspiration and hope, no matter what the challenge."
~ Ashi, Author of *Bless Your Mess*, Owner of Grace Your Space Productions

"A lovely collection of heartfelt stories to inspire and empower everyone!"
~Sharon Good, Good Life Coaching, Author, *The Tortoise Workbook: Strategies for Getting Ahead at Your Own Pace*

"A very rich, very lively compendium of women's life experiences and the wisdom earned!"
~ Sheila Bender, *A New Theology: Turning to Poetry in a Time of Grief* and WritingItReal.com

"This collection of personal stories is a brave and intimate look at the physical and emotional issues that challenge us all. There is something here for everyone, ranging from the importance of acknowledging your inner voice, to the transformative consequences of sharing a kind word when it is needed most. Kudos to all the contributors who so generously shared the details of their own painful journeys on these pages. I hope that reading this book will encourage other women to acknowledge their personal power and develop the courage to be true to themselves."
~ Sharon Gnatt Epel, CEO/Founder La Ishá, Inc.

"*Speaking Your Truth, Courageous Stories by Inspiring Women* is a book that will resonate with women and educate daughters. In telling the stories of so many extraordinarily ordinary women this powerful anthology captures the essence of womanhood: resilience, reflection, relation and re-creation. Story-telling has been a strong thread connecting generations for centuries...these her-stories will surely impact futures through the authentic sharing of pasts."
~ Gretchen Seefried, Founder and CEO, MidChix.com LLC

"*Speaking Your Truth* is an authentic celebration of courage and love. Each person's journey will inspire you to connect with your heart, discover your voice and speak your own truth."
~ Marie Kirkland, Spiritual Life Coach and Founder of Inner Alignment Living

"I found *Speaking Your Truth* overwhelmingly hopeful, inspiring and most of all something for every woman. When we know that there is hope for us in our journey, somehow it makes it that much easier to keep going because we are not alone. Much success in spreading happiness and hopefulness to all!
~ Tara Becker, Elle Group Founder and CEO

"The stories in this collection are full of heart and soul, seasoned with a dose of courage. Witnessing the deep truths of other's lives frees us all to become more of who we really are."
~ Linda Joy Myers, President of the National Association of Memoir Writers, author of *The Power of Memoir*.

"*Speaking Your Truth* shows through individual stories how embracing truth allows real healing and freedom to occur in your life. The truth we often hide from ourselves and others is the true doorway to life. *Speaking Your Truth* invites us to live more fully.
~ Lori A. Mateer, MA, LPC Littleton Colorado

"The women in *Speaking Your Truth* are all fearless and risk takers with their truth. All women, especially young women who are still searching for who they are, need to read these stories to share in the inspiration and wisdom of women who are achieving their dreams despite life's roadblocks. I thought of my young daughter as I was reading this book and thought that this book could be so healing when she encounters negativity. Thank you so much, writers, for sharing your words with us!"
~ Alice Osborn (http://aliceosborn.com) Writer, Editor, Speaker and Teacher

"In speaking our truth, we may not fully realize how deeply we must delve to reach that truth. Each of these women opened up their hearts from the deepest level to share their truth. The comfort, humor and rest I found in their stories will help me more confidently speak my own truth."
~ Connie Pshigoda, Speaker and Author of *The Wise Woman's Almanac*, WellnessForAllSeasons.com

"*Speaking Your Truth*" does just that. It captures the essence of the power, connection and healing that comes from us all sharing our truths, our pains, our loves, our struggles and our successes. It opens the door and gives us permission to speak our own truth and share our own story. I felt uniquely connected to each woman as they shared their deeply personal life experiences. They each became friends as I got to know the underlying story that made them distinctively who they are. This book is truly a gift and an inspiration. Thank you!"
~ Karen Sherwood, Founder of The Women's Small Biz Network
www.WSBizNetwork.com

"*Speaking Your Truth, Courageous Stories from Inspiring Women* is a must read anthology that offers messages of strength and hope as each writer reflects upon events from her past that shaped her personality and fired her passion. In telling their stories, the courageous women in *Speaking Your Truth* reveal their own gaping soul-wounds solely to encourage us to, likewise, speak our own so that we might become both healed and whole."
~ Jackie Dove-Miller, Writer, Spoken-Word Artist

"The book *Speaking Your Truth* will touch your heart. These diverse women share their personal and profound stories of how by honoring themselves they overcame great adversities."
~ Sheri Ruston, www.TheFlowDoctor.com

"In these many stories of encountering and surviving life's difficult moments, one reads of courage accompanied by fear, of determination followed by doubt, of hope aligning with despair. These are stories of doing what one must do, what the situation calls for. These stories point out once again that "life is not for sissies" and that only courage, determination, and hope will carry the day."
~ Denis Ledoux, author of *Turning Memories Into Memoirs, A Handbook for Writing Lifestories*

"Every woman will find more than one story in this book she relates to and learns from…We can only benefit from these words of experience in our quest for peace and happiness in this trying world."
~ Shelley Thompson, attorney at Allen & Vellone, P.C., Denver, Colorado

"WOW is an understatement for the amazing stories from the hearts of these women. What a blessing you have produced for all to read!"
~ Betsy Wiersma, Founder CampExperience™

"What a wonderful compilation of experiences by exceptional, yet very much like the rest of us, women! I cried and I laughed, related, and learned as I read through the stories. Sometimes it's nice to know that you are not alone in your struggles, but also wonderful to hear about women triumphing and rising above adversity, and this book is full of those inspirational stories!"
~ Lisa Huntington-Kinn, Founder and CEO of Open House with Style

"Aimed at women who on a daily basis need to know that we have collective stories and energy. It reads like personal journal entries with stories and thoughts we all have or will face in our lifetime. There is something to enlighten us in every story."
~ Mary Baum, BA&T President

"*Speaking Your Truth: Courageous Stories from Inspiring Women*, is powerfully written by many women who have faced life's challenges and learned the truth about themselves. I've loved reading these stories -- perfect length to read during lunchtime to lift the rest of my day. Thanks to all the generous authors for sharing their stories with the world."
~ Carol Johnson, Manager, Operations & Administration, Pittman Development Group

"Each of us has a story to tell and there is nothing quite as powerful as the written word - for both the writer and the reader. The wide scope of real life stories shared in this book is a learning journey of how we each have life events to share that create our core being."
~ Cheri Ruskus, Founder of the Victory Circles and Author of *Victory One Moment at a Time*

"The women in this book bravely offer stories of lives lived with passion, mindfulness, and perseverance. Their strength is humbling, and uplifting. Their stories are stimulating and inspiring, and they prove that we alone define ourselves and our place in this world."
~ Rachel Thompson, DVM Associate Veterinarian Minnesota Zoological Garden

"A suggested read for any woman. The stories of heartache, grief, and suffering that move into empowerment, self-love, and being authentic are truly amazing! This book will empower those who need it and support those who have been through similar events. It is a wonderful copulation of courageous woman truly speaking their truths!"
~ Christy Whitman, Bestselling Author, Creator of www.7essentiallaws.com

"We can see a little piece of ourselves in every story as we share the heartache but also the joy of remembering who we really are. Bravo to all these brave and beautiful women!"
~ Sherrie Scott, Singer/Songwriter, Filmmaker

"This is a wonderful collection of soul inspiring, spirit enriched stories of hope and love. These messages promote spiritual, emotional and physical healing via soul development. I validate this book as an empowering compilation of women's experiences in which they receive spiritual guidance to embrace their life lessons, providing the reader with an illumination of the soul's journey into ascension."
~ Sandy Guarnotta, Medium, Medical Intuitive and Visionary for the Planet

"I am so inspired by the truth, passion and journeys of the stories reflected in this book. I give these authors credit for being who they are and saying what they need to say to recreate their experiences for the readers. I would recommend this book to all of the women I know and work with through my organization and look forward to the next volume!"
~ Erin Seabold CEO, The Seed

"*Speaking Your Truth* will uplift you to envision the next best stage of your precious life! Each woman's story is an authentic inspiration for real change and meaning!"
~ Bernadette Hunter, LPC, P.C., Owner, Powerful Performance

"*Speaking Your Truth* will provide you a community which supports your "little voice" in its need to flick the on switch on the microphone and let everyone hear what she has to say. It's a green light to knowledge and introduce her to the world. Enjoy -- your inner voice will thank you!"
~ Liz MacNeill, Owner, Grace Mac LLC

"This book helps one feel empowered to take control of our own lives, see the gifts we are given along the way and have the strength to be the person we were meant to be. It gives hope and strength and support. I found each story quite touching and unique."
~ Lee Weisbard D.D.S., Excellence in Dental Health Care

"What a wonderful collection of stories and experiences!! Much wisdom, strength and courage is shared by the various authors in *Speaking Your Truth, Courageous Stories from Inspiring Women!* It took courage in itself to share some of these experiences! There is a warrior in all of these women. Everyone had varied experience but by telling their story these warriors have shown how individually they have become healed, whole, and equipped to show the way and help others become the best that they can be. There is literally a collage of experiences, but by sharing them, these women have put themselves in the position to make a difference in the lives of all they meet. "
~ Wilma Dunias, Independent Sales Director Mary Kay Cosmetics, Owner and Proprietor Baklava by Wilma

"What I believe that you will get from reading the incredible stories in this book, is a sense of the power of doing just what the title of this beautiful book suggests - *Speaking Your Truth.* This is because being aware of what is really true for you and being able to speak it out is a profound way for you to come into alignment with the unique possibilities that are waiting to be actualized in your own life. Perhaps you will find the courage to step into a life of even more full expression of who you really are from reading these inspiring stories. "
~ Tom Stone - CEO of Great Life Technologies and author of *Vaporize Your Anxiety without Drugs or Therapy* and *The Power of How.*

"I would like to thank all of these brave women. It takes a special kind of courage to share such personal stories with the world. Thank you for motivating me to try to better my own life."
~ Sandy Balanecki, Sydney, Australia

"Stories inspire us and they make us aware we are not alone in the world with our heartaches, problems and particular challenges. Through reading other women's words of wisdom in *Speaking Your Truth*, you may feel a calling from within to be brave and speak your own truth as you step into your power."
~ Kris Steinnes, best-selling author of *Women of Wisdom, Empowering the Dreams and Spirit of Women*

"I love reading stories about how people have overcome incredible odds and have risen to the challenges life puts in the path. This book did not disappoint. In story after story I felt inspired and grateful for a glimpse into the real lives of real women who have done amazing things in spite of obstacles. Well done."
~ Merit Gest, Creator of *Grow Up!* A philosophy of possibility

"I LOVE this book. When women tap into the core of their being to share what has given meaning to their life, they bravely demonstrate a powerful authenticity. One learns from another in the ancient tradition of wisdom teachin... You just have to read every word of these courageous and inspiring stories. What a gift!"
~ Donna DeNomme, Internationally-published, award-winning author of *Turtle Wisdom: Coming Home to Yourself* and *Ophelia's Oracle: Discovering the Healthy, Happy, Self-Aware, and Confident Girl in the Mirror.*

TABLE OF CONTENTS

PART ONE
SELF-DISCOVERY

PART TWO
FAMILY MATTERS

PART THREE
FAITH AND SPIRITUALITY

PART FOUR
LOVE AND ABUSE

PART FIVE
HEALTH AND HEALING

PART SIX
FINDING YOUR PATH

INTRODUCTION

I have been interested in supporting women in achieving self empowerment since my divorce in 1999. As I regained my self confidence and self esteem following that difficult time in my life, I encouraged other women to learn and grow from their unique challenges. Many women shared their stories with me through the years. I found them inspiring. I began to wonder if I could compile them into a book to help other women.

I began to mention the idea to the public early in 2009. Many women liked the idea, but no actual chapter submissions came in until the summertime of 2009. Andrea Costantine sent me her story, and it moved me to tears. I realized that the idea was worthy, and I began to work harder at promoting others to contribute.

Later that year as I got to know Andrea more, I pondered the idea of asking her to partner with me in the project. She agreed. She then scheduled a writing workshop in January of 2010 to help women write their stories and also began to help me with promotion and marketing of the concept. We set a deadline of submission for early February of 2010. I said I would like to see about 50 chapters in the book.

The submissions began to roll in, and we continued to work towards the completion of the project together. Some of our authors shared that they had not expressed their stories in words before. The exercise of putting their experiences on paper was sometimes transformational to them and further assisted them in healing.

In the fall of 2009, I saw the artwork of Janice Earhart and thought it might be a great addition to the book for illustrations. Her characters tell stories too, so I approached her with the idea of joining the project. I was excited to have her embrace our vision and add her characters to our cover and topic sections.

It is my hope that this collection of inspiring stories from courageous women will have a ripple effect in helping others speak their truths. Our personal experiences can be powerful when shared instead of hidden. I kept mine locked away for a long time. Expressing it has further assisted me in moving on and living a full life.

I would like to thank Andrea for joining me in this project. Her strengths of marketing, promotion, and advising have been invaluable to me. The most enjoyable part of having her join me was the friendship that developed between us. Our souls have similar callings, and it has been a partnership that has added to my life in a wonderful way. I am grateful for her contribution on so many levels, and I look forward to more collaborative ventures and projects in our futures.

Lastly, I dedicate this book to my two beautiful daughters Summer and Liberty. They are amazing beings who were the main reason I chose to live my best life. I also thank my mom, Norma Shultz, for her unwavering support of me. I am incredibly grateful for the life I am living.

~ Lisa Shultz

INTRODUCTION

When I first heard about a book project Lisa Shultz was putting together about inspiring women I knew I had to write my story. I had hidden behind my personal story professionally for many years, only letting close friends and colleagues know about the tragedy of my childhood.

Synchronistically, I had just worked with a business coach, Alexi Sebasttien who had helped me to share my story in a private and safe group setting so I could work through my memories of how they all tied into where I am in my life now. Prior to that experience I never saw the link between the events of my past and how they have influenced who I am today and the people who are attracted to me and my work. Alexi's coaching gave me the confidence to stand in my truth and revisit some darker parts of my path that I had always avoided sharing with others.

As I wrote my story in more detail than I ever had shared before, the tears poured out of me and I began to feel a huge weight lift off of my shoulders. A sense of freedom enveloped me in knowing that I didn't have to keep this bottled in anymore. The majority of the details in my submission had never been shared with others before. Not even my mother knew that I remembered parts of those events. I was excited to be a part of a book project where I was able to share my story and hopefully inspire other women to author their own story as well and choose their own destiny despite their path.

At the time of my submission I barely knew Lisa. The little I did know was that she was a powerful connector, well known in the community, and highly respected by others. I knew instantly from meeting her that she was doing big things with her life and it wasn't long before the two of us began to develop a partnership and a mutual respect for one another.

Months after my submission Lisa approached me about hosting a writing workshop to help the women who were interested in submitting chapters for the book. I excitedly agreed – I knew after writing my own story the power that could come with it and how much I enjoyed the process. When over

30 people registered we knew that the book project was on a roll and the women were getting excited. During this time Lisa approached me about collaborating on the book project with her, and without hesitation I said YES! We quickly set some deadlines for submissions, outlined the timeline and were shooting to have a finished book released in the fall of 2010.

As the stories began to pour in, we received over 50 submissions by the deadline – the specific number that Lisa had set as an intention just a few months earlier. When the book started we didn't have a working name, but as we read the stories we knew there was no other choice for a title than *Speaking Your Truth: Courageous Stories from Inspiring Women*.

My desire is that both the contributing authors and the readers of this project find hope, courage, and inspiration to share their stories and release the pains of the past in order to find a new direction that brings them joy, peace, and fulfillment into the life. My wish is that these stories empower others to let go of what's been holding them back in life, allow them to stand in their power, and ultimately speak their truth.

~ Andrea Costantine

FOREWORD

I am a complete advocate for speaking the truth. I believe that communicating from the authentic self sets us free. I am also aware that opening up and taking a stand for what we believe or know to be true for ourselves and others is not easy. I find this to be especially true for women. Historically, women who have stood up have been labeled witches, traders, dangerous and harlots, just to name a few. Women have been taught that it is completely possible to be outcast, left, tortured or killed if we speak up for our rights and ask to be heard or respected.

Powerful women have been maligned and misunderstood for centuries. In fact, our history books all too often do not speak of some of the incredible women that were pioneers in every area of life on this planet. We have struggled to find our voice and be heard. We have struggled to be recognized as equals. We have struggled to shine our lights for fear of being misunderstood or losing loved ones. It is no wonder that many of us have made choices out of a state of identity crisis and confusion.

The struggle to achieve equal rights for women is often thought to have begun, in the English-speaking world, with the publication of Mary Wollstonecraft's *A Vindication of the Rights of Woman* (1792). During the 19th century, as male suffrage was gradually extended in many countries, women became increasingly active in the quest for their own suffrage. Not until 1893, however, in New Zealand, did women achieve suffrage on the national level. Australia followed in 1902, but American, British, and Canadian women did not win the same rights until the end of World War I. In America, the first women's rights convention was held in Seneca Falls, New York. After 2 days of discussion and debate, 68 women and 32 men signed a Declaration of Sentiments, which outlined grievances and established the agenda for the women's rights movement. A set of 12 resolutions was adopted calling for equal treatment of women and men under the law and voting rights for women. This created quite a stir and many women lost families and went to jail fighting for these rights.

I share this information to bring to awareness that women have been awakening. All over the world women have been asking themselves "who am I?" and "why am I here?" They are asking to be considered as artists, writers, healers, teachers and leaders. They are asking for recognition as great minds and trendsetters. They are asking to get out of the box of limitations that have been placed on women. They are asking how to move beyond race, culture and misguided thinking. They are asking how to be wives, partners, mothers and friends while making a difference on this planet. They are asking how to use their gifts and still reflect the beauty of the divine feminine. This is so exciting to me because I have been in this area of questioning for years. Not just for me but for all of the women I support through classes, workshops and individual coaching.

I salute the women in this book. I celebrate their willingness to open and share from their hearts. I am thrilled that this book has the potential to support women into knowing that they are powerful and essential beings. As females, we are intuitive, compassionate and extraordinary guides to wholeness and oneness. When we stand in the power of the divinity that is our inherent nature great things begin to unfold. Bravo contributors! Bravo "courageous women" for inviting us into your private thoughts and experiences. Make no mistake. This will make a difference and change lives.

~ Cynthia James, Transformational Specialist/Speaker/Artist/Author

Self Discovery

Transcending Grief; Awakening Joy

Karen Mehringer

Spring was in full blossom with an explosion of green everywhere. Birds chirped wildly as they darted outside the hospital room. Life was in high gear outside, but winding down inside. It was the last day of my father's life. My sisters, brother, step-mother and I sat by his side, watching intently as his chest rose and fell with each breath, waiting for him to transition. As we watched and waited, the hospice nurse came in and monitored his progress. While rubbing his feet, she encouraged him by saying, "Go into the light Mr. Butler. Go into the light." Talking quietly, we shared memories of my father as tears fell down our faces.

My dad had been admitted to the hospital eight weeks prior. He was unable to keep any food down and was losing weight rapidly. Within days, cancer was found in his abdomen. Doctors were unable to locate its source, but decided to administer chemo therapy which landed him in the ICU with an infection and temperature of 105 degrees. We had a decision to make…should we let him go since the cancer would inevitably take his life, or should we put him on life support and pray for a miracle? The doctors suggested we let him go. We decided to keep him alive. It had been less than a week since the cancer was discovered and we weren't ready to say goodbye. Further, my father appeared terrified as he sat up in bed with an oxygen mask on, hooked up to monitors and IV tubes, laboring for each breath, fighting to stay alive. This was not how we wanted to remember him.

The next seven weeks were a roller coaster ride with miracles of healing and moments of hope alternating between set backs and feelings of deep despair. Ultimately, my dad was taken off life support and moved from ICU to the fourth floor of the hospital where he experienced drug-induced hallucinations and mental confusion for several weeks before being transferred to the VA Hospice in Palo Alto, California. Here he received excellent care and was more lucid due to better medication management, which allowed us to interact with him and experience closure before his death.

On that beautiful spring day in May, my father surrendered his life. He was surrounded by the love of family and died in peace at the age of sixty-four. Only three years earlier, almost to the day, my brother, Kyle, died from Cystic Fibrosis, a terminal genetic illness. He was only fifteen years old. Like Kyle, my dad was strong and brave as he fought for and eventually surrendered his life, but, before he let go, he left us with a final gift. Not being a religious man, he said, "God, there you are" several times and his last whispered word was "Kyle." He left us with the knowledge that he was safe and in good hands with his Creator and son.

My father gave me another gift...my passion for sailing. At his deathbed, I cried while uttering, "I will always remember you every time I step onto a sailboat." At the early age of four, he introduced me to sailing. We were on summer vacation at the Stanford Family Camp, near Lake Tahoe, California. Surrounded by pine trees, we sailed in the middle of a beautiful alpine lake aboard our 22-foot Catalina. Every time the boat heeled with the force of the wind, I was afraid it would tip over and capsize. My father reassured me that this would never happen.

My first cruising experience, at the age of ten, was with family friends on their 50-foot yacht. Heading out to sea past the Golden Gate Bridge at night, under a moonless sky, butterflies filled my belly as the boat glided into the dark, into the unknown. During our five day voyage, we experienced whales breaching near our boat and saw over a hundred sharks. Abundant sea life surrounded us!

Later, my dad sold his 22-foot Catalina and upgraded to a 31-foot Pearson which he moored at Pier 39 in the San Francisco Bay where the winds were stronger and the swells were larger than what I was used to. At the age of twelve, I was often assigned to the helm as my dad went forward to raise the sails. Anxiously, I held the boat steady into the wind fearful my father would fall overboard. Thankfully, he never did.

Over the years, my love for sailing grew, so much so, that my husband, John, and I, while taking a year off to re-invent our lives, decided to crew a 46-foot sailboat cruising from Fiji to Singapore for six-months. On our first ocean passage, sailing into open sea, away from the sight of land, I felt excited as if I were an explorer heading into uncharted waters. Dolphins playfully swam at the bow of the boat, escorting us on our grand adventure as the sun set ahead of us casting hues of bright orange and red on our path. Satisfied, I smiled with a deep sense of knowing that all was well.

Shortly after my father died, John and I made a commitment to follow our hearts and pursue a vision we had had during our one-year hiatus...to own a cabin in the mountains and a sailboat on the ocean.

Sitting aboard our 30-foot Catalina in our Oxnard, California marina slip, resting against a pillow, I noticed the sound of sea gulls; sea birds darted into the ocean attempting to make a catch; boats glided past on their way out to sea. A feeling of peace washed over me and then a thought surfaced, "I would not be experiencing this wondrous moment if it were not for my dad."

I began to cry, missing him. But as the tears rolled down my face, a deep feeling of gratitude welled up and a profound insight developed..."I would not be feeling this much grief if it were not for the depths of love I have felt for my father." It occurred to me that my grief was in direct proportion to the amount of love that we shared. I realized how blessed I was to have experienced so much love in one lifetime. In awe, I was transcended, as my grief was transformed into a deep well of joy that bubbled up to the surface of my being. In the moment, I was overcome by God's amazing grace.

Two years later, eating lunch at the kitchen table in our cozy mountain home in Evergreen, Colorado, I gazed out the window at the pine and aspen trees. Their beauty mesmerized me. Shocked out of my trance-like state by the loud bark of Rennie, our German Shepherd dog, I thought, "Someone must be at the front door." I looked up to find The UPS delivery man standing at the door with a surprise package for me. It was the cardboard version of my book cover – front and back! I had seen the front cover of Sail Into Your Dreams in an e-mail attachment, which I was very pleased with, but I hadn't seen the back cover yet with the blurbs, description of my book and life, my bio and picture. Reading the description, tears streamed down my face. In awe I thought, "Was this really me? Was this really my life?"

Soon I was bawling uncontrollably. The thoughts that ran through my mind were, "My life is so amazing. I can't believe how amazing my life is. Why didn't I see this before? My life is so amazing!" Next I questioned, "If my life is so amazing, then why am I crying uncontrollably?" It was as if tears of anguish were coming up from the depths of my soul. To make things even more confusing, I was simultaneously experiencing bliss.

I didn't get it right away. But, several days later it dawned on me…my life is so amazing today not despite the painful losses that I've experienced, but because of them. I wouldn't be the person I am today nor would I be living the life of my dreams if I hadn't weathered and transcended the storms in my life. The joy and bliss that I experienced were in direct proportion to the pain and suffering that had been transcended.

"When you are sorrowful look again in your heart, and you shall see that in truth you are weeping for that which has been your delight."
~ Kahil Gilbran, Poet

Karen is the author of Sail Into Your Dreams: 8 Steps to Living a More Purposeful Life, an inspirational speaker, Life Empowerment Coach, psychotherapist and the founder of Creative Transformations. She has over fifteen years of experience in the personal development field including a master's degree in marriage and family therapy and special training in energy transformations. Her specialties include: Life Purpose; Life Transitions; Personal Empowerment; Grief and Loss; and Relationship Issues. For more information about Karen and her work, please visit: www.LiveAPurposefulLife.com.

Say Yes to Me

Meenal Kelkar

In 2005, I took the drastic step of leaving all I knew by getting out of the corporate world. The stress I had taken on behalf of my clients had become too much to bear. With headaches that would last for days in a row, I couldn't sleep and had all sorts of stomach problems. Ten years prior my father had successful bypass surgery, and it was three years since my baby brother survived a heart attack one week after turning 32. Now, the final straw was the realization that I was becoming bitchy at home ... I didn't even want to be around myself. I can't imagine how my poor dog and husband felt! When I looked ahead ten years, I felt a stifling darkness envelop me. I saw myself in a prison, banging on the bars, screaming to be let out of that constricted space. So I decided to quit and take advantage of the fact that as a self-employed management consultant, I could just say no.

Jump ahead to 2009. I have transformed myself into an entrepreneur whose mind-body services meld the ancient practices of yoga therapy and meditation into modern-day tools that empower people to transform their stress into peace. My programs are highly successful in my local community: I am regularly called for speaking engagements; I serve on the advisory board of a local wellness magazine, and I have taken the step to expand into my own office space, which I will share with a close friend. I decided to transfer my programs into an on-line format to serve a larger audience. I am CEO, CFO, chief marketing officer, webmaster, graphics artist, copy writer and chief bottle-washer of my own creation. I am an empowered, powerful woman doing everything successfully.

Until I crashed ... and crashed again ... and yet again. Three times in four months. In bed, flat on my back, without the energy to move, for at least one full week each time. Actually the last time, it was more like four weeks. Cut off at the knees by an upper respiratory infection! Even now, I feel embarrassed at admitting that I could let that happen to me! Me, who has over 1,000 hours of training in yoga therapy, with a practice dedicated to teaching others how to tune into their bodies for signs of stress and who has a strong commitment to being proactive about health, successfully navigating the flu season with only a sniffle for four years!

More than the embarrassment was the underlying sense of betrayal directed inwards towards my body. How could this happen to me after all that I do to take care of myself? During my four week enforced bed rest, I could do nothing but ponder, "What can I do differently?" Hadn't the last two times I was sick taught me anything? Obviously not, because I could see the promises to change I had made to myself while on my back: hire an assistant, schedule more time for my self-care, plan and take regular breaks from the eight hours I can easily spend on the computer seven days per week. Promises that were quickly forgotten when I was on my feet, feeling healthy and back to my usual way of being. Each one of those promises meant that I would have to endure the challenge of paying more attention, rather than operate mindlessly on autopilot, getting things done the way I was used to.

Then I realized that was the problem ... all I did was do. You know that prison I saw ahead when I was at the end of my corporate rope? I had unknowingly found another route to it, walked right into it, locked the door and thrown away the key. This time I couldn't pin that on anyone else but myself. I had become addicted to living life in a state of overwhelm. Different reasons, but nonetheless the same patterns. It was much harder to see this time around, because it was masked by my genuine heart-felt desire to support people in their transformation.

So I asked myself the question: if, despite my best intentions, it is such a struggle for me to do differently, is there a way that I can simply be differently? In that one question lay all of my answers. Rather than try to figure out the specifics, I decided to take small steps to "just do it". Or maybe a better phrase is "just be it"?

When I woke up in the morning, rather than checking emails or watching the weather forecast, I chose to head straight into my yoga room to do moving meditation and breath work to strengthen my lungs and create new patterns in my nervous system. I started my day with my self-care, instead of bemoaning the fact that I couldn't fit it into my schedule once my day got started. While sick, when talking with clients and colleagues, I was forced to let go of my habitual, mindless "I'll be able to get to it tomorrow" reply because tomorrow would come and I might not have the energy to get out of bed. I taught myself to say "I am sorry. As much as I would like to help out, I can't take that on right now" or to ask for help to get it done because the stark reality was I didn't know when I would feel better. Rather than panic at the thought of an empty schedule and respond with habitual knee-jerk reaction to pile on new things, I gave myself permission to transform my perception of "empty" into "spacious." I took joy in the time, mindset and opportunity for inspiration, play and creativity; things I had long envied in others and craved for myself. I knew that exhausting myself would only prolong being sick, so I learned to check in with my energy levels throughout the day and take much needed rest breaks. I realized that the regular breaks were actually easier on my mind and my body than running on full throttle as I had done in the past.

Even as I write this, a part of me marvels "What revolutionary actions in this day and age!" Another part of me asks, "Why did you, a Mind-Body-Spirit Educator who understands how the body-mind works, have to hit a brick wall, not just once but three times in four months, to find a path of ease? A path that intuitively makes the most sense for your long-term well-being?"

Some of these things sound so simple and obvious you may wonder why I didn't conceive of them before. Seriously, when the only way I knew to approach my life was in a state of overwhelm, these options were so far out of the realm of possibilities for me I couldn't see them or take them in as solutions when suggested by others. I was so stuck in overwhelm as the only way to live life I couldn't even conceive of another way. For others, sure! But for me? I don't think so!

When locked into a state of worry or stress or in my case, overwhelm, the only option a person can see is to fight or flee, that is a physiological given. Our body-mind chemistry only supports these two options because they were only two available when confronted with a saber-toothed tiger. "Fight or flee" summarizes all of my previous actions. Every time I chose to take on something new, adding to my state of overwhelm, it was my attempt to fight. Every time my body collapsed, it was the only way I knew to flee.

This is an important concept, so it is worth repeating. When you are locked into a state of worry, stress or overwhelm, you are not physically or psychologically able to conceive of any other options because you are not meant to do so. The only way to change is to choose to be different in your life, by mindfully choosing actions that support an open, inspired, relaxed, easy way of being. By choosing to engage in those practices, finding more ways to bring them into your life, balance begins to emerge.

The new decade, 2010, marked forty-three years of selflessness, leaving my self out of the equation. I have successfully learned how to live life in a continual state of overwhelm. Now I choose differently. I started this year with a "Say Yes to Me" campaign. It scares me to even write that, as I imagine centuries of female ancestors frowning in disapproval at the implied selfishness. But you see, "Say Yes to Me" is not about selfishness, it is about self-fullness. If my genuine desire is to give to those around me, then I have to include myself in the equation. Simply stated, giving cannot happen without a giver. The giver is a valuable element in the act of giving and must be nurtured for giving to happen. Translation: if my intention is to live my life giving to others, I am a valuable element in that act of giving and must be nurtured for giving to happen. Radical concept, isn't it? I've always known that the simplest truths are the most transformative.

As I write this with tears in my eyes, I am aware of both a small voice within that still resists that simple truth, and the addiction to overwhelm arising within me. You see, overwhelm was more than just a state of being. My identity had been wrapped up in it; my reputation as someone who gets things done; my compulsion to have things be done a certain way; my pride in giving 150% at all times; my excuse for disappearing into my cave for a few weeks; my easy out when asked to do something I didn't really want to do. Overwhelm has been such a great smoke screen for me to hide behind. Without it, I stand exposed and vulnerable.

Unexpectedly, "Say Yes to Me" disrupted my belief system with tremendous aftershocks. I accomplish more when I honor my body's natural rhythms. I prefer the person I become when I say no, not adding to my To Do list, because I can freely say yes to being with friends. I become the person I want to be by regularly giving myself a computer-free day—one that is reserved exclusively for inspiration, connection and renewal. It is sobering to realize even all of these choices are not enough for me to whole-heartedly and easily "Say Yes to Me." So I am also grateful for the new voice within … that is slowly growing in volume every day … the one that says "YES! I think she's got it!"

I've taken the time to write a series of questions I have framed and posted on the wall next to my desk; questions intended to support me in following through on my "Say Yes to Me" campaign. These questions challenge me to bring mindfulness to my habits; to be patient and accepting when I stray from this fragile, new path; to reach out to my three K's (husband and two best friends whose names all begin with K) for support when I am on the verge of taking on too much, especially when those other options are exciting and fit perfectly with my values. I've transformed my relationship with overwhelm by listening to how my mind-body-spirit expresses overwhelm and to use those signs as a signal to pause, take a deep breath, step back from what I am doing and ask myself "What can I change here?"

Isn't that what all recovering addicts do? We wake up each day and recommit to practicing loving-kindness towards ourselves and to making more mindful, healthful, and hopefully self-full choices.

After 15 years in corporate finance and four years as an entrepreneur and holistic healer, Meenal Kelkar, MBA, CPRYT knows the pitfalls of living a life in a constant state of overwhelm. As a Mind-Body-Spirit Educator, Meenal teaches pragmatic approaches to breaking free of the cycles of stress-burnout and giving-depletion. She helps corporate executives and women entrepreneurs experience more ease, more calm and more balance in everyday life. These tools will soon be available as on-line programs through her website www.integrative-insight.com. In 2010, in conjunction with her "Say Yes to Me" campaign, Meenal launched www.YourBodyOfWisdom.com, where she will share her new insights and programs as they unfold.

Wings to Fly

Suzanne Simpson

I want to tell you the story of a young woman I knew many years ago. She was hired as a buyer for a well-known specialty store. She worked from morning until night, smoking cigarettes and drinking coffee to keep her going throughout the day so she would have enough energy to maintain her workload.

When she attended regular company meetings, she put on her confident face and wouldn't allow herself to be intimidated by the aggressive women in upper management. Inside she was dying from all the pressure placed on her to meet the bottom line profit expected for her department. Due to the expansion phase the company was in, she traveled often. In the evenings, to take away her loneliness, she ventured out to social gatherings in hope of finding that perfect mate who could fit into her busy lifestyle. Her parents were proud of her accomplishments and pushed her to continue succeeding.

It was no wonder that one day her health began to show signs of stress. She developed major allergies and often felt fatigued. She resorted to drinking more coffee to combat the fatigue. She thought that the problem was her career. So if she made a change that would be the answer. After continuing to push her limits, she eventually found herself in a counselor's office feeling insecure, drained, and not wanting to go on. Today, if I were to see this woman walking down the street I might not recognize her since she appears (and also feels) so calm and confident. You see, I was this young woman in my twenties.

During those years, I decided to buy a house and fix it up on my own. I found a house that appealed to me because of its Victorian style and front porch with a swing. Not only was the house affordable, it was in an area of town where real estate was starting to revive. People were restoring the old character to these neighborhood homes and improving their value. It felt like a wise thing to purchase this house with my mere little salary. After closing, my Dad came by to view it. He commented that it looked like the foundation was uneven and the house was slanting. His remark made me feel insecure, but I overlooked it and focused on all the plans I had for decorating and enhancing the looks of my house.

After a few years of living in the house, I began to notice the front wall of the living room was sloping more and more toward the street. I suddenly remembered Dad's comments about the foundation looking uneven. I wasn't too worried about it because I really loved the home and knew that this was a great gift—an affordable home of my own.

Actually, the house was a metaphor of my whole life. I was busy decorating outwardly, but didn't notice that my foundation wasn't sound. During these early years in my life, I drove myself to accomplish outward success only to realize that I was looking only on the outside. As a result of striving so hard, I began to experience chronic fatigue and some depression. This period of burnout left me feeling like I couldn't see any way out.

One day I got a message that came through with much clarity: my mission would be helping people mind, body, and spirit. What I didn't realize is that I would be embarking on a personal journey of healing myself so I would be able to best pass this knowledge on to others. I began traveling on this path, focusing on these three areas of mind, body, and spirit, not really knowing where it would take me. Thus I began to get my connection more internal rather than from the outside, opening up a whole new world of possibilities for growth in the spiritual side of my life.

One of my friends says, "In everything there is a gift." This truth became evident as I began to develop the part of me that had been neglected and pushed aside for many years. Let me describe the process that unfolded as I learned to allow healing to take place on its own timetable.

As I uncovered what was going on inside me, I realized that I didn't feel worthy and valuable unless I could perform well. During my early career, I tried to be successful through achievements, becoming a buyer for a world-renowned specialty store. I knew that my mother would be proud of me and think I was successful and had achieved status. She could tell all of her friends that her daughter worked for Neiman Marcus. Most people who I told what I did were in awe, thinking I had an exciting and glamorous career. What they didn't see was that behind the scenes I felt tremendous anxiety and was exhausted from the traveling and constant pressure to meet my monthly budget goals. I accomplished my goals, but paid a huge price.

Later I came to understand that I had many beliefs that didn't support me. I was overly focused on developing outside relationships, but I didn't know how to have a relationship with myself. I could no longer avoid listening to my feelings and paying attention to the kind of berating statements going on in my head. They began shouting loudly and the only way I knew how to shut them up was to start rewriting them in my mind. Even though I tried hard to make the thoughts more affirming and not such absolute black-and-white statements, they still seemed to show their ugly head. Some of these statements sounded like this:

"I am not smart enough," "I'm not worthy of having a voice and opinion," "People won't see what I have to offer," or "I am not worthy of success." It became a discipline to control these thoughts. Gradually, I began to feel much better about myself when I consciously rewrote these messages on a daily basis.

It wasn't until years later that I realized how toxic these beliefs had been, causing chronic fatigue and my immune system to be run down. I learned I have the traits of a highly sensitive person. A highly sensitive person tends to not filter information well and takes in things in a heightened way—much like someone who is fair-skinned going to the equator without sunscreen. I have to work extra hard to let go of personalizing so many things and adjust my thoughts.

On a physical level I began a process of detoxifying my body nutritionally and supporting many of the systems that were depleted from all of my striving. One of the systems I found to be particularly important was the adrenal system. When I was in a constant fight-or-flight mentality, it put undue stress on the adrenals, causing them to secrete high levels of Cortisol. Over time this Cortisol overload depleted a valuable hormone called DHEA leaving me with not much reserve to combat stress.

For some time my heart's desire was to find a partner with mutual values and faith. It seemed like I was single forever and Mr. Right wasn't showing up. I tried to get out as much as possible, going to groups for singles at churches and trying dating services, but I wasn't meeting guys who were open to growth and not too rigid in their spiritual beliefs. Everyone says you will find your mate when you aren't looking. That was a hard thing for me to follow, to fully let go and trust that I didn't have to be in just the right place to meet him. After many years of searching, I learned to look for someone I could enjoy being with and not necessarily marry. Eventually, the right guy did show up, however he was different from the image I had been programmed all of my life to value.

As I shared earlier, my parents raised me to believe that social status in life was quite important. That belief made it difficult to find a man who was genuinely spiritual, had a heart for God, and wasn't obsessed with working all the time. If I looked for someone like my Dad, I probably wouldn't see him very often and he might not be available to me emotionally. After kissing many frogs, I finally found a guy who was a great listener, strongly invested in his spiritual life, and had time for a relationship with me. That was encouraging. In the beginning of our relationship, he always said he wanted to get to know me. Wow! That was new. The past years that I had invested in learning to love myself paid off, since I was finally attracting someone who valued me on the inside!

Entering marriage for the first time at the age of fifty brought quite an adjustment. I had built up so many fantasy images of what I thought my husband would give me, as well as be for me. After years of counseling couples, I thought that marriage would be easy for me. I had worked through so much of my family baggage that I didn't think I would be like those couples I had counseled. What I became aware of early on is that I wanted my husband to be a certain way to make me feel good about myself. I also wanted him to be a clone of me with the same interests, hobbies, and habits. I quickly found out that my new marriage would not be so simple.

Even though I valued my husband's strong spiritual connection, I also wanted him to be successful in all those outward ways that I had learned to value. I was in for quite an adjustment. We got married a few weeks after 9/11 and my husband soon lost his insurance sales job, since the national uncertainty affected his ability to reach his quotas. Little did I know that over the next eight years he would be on a continual search to acquire all the training he needed as a financial advisor, generating very little income. This advanced training led to a considerable amount of debt, which certainly did not meet my image of a successful husband!

I was in daily anguish, feeling that he wasn't the husband who lived up to the expectations I had built up all those years of being single. One of my friends said, "Just divorce him," which offended me. I remember her saying, "It takes a strong person to get a divorce." I thought to myself, "It takes a strong person to stay in a marriage." I hadn't waited until I was fifty to get married and then divorced shortly after. I believed that I had made a commitment for life.

I had many frequent outbursts of anger that really surprised me and broke through my image of myself as the nice girl. I had always played this role and learned to stuff my negative emotions due to my family programming. Fortunately, my husband allowed me to get angry, which was very different from my family upbringing. He gave me tremendous support to go inside myself to discover the rooted beliefs I was feeling.

I finally figured out that my partner mirrored to me some of those same insecurities I felt in myself—not successful, not good enough. I used to have a plastic case that covered a mirror that I kept in my purse that kind of says it all: "There is really nobody out there. Everything we see on the outside is a reflection of what we see in ourselves—mirroring back to us." I needed to realize that being irritated with his behavior was a reflection of an issue I had within myself.

In addition, I had to come face to face with all my beliefs about money. Even though I grew up with a family that had money, I had tremendous fears of scarcity that there would not be enough. With much exploration I have been able to identify and release the beliefs that weren't supporting me so that I could move into more of a feeling of abundance. If my husband hadn't gone through all of this period of financial drought, I probably would not have identified all this fear inside me.

In hindsight, I can see the growth in me has been valuable—both spiritually and emotionally. I now can live more in a state of abundance—that there is enough of whatever I need. I have learned to go inside and see what really bothers me about situations that trigger my emotions. I now take more responsibility for my own feelings and changing myself rather than trying to change the outside or the other person.

Because of my experiences, I now emphasize to my clients that looking inside is the key to growth. Taking this approach I discovered how to work with emotional energy clearing methods to fully clear out my unconscious programming. This helped my healing and bringing my body back into balance. I am convinced that I feel really different and am able to move forward in ways that feel easier with less stress, reaching a new level of confidence and energy.

In closing, I would like to share the story of a butterfly's metamorphosis that I believe best illustrates what my journey has been. There once was a little boy who was fascinated with a caterpillar building a cocoon. He watched the cocoon daily, waiting for the butterfly to emerge. One day he saw the tiny butterfly struggling to come out. He was concerned that it was struggling so much and decided to help. The boy ran to get scissors. He snipped the cocoon to make the hole bigger and the butterfly quickly emerged. As the butterfly came out it had a small swollen body and shriveled wings. The butterfly spent the rest of its life crawling around, dragging its shriveled body and was never able to fly. As the boy tried to figure out what had gone wrong, he learned that a butterfly is supposed to struggle. In fact, the butterfly's struggle to push its way out of the cocoon pushes the fluid out of its body and into its wings. Without the struggle, a butterfly will never fly.

I can see how my struggles have allowed beauty within to unfold. I look forward to continuing each day to connect inwardly to that vital part of myself: my inner spirit. My hope for you is that through this snapshot into my life you will be inspired to develop the connection with yourself and work through your inner conflicts. I believe you can allow your own beautiful butterfly to emerge and soar with all the beauty your life deserves.

Suzanne Simpson, M.Ed, LPC, is owner of Inner-Connected Health, an integrative practice with expertise in women's wellness issues through mid-life. She is a Licensed Psychotherapist, Connection Coach, Author, and Workshop Facilitator helping those connect to their heart energy that has been locked up and blocking their success in relationships, career, and health. She provides life coaching, and emotional clearing tools, techniques and strategies through one-on-one or group teleclasses and workshops. She can be visited at www.inner-connectedhealth.com Email: suzanne@connectcoach.com (720) 981-0713.

I Choose Me

Ronda Wada

I was in love and that was no minor deal. Like so many of us, my heart had been broken before - badly. We're not just talking a crack or a fissure, but a deep crevice. But this; this was different. This was the first time I had truly FELT loved. It didn't feel like just any old kind of love, but true love - love where I was just me, and for once that seemed to be enough. Have you ever pretended to be something you weren't, or altered your behavior in order to get or keep love? Well, I sure had.

BUT this time was different. I had made a promise to myself that I would no longer accept being loved for being anything but the real me. So, I put myself out there and allowed myself to be vulnerable, and that was a pretty scary thing. I exposed all the soft and fragile bits, along with the hard, calloused, not-so-pretty bits. I put it all out there for him to see.

Yet he still seemed to love me. I had begun to really believe that I might be lovable after all. And I was ready to truly be loved. I felt safer, more accepted, and more appreciated than I had ever felt in my life. So I decided to get married. It was as much of a surprise to me as it was to everyone else in my life. It was an even bigger surprise than falling in love, and I certainly hadn't expected that!

We – well, I, really – set about planning a small intimate wedding in the very near future. The day arrived. It was glorious. We were joined by our parents and our respective children for the ceremony, which was followed by a small reception with close friends. Everything was perfect, and I couldn't possibly have been happier.

For our wedding night, we were staying at my favorite hotel – you know the one, the one with the heavenly beds. Oh, how I adore those beds! I could get in one of those beds and not come out for a week!

When we entered the honeymoon suite, I was on top of the world. I was thinking to myself, "I never knew I could be this happy!" As I prepared to make love with my husband for the first time as his wife, I was elated. We aren't talking just cloud nine here; I had sailed all the way to at least cloud 13! I crawled into the bed and sunk into the pile of feathers they call a comforter, and I remember thinking, "It just doesn't get any better than this."

I watched him as he crossed the room to join me. He wasn't walking but more like stalking toward the bed, with raw, masculine intention. Anticipation hung in the air as he climbed into bed. And then, hovering over me, he said, "You are now Mrs. SoAndSo, and you are mine." I can't say for sure if it was the words he spoke, the look in his eye, the intensity of his movements, or something less tangible that alerted me, but something was suddenly not right. In a split second, I went from the most joy I had ever felt to being stricken with complete panic. My entire body was on Threat Level Red. I was more terrified than I had ever been in my life, for no logical reason.

It took every ounce of willpower I had not to get up that moment and run from the room, to run for my life. "This just doesn't make sense," I thought. "Why in the world should I be afraid of the man that I love and who loves me more than anything? Where in the world could this be coming from?" I attempted to settle myself down and stay composed. I certainly didn't want to have to explain to him why his new wife was having a panic attack on our wedding night. I didn't understand it, but suddenly I had the strong sense that he wanted to completely possess me and wouldn't stop until he had succeeded. That sense that I was in danger really never went away.

For the next six months, I rode a roller-coaster of ecstasy and agony. There were periods of the thoughtful, loving, sweet man that I had fallen in love with, and then there were just as many visits from the possessive, needy stranger who had first appeared on our wedding night. Late one night, as I fled our bed to escape his now-familiar compulsive behavior, he followed with the same intention I had first seen in our honeymoon suite. In that moment, I knew that I had a choice to make. Could I admit that I had made a mistake by marrying him? Would I choose to live this way until it broke me, or would I choose me?

There is a vast intellect that resides in each of us. Women, in particular, are more receptive to the signs, nudges and whispers referred to as intuition. For the first time, I became completely aware of the gift my intuition had been giving me on our wedding night. It had been warning me of what was to come, and I chose to ignore it because it didn't make logical sense. How many other times in my life had I declined such gifts by ignoring the amazing wisdom of my body to guide me? And why had it taken me so long to trust my own inner voice? To trust that somewhere deep inside I always know what is right for me? The answer at that point didn't matter, because I realized that in each moment I have the power to make a new choice. I could continue to try to make this hasty marriage work or I could admit that I had made a grave error in judgment and move on from here. That night I made a new choice, the "right" choice, the one my intuition told me to: I chose me.

Today, I remain single. Not out of fear created from this experience but from liberation created from this experience. You see, each day I renew my commitment to choose me. Choosing me means being clear on what I want out of life including what I want out of a relationship. I look forward to the day that I might once again share my life with someone. Yet, I know at what cost that can come. My experience has taught me that I am better off being alone than I am being with someone who doesn't love me just for me.

Ronda Wada guides teens and women to become the expert in their own lives by learning to trust themselves. Through writing, workshops, tele-classes and one-on-one coaching, Ronda empowers you to design a life you love, live from inspiration and follow that still small voice inside. Ronda can be reached at Ronda@RondaWada.com.

From Bricks to Roses

Alyssa Sharon

F-E-A-R, this four-letter word seemed to be my name as a child and this same word holds a lot of people back in many areas of their lives. The word fear can stand for many things, such as: **F**alse **E**vidence **A**ppearing **R**eal or **F**orgetting **E**verything's **A**ll **R**ight. Fear can take hold of your soul like cold air sucks the breath right from your lungs. Every human being experiences fear within their first moments of life. Some people are able to push through it as they develop and some live in fear their whole existence. This is not just the story of my frightful childhood, but how I overcame my fear and bloomed into a vivacious young woman.

I was pondering over a section in the book *Bumper Stickers* by Bob Meehan where he explains that when people think aliens abducted them, they were really just having flashbacks of being born. If you think about it, it makes sense. I can picture being a baby nestled peacefully inside my mother's womb when, all of a sudden, I am in this unfamiliar, uncomfortable, cold room with blindingly bright lights and stark white walls. The first thing I see is the doctor who has a mask covering his mouth, so the only visible things are two big eyes staring back at me. Various strangers are prodding me with all kinds of metal tools and passing me from one pair of gloved hands to another. I am completely disoriented, and I just can't stop screaming. This traumatic experience aligns with most people's perception of what it must feel like to be abducted by aliens.

According to my mother, however, my birthing was very peaceful. She said that since I was her third child, she knew what to do by the time I came. Meditation and breathing guided me out in a silent, gentle manner. I'm sure coming out of the womb was still very overwhelming and terrifying for me but not nearly as much so because my mom stayed so calm.

I have lived in the same house my whole life, and the house has changed with me through my development. I can still remember how my home looked through my awe filled eyes as a child. At a very young age, I always wanted to spend time with my mom, but she was busy working, so I spent my time with babysitters instead. When preschool started, I didn't want to let go of my mom. I felt abandoned, and I didn't understand why my parents were trying to get rid of me.

On the first day of kindergarten, when I stepped into the big classroom, my body felt weak and naked as my heart pounded under my little pink t-shirt. My classmates were chatting with each other about their summer adventures, and I didn't want to have anything to do with it. I sat alone, separate from the crowd. I had nothing to say. A part of me shut down, and I decided not to talk to anyone, including my teacher. I think it was partly out of spite towards my parents and partly out of fear of growing up. The teacher called roll, and when it came to me, I was silent. I wanted to disappear into the walls. "Alyssa Sharon?" I lifted my hand just enough to catch my teacher's eye. She marked me present although I felt absent to the world.

This state of feeling absent became my way of life. I refused to speak to anyone with authority. It had gone beyond rebellion; it was purely habit by that point. I was terrified to say a word because I knew that everyone would notice me if I did. I struggled so much that my parents took me to a counselor who helped us all to understand that I had developed selective mutism.

According to the Selective Mutism Foundation, Inc., "Selective mutism is a psychiatric disorder most commonly found in children, characterized by a persistent failure to speak in select settings, which continues for more than one month. These children understand spoken language and have the ability to speak normally. In typical cases, they speak to their parents and a few selected others." From ages four to nine, I fit this description.

In the summer after 3rd grade something shifted inside me; I was ready to speak. My parents decided to take me to see a psychiatrist to help me make the transition from the selectively mute child to a blooming flower. I felt myself open up to a stranger for the first time. The psychiatrist related to me and knew how to assist me in lifting the veil I had been hiding behind for the four prior years.

As I entered my 4th grade classroom on the first day of school, my mom's hand in mine, a wave of nervousness washed over my body. My teacher, Ms. Wood, told the class to sit in a circle on the carpet. I joined my classmates and my mom sat behind me.

"Ok, class, let's get to know each other!" Ms. Wood said enthusiastically. "I want you to go around the circle and say your name and an animal whose name starts with the same letter as yours."

"How about orangutan; I love monkeys." I whispered to my mom. She giggled. "Ok, honey, sounds good."

It was getting close to my turn. Passing out would not have been unexpected for me at that moment. Taking a deep breath, I looked at my mom one more time; she squeezed my hand gently.

The girl to my right said, "My name is Kelsey, and I like kangaroos!" I stopped breathing and looked down at the floor. I wanted to just run out of the room or curl up in a ball in a dark corner somewhere, giving up. My body felt as heavy as a bag of bricks. "Just do it," my mind tried to motivate my mouth to open. "I'm Alyssa...and I-I-I like o-orangutans." The words finally stumbled out my lips as quickly as possible.

The bag of bricks opened up, the bricks tumbled out of my body and in its place, a garden of roses began stemming from my skin. A huge weight had been lifted from me. I turned to see my mom smiling. With tears in her eyes she looked as relieved as I did.

As the year progressed, speaking became more and more natural. By 5th grade, I walked into the classroom with ease. To my surprise, none of my peers judged me at all. I realized this scenario of everyone making a big deal about me talking ended up being fictional. It was just **F**alse **E**vidence **A**ppearing **R**eal. Everyone just wanted to get to know me. I received straight A's on all my oral presentations and written pieces that year.

For my Continuation ceremony at the end of elementary school, everyone had to write a short speech to present in front of all of our families, friends and teachers. I got up on the stage, walked up to the microphone and delivered a powerful speech to the audience about my elementary school experience. The crowd had tears in their eyes. These people were not my enemies; they were here supporting me all along. My fear and anxiety had masked these friendly faces, making them seem terrifying. When I looked out at all the people around me on my last day of elementary school, their masks fell to the ground, and I had a new perspective on life.

This perspective carried me through the past years with a confidence I never had before. When I entered high school, I felt ready to take on the world. My struggles through elementary school gave me great strength and discipline. It wasn't easy keeping track of who I could and could not speak to. Keeping my lips sealed all those years caused me to burst out by high school. Friends were not hard to make and participating in class was not nearly as scary. I knew I could flourish as an independent adult.

Everyone has to face some sort of difficulty or setback in life, whether a physical or mental disability, discrimination, poverty, or a broken home. It takes a tremendous amount of strength to overcome these challenges in our lives. It took a lot of discipline to decide who was allowed to hear my voice and whom I would allow into my secretive world. However, it took much more strength and willpower to push through my fear of speaking, opening up to the world around me. I hope to inspire people who are holding themselves back because of fear or lack of motivation. I believe it is possible to overcome any challenge with the right amount of determination and support.

The reward of pushing through my extreme anxiety was my ability to share myself with other people. If I still had my jaw clenched shut today, nobody would know about my passion for life. I write poetry. I am interested in philosophy and art. I love to delve into deep conversations with people about my theories on life. I can't imagine still being stuck in my little world of insecurities, but as a child I never thought I would blossom into the outspoken, witty, creative woman I am today.

I will carry my experiences with selective mutism with me in my heart my entire life. I won't be ashamed to share them because I know they've made a positive impact on the person I am today. I would not trade those difficult years of my life for anything.

Alyssa Sharon lives in Denver and is currently in the Yoga Teacher Training program at Samadhi Yoga Center. Her passion is strengthening her body, mind and spirit from the inside out through yoga and mediation. She looks forward to helping others do the same when she is a certified yoga instructor. Her dream is to become a healer, giving people a safe place to explore themselves through art, yoga, dance, and meditation. She is uncovering more and more layers of herself each day to reveal the brilliant light that shines within her. Contact Alyssa to hear more about her success story or if you live near the Denver Metro area and want to practice yoga/mediation with her. Email: alyssasharon@yahoo.com Facebook: www.facebook.com/alysharon

The Year of the Tiger

Judith Wade

I was traveling down Santa Fe Drive near the I-25 interchange at dusk when I lifted up my eyes for a moment. And there it was on a billboard under those tiny spotlights, their glow adding to the magic, "TOPLESS SHOWS...FORMERLY THE PAPER TIGER." Yes, of course. This was my sign. My friend Sally does shaman work and we journeyed to the lower Earth where she saw a Tiger as my power animal. She told me to watch for signs from the universe.

"Fierce love," she said. "Over the next few days look for ways the Tiger shows up in your life." Now this didn't mean I was supposed to become a show girl. No, the topless for me was more a reference to being exposed. Showing the world who I really am. Fierce love that is intensely eager about being authentic.

"I love you, and because I love you, I would sooner have you hate me for telling you the truth than adore me for telling you lies" (Pietro Aretino). I've found this in relationship with my boyfriend. It's been quite a feeling of freedom to speak what's on my mind, instead of holding it down like an oversized beach ball under the water, squirming and throwing you off balance, exploding out of the water hitting young children and that 82 year-old grandma who just wanted to turn her face upwards towards the sun and soak in the rays. Sometimes the words ricochet out of my mouth giving me time to think before I say them, but recently just flew straight out as if they were channeled from the part of me who has been hurt in the past and really knows how I feel. This was unlike how I've spoken in past relationships.

My boyfriend promised me a two hour massage and the thought of being pampered and receiving the treatment I see him give his clients made me feel grateful, appreciated, acknowledged. I get massaged by him all time, fifteen minutes here, and ten minutes there. I know it's all added up to much more than two hours but it was the thought of him stopping his life for a complete two hours of quality time, not sharing it with the TV or watching a movie, just our essence moving together a back and forth movement of breath, spirit and attention. It made me feel giddy, like when we first dated.

"I'm going to a friend's house first for dinner. She's going through a tough time and needs someone to listen. But I'll be back for the massage. This is definitely going to happen tonight," he said.

I start my dinner, a nice aromatic chicken curry with basmati rice (sounds nurturing, I thought), and then get some writing done while I have some alone time. Later I look up away from my writing and notice it's 9 p.m. I start wrapping things up in anticipation of a late night, roll-into-bed massage. I wish I could call him but his phone isn't working right now. I look at the clock – 9:30. . . 10:00 . . .10:30 . . . at each interval I become more angry and more disappointed. I feel like the child of a divorced couple. It's visitation weekend and the parent picking me up is so caught up in work, that it's hours later before someone comes, and the ballgame is over with only empty popcorn boxes blowing about.

At 11 p.m., I hear the crunch of tires as he pulls into the driveway, headlights straight on like my anger. Leaning in to give me a big kiss he says, "Hello Dear." Had he forgotten the massage or thought I wouldn't notice? As I walk away, spoken under my breath, but heard in my trail, "Maybe it's best you don't make promises to me. You seem to forget and I'd rather not be disappointed."

"I'm sorry. I got so caught up in helping my friend, I didn't notice the time. People are telling me how wonderful I am. It feels good to be needed. "

"Well, it didn't feel good to be forgotten," I say.

It flew out of my mouth without searching for the perfect words or recalling all my counseling sessions "remember to use I statements." No, it was raw and real and evidently a part of me. I stood there staring at my boyfriend my eyes moist with emotions, the statement suspended by my anger and disappointment.

Both of our insecurities were coming to the surface. His mommy issues, not feeling loved by her, looking outside for reassurance that he is accepted. My abandonment issues, with the most vibrant memory as a two-year-old when I had a kidney infection and stayed in the hospital for a week. Each day my pink fluffy robe wrapped around me like a security blanket, as I watched my dad walk down the long hospital corridor away from me, out the door, my lower lip curled outward heavy with sadness and disbelief that he wasn't taking me home. I continued to look at my boyfriend: the distance between us seemed as long as that corridor.

Before speaking any further, I go inward and ask myself, "How have I been abandoning myself lately?" How have I been giving up my authenticity? Was I forgetting how much gratitude my body has for my morning meditation and afternoon runs? Not spending enough time alone, giving into the requests of others for time and attention, worried people would think I was selfish if I wasn't always giving? Saying yes when I wanted to say no? Not setting boundaries with people in order to widen the area so acceptance can come into my life any way possible, even if it means losing a part of me in the process. Losing myself lately and realizing my boyfriend was just being a mirror for me? How could I let this happen?

I reminded myself there are bound to be setbacks on the path to self-growth and awareness. We get our smooth patches and the parts of the trail with the fallen tree blocking our path making us stop, re-direct. I sometimes try to be perfect, but perfection doesn't mean without mistakes, it means wholeness, accepting all parts of ourselves.

One theme of mine has been to become who I thought my partner wanted me to be, losing my center, falling away like apple pieces after slicing it with a de-corer. I was determined in this relationship not to lose myself. However, it was difficult having to discern if I was standing up for myself or saying "you can't control me;" knowing when to be sturdy like the trunk of an oak tree and when to compromise and be flexible like the leaves in the wind. Going into it with the courage of letting myself be enough. Of course there is bound to be some fear that goes along with that, but as Greg Mooers, founder and president of LifeCamp (Discover Your Heart Virtue workshop) says, "No, no, it's not really fear; it's excitement."

I have my own style. Taking on my boyfriend's style only waters me down or evaporates me altogether. I've learned I don't have to become him, but can learn from him. I can step into his world and what fits, I can keep. He likes McDonald's. I usually like healthy food but can certainly give into having a piece of carrot cake or a cheese-oozing, overstuffed panini. He speaks in the length of novels. I speak in the conciseness of poetry. He thinks coffee and smoking is the breakfast of champions. I'll stick with my oatmeal and prefer tea, but sometimes a strong black cup of coffee, stream rolling into sunrise, is the perfect accompaniment to morning. He's doesn't like to plan and prefers spontaneity. I find comfort in organization and structure, a foundation, like South Dakota soil under your feet. Even I, however, take a break from my structured existence. For example, a few years ago I decided to go on a trip to Italy – the out-of-the-ordinary thing about my decision was that I made it in only ten minutes. Booked a flight with a friend, without knowing if my boss would give me time off. I also decided at the last minute to drive to the east coast with a couple of friends without booking any hotels, taking any maps, just letting one turn into the next decide which way our journey would take us. Sometimes I like knowing in the relationship and sometimes I just let one turn decide the next.

I've had a tendency to choose guys who aren't emotionally available or who are only available for a short period of time, never making it much past the one year mark. Maybe I choose these men from a place of fear, afraid to love fully. I think it started back in third grade. I had a boyfriend who was my best friend. He chased me around at recess and gave me slobbery kisses on the cheek. We talked about everything from our favorite books and animals at the zoo to what we had for dinner and we shared our deepest secrets. Then one day at a science field trip to a nature center at a city park, he turned and looked at me, pointed to her, and said, "I like Gina better." I was shocked. I looked at Gina and thought of course he likes her better. She's prettier, probably smarter, and more fun. After that, I always thought that whoever I loved would find someone else. I think I chose people who would leave anyway or who never really arrived. At least I knew the outcome and it was safe, better than the unknown but sometimes the unknown can be an invitation to happiness, as Greg Mooers says.

I sometimes have a hard time admitting my profound gratitude for our relationship to my current boyfriend. He says it's the easiest relationship he's ever been in. For me, it's been challenging but also rewarding. Aside from the fact he'll do my nails, clean the snow off my car, fold my laundry, and make me dinner if I ask, the rewards have been personal transformation and growth. I've had the courage to speak my truth, set my boundaries, remain an individual within the perimeters of a "we," not settle for less than I value, and allow myself to be vulnerable. One of my messages from an intuitive woman was "be brave enough to be loved." When she said this I realized even with all my recent self-discovery and self worth, I hadn't fully let myself into this relationship yet. A part of me had remained outside peering through a looking glass, separated, yet I could see everything.

I sometimes start to express my appreciation and then there is this catch, like getting tripped up on carpet, falling upstairs. I put my arms out to avoid a perceived fall and I'm safe again. But then it happened. Without even realizing it, I was out on the edge of a cliff, with one foot taking a step onto air because I wasn't looking down but straight ahead. He was working in the kitchen and I was in my office. We were both absorbed in our own worlds but seemed to share a common one. I heard him stand up.

"I'm getting ready to leave. I need to go run some errands and then I have a massage to give," he said.

I put my arms around him, leaned into him, and just rested on his chest for a minute feeling his pulse synchronize with mine, "I wish you didn't need to go. I know we are in separate rooms doing our own things but just feeling you in the next room is nice."

It was simple, not elegant. Sometimes though, a simple admittance can seem out of reach for a cautious heart especially when you know you can't take it back and there is the ever-present fear that it might turn out the same as it always has in the past.

"You admitted something," he said and pulled me in closer.

"I did," I said surprised. And it wasn't scary like I thought it would be. Just like the time I held the snake. It was soft not slimy, not exactly a kitten, but at that moment there was some sort of peacefulness about the snake and I felt safe.

David is always giving me compliments, proclaiming his adoration and appreciation – sometimes like a sensual Pablo Neruda poem and sometimes soft like a gentle hand stroking my hair.

We don't realize what a huge impact we can have on people with what we say. Not saying what we think we should say, just whatever is coming from within, and then poof it's gone – like the fire of a magician on stage, the magic remembered long after the flame has died.

Now there is no turning back. I've admitted I like his hat.

Judith Wade lives in Colorado. Her business is Kaleidoscope Insights & Healing. Besides being a creative writer, focusing on non-fiction and poetry, Judith is also a professional animal communicator, healer, spiritual teacher, and intuitive. As a Usui Reiki Master/Teacher and Kundalini Reiki Master/Teacher, Judith teaches healing classes, animal communication and offers animal communication sessions, intuitive energy sessions, readings, and energy drawings. Judith can be reached at judithw44@ hotmail.com or 720.377.5567.

Finding My True Self

Kate Heartsong

Having grown up with a cynical and mentally ill father who always told my siblings and me not to trust anyone, and to always double check myself, I grew up not trusting the world, Spirit (God), myself and others. On top of what my father told us, my mother, whose horrific marriage to my father led her to believe men can't be trusted, shared this view with us children as well. She also lost most of her self-confidence, mainly due to the emotional abuse from her husband, my father. I believe that due to this, she felt she didn't have any skills to go out and find a job in order to get out of this marriage (although she had many wonderful skills such as being an excellent seamstress and gardener). I imagine she felt locked in this marriage and stayed with my father for the sake of her three children. Having this environment as the conditioning of my self-image, plus having a hearing loss from the age of two, and feeling so ashamed of it, I had no self-esteem. I felt I was a mistake and that I didn't matter. I thought everything was my fault. One example of this is when I was around eleven years old; I was asked why the traffic lights in my neighborhood were in the middle of the street rather than being at the intersection of two streets. I said I didn't know, but deep inside I felt somehow responsible for those traffic lights and I felt ashamed. Other perceptions I had about myself and my life included feelings of being helpless and powerless because my experiences in my very young life were that if I wanted something, I didn't get it, or if I took action on something, it would make no difference to the situation.

I look back now as I write this and realize once again the huge transformation I experienced and that due to this, I am now, and have been for several years, a happy, confident and outgoing person. I am *completely* opposite of what and who I was as a child and a young adult. What an enormous blessing to have found my true self!

How did I transcend the childhood trauma, the negative self-esteem, the shyness and the shameful feelings I had? I started my healing journey in 1997, while going through my divorce, with our two young children going through this as well. Often huge life changes will be the impetus to create change, and this was certainly true with me. Through this most turbulent time, when I also became unemployed, I was so fearful and didn't have a strong religious or spiritual foundation to find comfort in. And because I was taught not to trust anything or anyone, I always felt I had to control everything and do everything, resulting in even more stress in my life. However, there was an underlying strength that was stirring in me, the same strength that created the clarity I needed to file for divorce. This inner stirring became more evident to me and I slowly began to have a bit more self-confidence.

I believe that it was this beginning stage of gaining self-confidence and also my intuition that led me to beginning to recognize my true self. What I mean by "true self" is my inner divine nature, my inner light that was covered up by all the false beliefs that I took on as a child. My true self is that part of me that needs to express in order for me to live authentically, that is, to be the person I am meant to be. Perhaps one could even say it was/is my higher self or my soul. And I believe it was this part of me that helped me hear my inner guidance.

Among other things, this inner guidance led me to find a women's metaphysical support group. I resonated with the topics we spoke about and with the women there. Through this, I was introduced to a wonderful nondenominational church, Mile Hi Church, which is part of the United Center for Spiritual Living, and I felt I had "come home." This church offered many different classes, which I welcomed, many focusing on our inner power, our divine nature and how we create our own life through our thoughts and feelings. These teachings were as different as night and day to what I had grown up with. I thought to myself "What do you mean, I am a divine and special person"? "I create my own reality?" "I am important to the world?" But I came to realize these concepts were indeed true!

I remember a powerful healing weekend workshop that dealt with my inner child. In this workshop, I was able to break through some of the big misconceptions about not being deserving of happiness in life. I also came to realize that I, too, am important. I already knew everyone else was, and through this workshop, came to realize that since this is true for everyone else, of course it's also true for me. I also attended various workshops, experienced various non-traditional energy healings and became a Reiki Master and Teacher. I became (and still am) very spiritual, praying and meditating on a regular basis, and also attended various spiritual activities such as the Dances of Universal Peace and Kirtans. In addition, I attended talks given by many of the major spiritual leaders of today. Spirit and my connection with Spirit became, and still is, a major part of my life.

Other practices I took on, that have since become part of my daily life, include thinking positively, being aware of my thoughts and feelings, using positive affirmations, associating with positive people and being involved with several spiritual communities. Over time, my self-esteem and self-confidence increased; I began to peel away the layers of the false beliefs from childhood that had encased me for so long. I started to feel more empowered, happier and relaxed with life. Over the years, challenges would still come up, as they do for anyone, but I was and am able to handle these challenges with confidence and trust, having learned years ago that there are always reasons why these challenges arise, and I am all the wiser and experienced because of these challenges.

It took having my own life experiences and the various healing activities I just mentioned, to come to a place of recognizing there are many situations and people that can be trusted, and that I can trust myself. When I started building my self-esteem and self-confidence, I started to trust others more, as well as myself. I've also come to trust Spirit through prayers, meditation and other spiritual practices I started years ago and still practice regularly today.

A wonderful example of my increased level of trust is in what I call automatic writing. In 2003, while doing my daily meditation, I felt a pull to take a spiral notebook and pen and write down words I felt were coming through me in my meditation. These words were very loving and peaceful and gave me simple and divine guidance. I thought they were from my angels, but didn't feel I could completely trust them. I received this divine guidance consistently many times in the following seven years (and continue to do so today) and in time began to really trust the divine guidance. Now I'm at the place of recognizing this as a special gift and I share this with others as well. For example, I published my first spiritual self-help book entitled Deeply We Are One.

I have come to recognize that there were many blessings and gifts that came from my childhood. Since I've taken on this perspective, I have more joy and comfort in my life. Some of the greatest gifts I have seen include the gift of compassion for others, especially my parents, recognizing my own strength, fortitude, and courage, the ability to have more empathy for others, and a deeper understanding of my self-knowing.

I treat others with more respect, appreciation, support and kindness, because I now treat myself in this manner. This is because I recognize I am of the same divine nature as everyone else and of the same divine nature as Spirit. And what I have inside of me is what I can give, and therefore I am able to treat others in the same way as I treat myself. It's so wonderful to be able to give!

Today, I am a compassionate, kind and loving person doing the best I can. I realize that the past has already happened and the future is yet to come, so the only "real" place to live is in the present moment. I have more harmonious relationships. I know myself well enough to understand why I act and react to others or to life's opportunities or challenges. I realize all is well in my life, even in difficult times. Sometimes I need to dig deep into the very essence of my divine being to remind myself that all really is in divine right order. I realize that everything I experience is for a good reason and that reason is for my continual growth. In this expansion, I am better able to live more authentically; that is, to live in tandem with the inner expression of who I am that *needs* to express as Kate.

I recognize the unique gifts and talents I have to offer the world and in this, I better appreciate and acknowledge myself. It is because of this that I am now more able to appreciate and acknowledge others and all of life. I understand the vital role that each one of us plays on our dear Mother Earth. I know I am a divine being and it is in this knowing that I am delightfully able to know this to be true for *all* people, and for that matter, *all* of life. For what we have inside of us is what we are able to see in other people. It is through this portal that I now better understand, embrace and *feel* the interconnectivity of all of life, that each one of us is, on a deep level, connected with everyone else, and with all of life. *All* is divine, for everyone and everything is created from the same source of life, the great creator of all, Spirit. I have come to know that what I say, feel, think and do has an effect on others around me and on the collective consciousness as a whole because of our interconnectivity. Not only do I enjoy my life better by being more peaceful and happy, but I am also contributing, in a small way, to the possibility of a more peaceful world.

I am even all the more connected with Spirit and in feeling this connection I am reassured that I, along with everyone, am always held in the loving embrace of Spirit and that I am always provided for.

As a result of transcending my painful childhood and due to my transformation, I am better able to shine my inner light now. This radiates out to others in a positive way and I like to think that I am making a positive difference for many others by living my life the best way I know how, by sharing my love, compassion and kindness, and by being my true self. Thank you Spirit! I found my true self and am able to share this with others!

Kate Heartsong is one of today's newest international authors. She is also a gifted speaker, empowering and inspiring many. Kate holds a BS in Business Administration from Columbia College and also a BA in Psychology from the University of Colorado. She has used those degrees in combination with her dynamic life experiences, deep understanding and intuition to encourage and empower individuals in knowing their own unique worth. Her new book, Deeply We Are One, shares her intuitive guidance with others, assisting them in recognizing their divine nature and true connection with all of life through simple but profound life-enhancing tools, exercises and meditations. To learn more and also read Kate's blog, go to www.JoyfulRadiance.com.

Healing the Planet

Debbie Sloan

I received a phone call from my very first client and dear friend, Susee. She needed to cancel her massage appointment with me because her daughter, Margot, was in labor. At that time I had known the family for about three years. I worked in their restaurant during massage school and they were the source of a large part of my massage clientele and close network of friends. I offered to come over to see if I could help out.

Margot had been up most of the night and was getting pretty weary of the labor's progress. When I got to Susee's house I had no plan of how to help or intention of assisting in Margot's birth. My experience at this time had only been as a massage therapist for two years and having birthed three of my five babies. I asked if she wanted me to help her get some rest or speed things up to get the birth process going. She said she wanted to get the process going. Four hours later, with no medical interventions, Alicia came into the world; eyes open, looking right at her Nana, Susee.

As cliché as it sounds, leaving the hospital that evening, I felt I was walking on a cloud. I had had a full day of appointments at work before I went over to help out Margot and was still full of energy. Besides the amazing feeling I was experiencing after the birth I had been very aware of the connection between Margot and me as soon as I walked into their home. She was attended to by family and at the hospital had more family and friends waiting in support. But it seemed that we were in our own little bubble; she trusted that I was there to help her and I was confident that I could.

My experiences with my own natural births and Margot's gave me the notion that I had a knack for this kind of work. My massage school was offering Doula training classes. I called KC, the owner and inspiring mentor and told her of my experience assisting Margot. She gifted the tuition for the class as a way to promote the program and the mission of a doula. I felt she had appointed me as Doula Ambassador and I took in the motto of the program, "Healing the Planet One Birth at a Time."

Going back 13 years prior to Alicia's birth, I had an unplanned pregnancy my first year of college. I also had an unplanned natural birth. While I was pregnant I was a freshman biology student and naturally interested in the developmental process. So I was pretty well self-educated about what was happening to me and to the baby growing inside me. I was also putting the baby up for adoption. That choice empowered me as an advocate, for my situation, myself and my unborn child.

My expectation for my birth experience was something I would suffer through, in order to move on and to continue my life and education. I fully expected hours of tortuous labor, ending in a caesarean, with weeks of recovery ahead. But what ended up happening was, my labor was less painful and much more manageable than menstrual cramps. There were breaks from the pain, with the natural ebbs and flows of the contractions. By the time I asked for the relief of medications, six hours after the onset of productive labor, I was fully dilated and ready to go to the delivery room. Steve was born after 15 minutes of pushing and I was back in classes 4 days later. (As an aside, Steve contacted me over four years ago and we have an open, goofy, honest mother/son relationship.)

I am ready to use these experiences, my other successes as a doula, my expertise as a massage therapist/wellness advocate and my personal experiences as a birthing mom of five kids to become a professional doula. I am very sincere about the motto of Healing the Planet One Birth at a Time.

Through pregnancy and labor, doulas offer education, emotional support, guidance in making decisions, creating a birth plan, advocating for that birth plan and even in retelling the birth story. Numerous studies have shown the positive benefits of a doula's presence at birth, for the parents and their babies. Benefits extend to the hospital staff and also by decreasing costs. Specific benefits include a decreased incidence of caesarean sections, need for vacuum extraction, forceps and pain medications. Moms report a more satisfying birth experience, less anxiety and depression. They are shown to have increased self-esteem, are more affectionate towards their babies and are more likely to breastfeed.

Benefits to dad, partners and/or family members have to be mentioned. The reality of labor can be very difficult for the mom's support person. Parents going through childbirth classes are taught techniques to help through labor. Sometimes, based on my own experiences, those techniques do not work. For example, lavender oil may smell great and relaxing during practice. But to a nauseous, laboring mother, it may not work so well. Moms may also be touch sensitive, negating massage techniques learned. Untrained partners may not have the skills to find useful alternatives and suggestions. Doulas have many tools based on education and previous birth experiences. Offering dads or partners the opportunity to step out of the labor room for a break, has always been met with appreciation. Moms appreciate the break too. Often times, they have been together for hours and need some breathing room. Moms are concerned for the dad's welfare, as well. The break gives the dads, or partners, time to regroup and they return refreshed and ready for the final hours of labor.

The special techniques and suggestions I use have been developed by my experience and creativity, a bit of knowledge, and a lot of confidence in knowing that the suggestions will work. Expressing that effectively to the medical staff has always worked for me and ultimately has saved the mom from a seemingly unnecessary medical intervention or enhanced her birth experience. I suggest to moms, going through transition, the hardest part of labor, that they sit in a shower. The mom comes from the shower more relaxed and fully dilated. It is time to push the baby out, with an epidural and its complications avoided. I advocate for the baby to be laid on mom's chest, skin to skin as immediately after birth as the staff will allow. Mom can warm the baby and bonding is enhanced. It also creates, for mom, the sense of being exactly what her baby needs, without the help of fetal warmers and monitors. As a massage therapist, I massage moms through their labor. I have the stamina for that and it is what I know to do best. The labors I have attended have been two to six hours long. A relaxed, focused mom is an effective, laboring mom. I have attended births at hospitals and birthing centers, with and without epidurals.

Besides increased patient satisfaction, a potential marketing piece, hospitals benefit by reduced costs. The doula's role of attending to the laboring mom's non-clinical needs allows the medical staff to attend to her clinical needs and focus on other laboring parents.

The medical community with all their resources, education and protocols often times steal the birth experience from the expectant and birthing parents. This is an observation of mine over the years, but not my personal experience. It is not my experience simply because I educated myself and felt empowered and thus was in control of each of my birth experiences. It has not been the experience of my previous doula clients as my support created for them a calmer, empowered and healing birth experience. An unspoken intention I have held has been to offer to moms, healing from previous birth trauma. I was almost unaware of this until my sister-in-law told me how she felt more at peace with her first birth after I attended her second. I remembered then, a friend saying the same after I attended her third birth. Healing the planet one birth at a time has a ripple effect on everyone involved, mom, dad, babies, family medical staff and even myself.

Debbie is a native of Colorado and the mom of 5 kids, two sons and three daughters. She studied Biology at CU- Boulder, but was lured by the Holistic Health and Wellness program at Metropolitan State College of Denver. Debbie also earned a BA in psychology, has attended massage school and is a licensed esthetician. She expects to be certified as a professional doula in summer 2010. Debbie's hobbies include, listening to music and seeing live shows, reading, hanging out in nature and with her kids. She has volunteered extensively at her kids' schools and church. She hopes to travel more, in the states and abroad, spending more time with those she loves. She can be reached at deb37@bmail.com, www.atouch4wellness.info or 303-995-9919.

Family Matters

The Appearance of Layla and Shaddai

Ruth Sharon

I took a deep satisfying breath. After a delicious picnic lunch at the Colorado National Monument, I meditated for a quiet moment, receiving the glory and beauty of the summer-filled, natural world around me. My husband, Jim and our four-year old daughter, Alaina, quietly started off to explore the dusty path to the left. Needing some time alone, I told them I would be back after I walked off to the right.

"What a peaceful place this is," I thought as I strolled along on the path. Approaching an expansive rocky canyon on my left side, I heard a calm voice say, "Welcome, we've been waiting for you."

Startled, I gasped, "Who is talking to me?" I looked around. The comforting male voice continued, "Please sit down here." I obeyed and sat cross-legged on a large, flat rock in the bright sun. In an instant, a spirited energy emerged from the canyon! I felt a grabbing sensation in my chest. Tears burst from my eyes uncontrollably.

I surprised myself as I uttered, "I have missed you," unaware of who or what this energy was.

"I have been with you all along," a kind strong female voice reminded me. "We have always been together."

"Who are you?" I wondered. "What is this place? What is happening?" My racing mind filled with so many questions; I had never experienced anything like this before.

"We are the Ancient Ones; we have been guardians of the Earth since the beginning. This is a gathering place where we hold council and guide the Earth Beings."

She continued with descriptions of past Earth ages and prophecies for the coming time periods. She also informed me of what we, as humans, must learn to survive. She described the next stages of human development.

I listened at a deep, non-verbal level. My soul resonated with the truth of her words. My heart trembled, yet I felt very calm and oh so awake! She shared mystical techniques and ancient stories. I was in a timeless suspension. A great peace nourished every cell of my enlivened being. I asked her what I can call her and if I could stay connected to her.

"Layyyyy-la," she exhaled the sounds. "I will be, and always have been, connected to you."

I breathed in her name, "Layyyyyy-la," scooping up her essence in my energized hands and gently placing her deep in my heart.

"What does your name mean?" She began describing in pictures that told an ancient story, "Goddess ...Guardian ....Mistress of the Night... of the Darkness, of the Unknown Mystery...…" She was expressing aspects of the Divine Feminine that I would learn about much later in my life. In that moment I nodded, as if I understood, but I truly knew so little of what she spoke about in her mystical wisdom.

Layla then asked me if I was willing to meet someone very special to her.

I said, "Of course," looking around eagerly, waiting for who would appear....

"Later," she simply replied and paused. In the sacred stillness, I knew my life was about to change in ways I could not comprehend. I bowed to her with my hands still palmed over my heart.

"Thank you." I wept profusely, feeling the tight skin of my ego shed off to allow my quickly-expanding soul space to breathe in the mysterious encounter with the Ancient One. Suddenly my body ached to move. I stood up and stretched, yawned, sighed and wiped my tears. "Wow, that was amazing!" My being was light and buoyant.

I floated back to our picnic area to find Jim and Alaina, who had just finished their exploration of the canyon. We were invigorated by our adventures and climbed in the car to head west to our psychology conference at UCLA.

I was silent as I closed my eyes and sighed. I couldn't talk to them. The spiritual conversations kept replaying in my mind. Then a sudden pang of terror attacked my reverie. "Was I imagining the whole thing? Did someone really talk to me? Am I dreaming? What is going to happen next?? Is this for real? Did I really know Layla before? Who was that male voice at the beginning that welcomed me?" My rational mind searched for files to store this new information in...none existed. I was in virgin territory.

Finally, many miles later, my voice broke the silence as I recounted to Jim what had transpired. Precious Alaina napped in the back seat. What a sweet moment! My molecules were being rearranged by a Reality greater than anything I could imagine.

One morning, later that summer of 1981, I awoke with a smile, feeling someone in my room. I sat up and felt Layla instantly. "How did ...did you... find me? I stuttered in amazement.

"I am always with you, remember?"

Then I sensed another energy in the room.

"Who else is here?" I asked her.

"This is who I want you to meet."

As I turned to fix my gaze, he kept shifting out of my range of vision. Otherworldly utterances came from behind me as he and Layla discussed something.

"What's going on?" I could not understand his very strange collection of sounds.

She began to translate his language, reassuring me he was from another level of consciousness. I sat on my bed wide-eyed listening. They talked for quite awhile. Am I hallucinating? Am I still sleeping and dreaming all this? My mind started to race again. I settled my breath, and they were gone. I went about my day, teaching college psychology courses and seeing counseling clients.

As I gradually, yet steadily, learned the practice of meditation and inner silence, I often heard Layla and him converse. I prayed to be open to what was happening and slowly began to understand his utterances without Layla's interpretation. He came alone once I could communicate with him. He told me his name, but I had trouble deciphering whether it was Shaddai or Jaddai. Whenever he came around me I felt ecstatic; my heart and soul were awakening. Months later he asked me a question that would completely reshape my life.

"Will you host me?" I sat stunned. He continued, "I am to come to Earth. I need to learn to maintain a spirit of unconditional love on this dense creation of Earth. Where I come from, the reality is all love, light and peace. We do not know separation and darkness. My soul's journey is to come to this sphere of reality and stay true to this unconditional love, light and peace. Will you host me for doing so?"

"Me? How did you pick me? How does this work? Why me? Am I worthy of this great honor? How can I do this?" My questions gushed forth to fill my bedroom. His only response was deep, unearthly laughter!

The resonance of this joyful sound cleared my mind immediately. My heart and soul whooshed to an expanded reality. I realized at once that my version of life was way too controlled, restricted, limited, narrow, and fearful. I knew that this mysterious being, who was manifesting in my life now, would open a new way of living. I realized my life, as I knew it, was over. With a huge sigh of relief, I shouted inside myself: "YES, YES, YES! I will host you. "

I told Jim that I had agreed to mother a child and asked if he was okay with that.

"Yes!" He responded eagerly…."a son!" Then he hesitated, "What or who am I agreeing to?" We cried in each other's arms, knowing our love would be shared in ways we could not imagine.

This mysterious covenant lingered in me for many years; the laughter expanded in my soul. I felt this great secret tickling me constantly. I couldn't wait for him to come.

A year or so later, I met an inspirational spiritual teacher who asked me, "Who is hanging around you?"

My inner judge jumped to life, "Is this really weird? Should I speak about this? Is it safe? Will he think I am crazy? Would anyone understand that I am in contact with a soul that wants to come in through me?"

I took a deep breath and said timidly, "A soul wants to come in."

He was silent for a moment, as if he was listening to someone unseen. "That's quite a laugh he has!"

I exhaled. "Wow, someone else can hear his laugh. I am not imagining things! This is real!"

I simply replied, "I know!"

Layla and Shaddai/Jaddai, the "dynamic duo" of my universe were my ever-present companions. They entered my dreams, meditations and journal writing. I still did not feel safe to speak to many others about them. This was the "secret of secrets" in my heart.

Several years later, after being separated from Jim and facing many challenges, we decided to move to Denver to reunite and start a new life together. With a mounting passion to offer peacemaking education, I gathered a talented group of people to launch a huge conflict resolution project. During this creative process I became pregnant!

What a thrill! With such great joy I announced to the world that a baby was coming! I read pregnancy books showing the baby's development unfold week-by-week in color photos. I imagined fingernails and eyelashes as my belly swelled. I bought maternity clothes and strutted proudly.

Then one summer night in a mountain hotel where I was leading a seminar, I started to bleed. I bled so much that I had to be rushed to Denver in an ambulance. The doctor in the emergency room showed me the bloody mass of dead tissue that had never really formed as a baby. I was devastated to lose the baby, and even more shocked that I had imagined the details of this baby that never existed. The mind can certainly play tricks on us!

After a full year of recovery, I became pregnant again, and lost the baby again. What a painful process of feeling such disappointment, uncertainty, anxiety and challenge.

Jim and I continued to build our relationship, using the skills and attitudes we shared as therapists. We felt strong enough to hold a baby. Consciously, we conceived our boy at a marriage retreat we conducted for other couples! My pregnancy, labor and delivery were joyful and gentle. I was hearing the laughter again.

Shaddai/Jaddai appeared on earth as Michael David Sharon, born on

June 20, 1988 when I was forty years old! (I had met him in the spirit form seven years earlier).

A sense of completion, satisfaction, accomplishment and sheer exhaustion hovered over the hospital bed. Ahhh! He finally arrived. The labor and natural delivery was powerful. Jim, Alaina, all 4 out-of-state grandparents, many relatives and friends gathered to celebrate his appearance in our family. We held the traditional bris to honor our Jewish covenant with God.

At a mystical Judaism class several months later I learned that Shaddai is a Hebrew name for the attribute of God's Almighty Power. Several years later, as I studied mystical Islam, I found out that Jaddai means the same. Just his name alone was a true testimony of the Reality greater than we can fathom. Such a humble quivering in my being!

We slowly adjusted to the new schedule and way of life. As a mother of a pre-teen and a baby, a professional counselor, a project director/author/trainer, I felt very fulfilled. Just as I was gaining strength and feeling more rested, several major events dramatically shifted our lives. Jim and I were in a terrible car accident that left me injured, in debilitating pain, needing many treatments and therapies. My dear friend died of cancer. My mother had a heart attack. My father-in-law was diagnosed with acute leukemia and died within 3 months. My maternal aunt (second mother) died three weeks later.

What a sleep-deprived, grief-stricken, pain-filled, overwhelming time that was. Meditation was my warm, safe and rejuvenating sanctuary. My spiritual faith, love of God and supportive community sustained me. Alaina at 12 was a great helper with Michael; Jim dedicated his efforts to the smooth running of the household. Life somehow proceeded on day after day.

One peaceful cool morning, I was nursing Michael on my family room couch. I opened my eyes to see the tiny new blossoms signaling Spring. Ah, peace! Layla was present, as she often was. "I'm here!" she announced. "I know, hello," I replied. "No, I mean I am here in your body, you are pregnant."

"What? You didn't ask. Are you trying to kill me? How can I survive this?" I panicked.

"You'll see, it'll be fine. Relax. Just take really good care of yourself. I love you. I need to be with you ...and Shaddai." She beamed rays of happiness into my heart and soul.

Stunned, I told Jim and then took a pregnancy test. Layla was right. My life as I knew it began unraveling. I had just been getting stronger and healing; I had plans, projects, places to go, people to meet—how can I be in control of my life? A power greater than me was definitely in charge. I knew I was being used as a conduit for the appearance of Layla! The pregnancy was delightful. The delivery room nurses and doctor were amazed by the ecstasy I experienced, consciously riding the waves of the contractions. Alyssa Danielle appeared at 3:03 pm on December 31, 1989, when I was forty-one and a half! Her luminescence, beauty and gentleness touched all who met her.

My usual busy pace and drive for accomplishments gradually gave way to a quieter lifestyle of resting, pacing myself, seeking support from friends, family and spiritual leaders/teachers, and learning to receive healing. Yoga, meditation, prayer, and spiritual study became my saving Grace. A dear spiritual teacher came into my life. Through renewed devotion to peace I allowed the softening, loosening, shedding of the ego and the transformation of my life. Jim, our three children and I were enveloped in Love.

With the kind guidance of our spiritual (Sufi) teacher and our rabbi, we simplified our lives. We reduced the marketing of our seminars and train the trainers program, moved our counseling offices to our house, organized our household with family meetings and hosted many peacemaking/meditation gatherings. As a Jewish Sufi, the healing of the "family of Abraham" became my focus. Michael's name as Shaddai (Hebrew) and Jaddai(Arabic) stirred my awakening as a conscious participant in ongoing Jewish-Muslim dialogues in Denver. Praying in Hebrew, Arabic, English and Sanskrit (yoga) expands my consciousness!

As they develop into adults, Alyssa and Michael, very aware of the Layla and Shaddai/Jaddai soul communication with me, are continually clarifying their life purpose. Through our struggles, hardships, challenges, conflicts, joys and triumphs, we have a great respect for each other and our soul purpose as a family. The appearance of Layla and Shaddai has brought great blessings.

Ruth Sharon, M.S., is a Licensed Professional Counselor, Wellness Coach and Consultant, Yoga and Meditation Teacher, Speaker and Team INA Independent Business Owner.

For more information: www.energyforlife.us. Contact her at energyforlife111@ yahoo.com.

The Power of Positive Thinking

Ginny Brannon

I'm not sure how old I was when I understood that my mom was mentally ill, but certainly no later than the age of four. I would later come to know that she was diagnosed as paranoid schizophrenic. But as a very young child, I couldn't comprehend why she spent hours pacing back and forth, sometimes muttering, but completely oblivious to the world around her. Having fought constantly, she and my dad eventually separated and the voices told her to take to the road. We didn't know where we were going. She threw away money if anyone touched her hand when giving her change. My older brother would go to the trash bin and try to retrieve it but was not always able to. After living out of the VW Bug for a while, we finally ended up in a small apartment in Los Angeles. She didn't have a job and there often wasn't any food, but I can't remember if that was because she didn't have money or just hadn't made it to the grocery store. I do remember the feeling of being hungry and of not being sure when I would eat next.

She stayed in her bedroom most of the time. We were enrolled in school, but sometimes the voices told her we shouldn't go, and so we stayed out. One day I recall driving by the school. They were playing Red Rover Red Rover on the playground. How I wanted to join them, but instead was trapped in a confused world dictated by voices I couldn't hear.

Again guided by those voices, we went back on the road without ever knowing where we were going or how long it would take. We lived largely out of the car, which she rolled while trying to make a peanut butter and jelly sandwich while driving. I ended up with a broken wrist. Not surprisingly, the police noticed she was "off" and managed to track down my dad. He came and took us to live with him in a tiny house in China Lake, California where I slept on a cot in the kitchen. It was much better there, but he had problems, including numerous ad-dictions, and would tell us that we were the only reason he didn't commit suicide. An older boy lived next door. He sexually molested me, but I never told. Guess I was embarrassed or just didn't know what to say or what the reaction would be.

Finally, my Aunt Virginia showed up from Colorado and talked my dad into letting us live with her. He agreed and so we moved to her house in Broomfield.

By then I was six or seven and in first grade, but didn't know how to read. We were a bit too much for my Aunt who had never been around children, and we came between her and my Uncle, who was not at all into raising kids. So, after my Uncle moved out, my grandparents stepped in.

My mom's parents were wealthy and so we moved to a beautiful storybook house in the Denver neighborhood of Washington Park. Although Denver schools had a solid reputation, Grandma was concerned about our academics and had heard good things about the Cherry Creek School District and so, after about a year, she and my Grandpa decided we would move to Cherry Hills Village. By the fourth grade, I was almost caught up. It was during those early years that I formed friendships that became my rock, and more than 35 years later, are still my family.

During my junior high school years, my Grandpa moved out of the house. Like my Uncle, he had never fully signed on to raising two more kids, and he and Grandma were arguing fiercely. After he left, Grandma became somewhat unstable and would accuse my brother and I of things we hadn't done. She resented being saddled with the responsibility of raising us and would say so on occasion. Anyway, the punishment for lying was worse than the alleged act, and so I'd admit to things I hadn't done. But at the same time, she could be very loving and supportive and we were in an affluent environment with stable families around us and getting a good education.

While I was still in Junior High School, mom came to live with us after a long stint at the mental health facility at Fort Logan. She did crazy stuff, the list too long to recount. She had to take her meds every day and, when she refused, my brother and I would pin her down on the ground and shove them down her throat.

In spite of all that, between my friends, their parents, and Grandma's good intentions and more sane moments, I had enough support to get through, and even some very happy times during junior high and high school. Still, when the time came to go to college and get out of there, I was thrilled. Grandma set mom up in an apartment and moved to the mountains. My brother and I would drive to Denver from Colorado College in Colorado Springs every week to take mom in to get her shot, but even on meds, she couldn't handle living alone in an apartment. She ended up at the mental hospital in Pueblo and, after a couple of years, they finally said there was nothing anyone could do for her and that she needed to be institutionalized. She spent the rest of her life in a nursing home in Brighton that caters to the mentally ill.

From the age of 18, I was my mom's legal guardian and responsible for her needs beyond her care at the nursing home. She died when I was 39, the first year of my life that I felt truly free.

Now, at age 46, I find myself basically happy. Divorced once but still friends with my ex-husband, no children, great career, and living a fairly carefree life in a loft in downtown Denver. I was lucky that my Grandma afforded me the basic foundation from which to get my bearings and eventually succeed. I am also fortunate to have a family of my own creation. And I survived, even thrived at times growing up, in part because I understood that how we think about what is happening and what will happen largely shapes our experiences. Norman Vincent Peale introduced to me to this notion with his book The Power of Positive Thinking. The lessons in Peale's book are not as trite as looking on the bright side or 'glass half full,' nor are they a call to be happy about everything all the time. It's more like a mode of existence that embraces the notion that thoughts have real power and, in fact, shape our energy, frequency and reality.

Ginny is a natural resources lawyer and lives with her feline companion, "Kitty," in downtown Denver.

Remembering Lily, Remembering Love

Tambra Harck

No one spoke of Alzheimer's back then - if that's what it was. Dementia had been taking moments of her awareness and memory, amplifying her suspicion and anger for years.

How could she not know me? She was the first member of my family to see me, even before my mother. I'd heard the story of my frighteningly frantic birth, "I want you to show her baby to her right now!" my Grandma demanded of the hospital staff. "My daughter is afraid something's wrong with her baby!" I was in another room when my mother awoke from gas they'd forced on her midway through my arrival.

How could she not know me?

Grandma Lily's cognitive function was unpredictable, as memories and know-ing slowly slipped away from her. One day when she lived with my parents, I stopped by for a visit. She led me into her room, showing me photos, telling me remembrances. I didn't know what to say or feel when she picked up a picture of me and said "That's my grand-daughter, Tammie." No one had called me that since I was 10, but something else upset me. She was looking right at me, standing beside me and didn't know it was me she was talking about. Inside I was crying, "I know, Grandma, it's me!" A moment later, she knew, but not because of a photo and not because I said a word. She was back in time, then here, now, with me, knowing.

A year or so later at a hospital visit, I came to be with her moments before she was scheduled for surgery on her broken hip. She was in so much pain. I'd never seen her show pain. Never. Lily was the strongest, most determined force of a woman I'd ever known.

Her physician stopped her pain meds that morning, anticipating she would soon be under anesthesia. Then something happened. A multiple-car accident – ambu-lances with patients whose needs were more urgent than an elderly woman with a broken bone and a waning mind. Other peoples' bodies claimed the operating staff and rooms. She remained in bed for hours. The pain of a broken body unmasked.

When I returned after her surgery, she had no idea who I was. She spoke as if I was a nice woman she'd just met. Was it 1930-something in her mind? Had she just arrived in California? Perhaps that's where she was when she told me, "It is beautiful country here. Maybe I will stay here." She told me that she came out from Oklahoma where most of her big family remained. The oldest of 10 siblings, like many first-born, she was a parent figure to most of them. Now that they were grown, she may stay in this new land.

I left her hospital recovery room, numb. Alone in my car I let myself feel my hurt and confusion. How could she not know me? She had been such a powerful influence in my life. I knew my pain was self-enhanced, thinking of losing her wasn't about her, but I couldn't break free. The spiraling eddy of thoughts and emotions wouldn't release me, dragging me into the muck and mire of my selfish suffering. There, on the ocean floor of my heart, I drove a wedge deep in my chest. Love I felt for her could not be reached or remembered without tugging on my wounded heart.

Love doesn't do that. It doesn't hurt like that. Love doesn't torture us. We do that to ourselves with resistance and unconscious expectations. What did I know of love then?

Clinging to an idea that Lily would be a presence in my life forever, I wanted her to be different with me. I wanted to be as special in her mind as she was in mine, maybe more. Dementia had taken her mind. Soon it would also take her words and freedom.

For the next six years I did something even crueler than dementia ever could. I banished her from my awareness. I did not write, call or visit her. I successfully avoided conversations and memories of her. If my mother, aunt or cousin talked about Lily, I absorbed their ideas and beliefs, having completely abandoned my own.

I was smart - I knew exactly how to close off my heart. I avoided loving stories and caring visits, whatever the cost. This was the best plan ever. I committed to walling myself off from all experiences of intimacy, joyous connection, love and belonging. Selfish self-preservation was my solution. Looking back, I see my soul longed for me to uncover my heart, calling me to release myself from this self-imposed prison. Stubborn and pitiful, I refused to hear the calls for six years.

In the fall of 1995 I lived in my beloved city, San Francisco. A person I met gave me a personal challenge. I sensed judgment in their words. Funny how that is sometimes, a potent message makes its way into consciousness, but the messenger is lost in the fog. The messenger said, "Lovingly communicate with someone for 30 minutes without speaking." I thought, "Pefh, I am an ardent, passionate lover. What do you know?! I do that all the time! That's not a challenge for me. Just ask the man in my life! You'll have to do better than that to challenge me!" For days the words teased me, "lovingly communicate with someone without speaking." Calling to me: Listen. Really listen. My heart wound softened to the sound of the call. I remembered Lily.

By this time she was in a nursing home in Marin County, about 25 miles north of my apartment. I asked my mom how to find her. Sunday afternoon I drove there, alone. I've driven that stretch of Highway 101 thousands of times. Crossing the Golden Gate Bridge, I started thinking of her: Lily, my grandmother, the woman who chose to be mother to my mother and to my aunt. Lily, whose home I lived in as a baby; Lily, who for years now, I knew only through the stories of others.

My drive became a meditation of remembrance and appreciation. I remember it distinctly. I was in ritual. Rituals involve a time when you're gathering energies, preparing for transformation that will come as you emerge on the other side. I drove through Marin, remembering Lily – whose life was bigger than I'd ever fully appreciated.

I reflected on stories I'd heard about her. I pictured her starting that first restaurant in their house with the orange orchard in Ventura County. That was when Grandpa, formerly widowed and with two young daughters, now weak in his organs, became ill, just a few years after they married. She marched down to the bank. "My husband may never work again," she told them, "I have two babies to take care of." They needed to give her a loan so she could convert part of her home into a restaurant. She would call it The Arbor.

Even then, in the 1940's, they lent her the money. She told me this story when I was a teenager, explaining why she never "believed in women's lib." "What's to believe in?" I asked. "It is a movement, not a faith." Clearly, I didn't understand the life she'd led. Women could do what they wanted. She always had. Besides, why would she ever want to burn her bra?

She was not the stereotype of a woman who gave up her identity and personal power to raise her family. That was one of many tales, a series of chapters in a life that involved my mother, aunt, grandfather, and countless other families.

Driving to visit her, all these years later, I could sense the force and fierceness that was this woman who had chosen to be my grandmother. My ritual-remembrance continued.

Tears and laughter accompanied my ritual-remembrance. I remembered more about her than I'd ever known. I must have been in a safe, traveling haven. Driving a motor vehicle while in ritual is not something I recommend! Still, I continued.

I went back to a summer I visited them in the desert. "You don't know what love is!" Her words struck me. I didn't want to remember this moment. Let's remember the gift she was, the joy she brought. Please! But she'd said it. I'd felt it. At nineteen, I was mature in so many ways. Love wasn't one of them. She knew it and called me on it.

Love meant something I could do for someone or something they would give me. It meant duty and living up to expectations. It meant keeping secrets. What I thought of love was a distorted version of cause-and-effect that went something like this:

Cause: If I was strong, smart, productive, frugal, creative, driven, resourceful, talented, pretty, successful and only let them see me in the best light possible, then:

Effect (with Conditions): I could hope that the love someone had to offer would get me something: a job, a boyfriend, some money, a client, an invitation to dance, a role in a play, a roll in the hay. (Effect required me to do my part just right... and then say yes to their offers in just the right way. Then when love did come my way, it would have to be secret.)

"You don't know what love is," she said. I thought she was being intentionally hurtful. It feels that way when truth is said bluntly and in your face. My ritual-remembrance brought new light to her words. Hurt transformed into understanding.

As I drove and remembered, weight that once bore heavy in my heart began to lift. You've heard of skies parting, angels singing, hearts spontaneously bursting open. This was not one of those moments. I'd like to tell you that clogged chambers of my heart broke open, that love coursed through me, source-energy informed, healed and illuminated my being and beyond. It didn't. The opening was subtle. It was one of many moments, over many years that led me to see through eyes of love. I thanked Lily for what she'd tried to show me oh-so-many years before.

When I arrived at her bedside, I was sad to see her. The years had taken her able body, her voice and her vitality. How long had she been here like this? Had this been her life for the past six years? I place my hand on hers and began to lovingly communicate with her without speaking. "I am sorry I forgot you, that I have been afraid of you. I am sorry I didn't come to visit, bring flowers or tell you stories of men - I know you loved them so!" I offered to be her memory, to carry it for both of us, for everyone.

On behalf of the hundreds of families she fed and welcomed in her restaurants, all those men who drove trucks, long away from home, tired and hungry, who found comfort and nourishment in her domain, I thanked her. I celebrated her, the courageous, stubborn, caring, generous, forthright, industrious, creative woman that she was. I honored her roots that were so different from the rest of our family. She was part Cherokee, from a big family, from the South, and so proud of where she came from. I appreciated that she stayed friends with her ex-husband. I didn't know anyone who had done that. I remembered him too, Whitey. He gave us rides in the boot of his back-hoe-such and adventure!

I thanked her for championing me from the start, for teaching and challenging me. I thanked her for choosing to be mother to my motherless mother. How long was I there, gazing in her blue eyes, loving her?

At one point I went into the bathroom, shut the door and cried. A heart that has been closed hurts when it begins to open, discovering how to unfurl, to beat and flow again. Returning to her, I honored my beloved Grandma Lily for showing me just how magical it is when one life touches the lives of everyone around them, and ripples out to the people far beyond their individual reach. Lily's reach extended to family and friends, into communities and beyond. Before I left her side, I sang the song she sang to me all my life, in my mind. It wasn't special for me - and wasn't just for children. She would have taken you onto her lap - or if you were bigger, next to her on the couch - and rocked while she sang it to you, too. You would have loved feeling that loved!

"You are my sunshine, my only sunshine.
You make me happy when skies are grey.
You'll never know dear how much I love you.
Please don't take my sunshine away."

As I silently sang, for the first time since I arrived, she was looking at me, into my eyes. Her watering eyes glistened. I knew in that moment she'd known me all along. She heard the song, a siren, calling her back to herself. I heard it too, calling out from my own heart.

Six weeks after our visit, Lily died. I stood with my mother and aunt around her bed as we sensed her soul leave her body. Even though Lily was not the same bloodline as my mother, aunt, cousin, sisters or me, she is our ancestor. In that room I realized that I am a woman of a lineage of women. I am a healing presence among women who are healers themselves.

Over time I learned to offer my words, voice, touch and intent, even my presence, as I guide others to open their hearts to love. I heal closed hearts, disconnected souls. Men and women who are lost, alone, afraid, enraged, stubborn or confused, calling them back to love. I wonder what Lily would think if she heard me say, "Love is one energy with limitless expressions," as I do each week on my radio show.

There is a camellia outside my front door that produces bright pink blossoms, a gift in remembrance of Lily. Its new buds twist open, showing their color, just as our hearts do when we open to our true selves and to love.

Sometimes I'm aware of her presence, reminding me to be fiercely committed to the choices I make, to stand in my power. Hers is the steady voice that says, "Stories and circumstances of your life do not excuse you from living your greatness. There are people who need you."

I love you, Lily. I am grateful for the gift you were to our family, this world and me.

Tambra Harck is a spiritual teacher who faciliates people to a profound connection to their essential self, their soul. For the past twenty-four years, she has been developing and sharing a message of spiritual and practical wellbeing. Through her speaking, writing, leading retreats and private consultations, she promotes joy, unconditional love and everyday fulfillment. Listen as Tambra engages with spiritual leaders in intimate conversations they openly offer their wealth of wisdom and experience on Joy of Love and Life radio. http://JoyofLoveandLife.com Her new book, Sacred Truths is due for release in Spring 2010. Tambra lives in Benicia, California, and is known for sharing her warm, insightful, trusting nature with her audiences and clients.

Author of My Own Story

Andrea Costantine

Everyone has a story. It's whether we choose to live that story over and over again, or if we choose to create a new story that really makes the difference in how we live our lives. My life was seemingly perfect and happy from my perspective, up until the age of five, when the direction of my story changed forever.

We were living in a small rural community about two hours north of Orlando, Florida. The roads leading to our home were unpaved; the houses sprawled out, each sitting on a few acres of land. My younger brother, older sister, and I would spend our days having fun, playing outside, and running around. We played with our Matchbox cars in the long dirt driveway for hours, driving them back and forth and up and down. Our lives were very care free, roaming around with the other neighborhood kids.

Our mom stayed home with us while our dad worked at the family business, a fast-food-fried chicken restaurant. My parents were young; my dad was barely thirty with three kids and a big responsibility weighing on his shoulders. The business was new, it was slow, and it was not bringing in as much money as anticipated.

Even though my dad worked long hours he would still take me everywhere with him, to work, to baseball games, and other fun places. The family restaurant closed late at night, but we would fight to stay awake as long as we could, waiting for our dad to come home. While we waited the three of us slept on the living room floor, as close as possible to the television as our mom would allow us to get. Then, he'd sneak around to the back door late at night and scare us. "Ahhhhh" we'd all scream in fear and excitement. He'd have a box of left-over's from the restaurant, usually fried chicken livers which was always such a treat; they were eagerly devoured.

He was a gentle, but strong man. Over six-feet tall he towered over my mother, had a large build, wavy brown hair, and crystal clear blue eyes. He was handsome and my mother quite beautiful. People used to say she looked like Olivia Newton-John, and she still does to this day. My mother was quiet; she loved her animals, us kids, and did what she had to do to raise us. She worked hard to take care of the house and run it under a tight budget and limited resources.

Thursday, February 3, 1983, started off as any normal day. It was exactly one month until my fifth birthday. I had a house that appeared full of love and life, but I had no idea that this normal day would end in tragedy, forever changing my destiny. I attended school that morning, worked on counting to 100, tying my shoes, and the typical arts and crafts that a kindergartner does to fill their days. I had dinner with my mom and siblings and was watching the television before going to bed, that's when it all changed.

My father was at work as we were once again gathered in the living room watching some bedtime television. It was late, so it was not unusual that my dad was still at work. Suddenly, my grandparents showed up at our door. Needless to say, my mother was extremely surprised, it was an hour drive from where they lived, and they hadn't called to say that they were coming. I could tell by my mother's expression that this wasn't a typical visit from my grandparents. I remember my grandmother's presence. She appeared as a solid structure, with a look of care and concern in her eyes that I had never seen before. The moments right after that are still a blur to me. The next thing I remember is that we had made the one hour drive back to their home, were dressed in our pajamas and on the sleeper sofa in my grandparent's living room.

We were told to lie down and go to sleep, but the tension in the home was unbearable. At eight, five, and three we all knew something very important was transpiring. Trying to behave, but feeling the tension, we couldn't help but jump around on the sleeper-sofa as we peered out into the family room where my mother and grandparents were gathered.

A man rang the doorbell and entered into my grandparent's home. He sat down on the couch next to my mother, put his arm around her, and she just wept. My grandmother sat on the other side of her, comforting her, all of their heads turned downwards.

From the other room, I felt my mother's pain. I looked at my siblings with curiosity and wondered what could possibly be so wrong that she seemed so sad. Soon after, she joined us in the living room. Tearful, sad, and heavy, she sat down next to us on the pull-out couch. She held us and cried. Then she told us the news. Our father passed away. He wasn't going to be coming home. Ever. He was gone. His life was over. It was just the four of us now.

More than anything, I didn't understand the severity of what that meant, but what I did know was that my always smiling mother was unbearably sad.

The days following were a blur. At the funeral home I wore a beautiful dress, stockings, and white shiny dress shoes. I watched the hundreds of visitors overcome with sadness as they passed me by, expressing their sorrow. Their sadness was contagious. I accepted the many hugs and kisses and love that were passed out that day, each one more saddening than the next. My head stayed focused on the ground beneath me; the look on their faces was too painful.

Soon after his death, his name was barely whispered, his memories slowly removed. My mother coped in the only way she knew how, never talking about him or what happened, and doing what she could to move on. For months we stayed with my grandparents, then my aunt and uncle, then finally moving out of our home to be closer to family. We never returned to the gravesite, and we never asked any questions. That part of our life was over.

At some point in my life I discovered my father didn't die from a car crash, a heart attack, or an accidental death. He took his own life. He left work that day, drove to his parent's home, took their gun, pointed it to his chest and ended his life. He chose to say no to the life he was living and in doing so, left his wife and three young children behind.

Now closer to family, we started a new school, and a new life. My mom was able to continue to stay home with us; using the income she received from the house and social security to support the family. She started dating again, and we'd stay the night at my grandmother's house (just a few minutes' drive away) on the nights she went out.

Before long, she fell in love again. She started dating a man she knew from high school. He was recently divorced, and they instantly hit it off. He soon moved in with us and one night right after dinner they made their big announcement: they were getting married. This didn't go over well. My older sister broke into hysterics, and my brother and I soon followed. What did this mean for us? Was he replacing our already forgotten about father? We were scared and confused, but they did their best to console us.

Once again my life dramatically changed. When they made the decision to marry, my mother also handed over the control of the family to our new stepfather. His parenting style was vastly different from what we were used to. Household chores, yard work, and strictly enforced rules were the predominant theme of the new household.

We moved to a newer and bigger home. They were excited to start their new life together. Unfortunately, as we grew older the tension in the household grew stronger. My oldest sister led the way, rebelling against him every chance she got, leaving many arguments, tears and turmoil.

My step-father also liked to drink. He'd easily finish a twelve-pack of Bud Light a night. I quickly learned that keeping peace was a priority, and as the cans stacked up on the counter waiting to be crushed for recycling, I took it as a cue to mind my P&Q's. My sister felt the opposite. There were many nights when the tension in the house could be cut with a knife. One wrong word could lead to a full-fledged blowout or explosion. At sixteen, my sister left home. She and my step-father came to the conclusion they couldn't get along, and she moved on.

That was a tough time for me. I looked up to my sister, but knew I couldn't follow in her footsteps if I wanted to make it until I was eighteen under their roof. I found a secure place as the peacemaker in the family, knowing exactly how to make my way out of trouble. For the most part, I was able to manage getting along.

As soon as I turned eighteen I moved out of the house. I had two months left to finish high school and moved in with my best friend. After I moved out, my relationship with my step-father began to change for the better.

When times were tough I often wondered why my father left us. Why did he choose the path he did? I don't believe what my father did was wrong; it was a choice he made without the awareness that another path could unfold for him. He was always in my thoughts growing up; despite his death I felt a strong connection to him. I believed he was watching over me. Even though his death was a tragedy, gifts came from it as well. I frequently talked with my brother and sister about how different our lives would have been if we stayed in that rural community. We all believed that regardless of the tragedy, our path was leading us to the place we needed to be.

During my early twenties, I struggled to find my identity, meaning and purpose in my life, and the reasons why I was living. I worked in a job I hated, growing more and more depressed, confused, and lost by the day. In a search for something, I got deep into personal growth and development, went back to school, and sought out new opportunities and experiences. Many people couldn't understand how I wasn't okay with just living a regular mediocre and status-quo life. Stuck in a job I hated, and feeling imprisoned by life, I sunk into a depression yet had a deep desire for something more.

In a desperate search, I jumped around from idea to idea, and job to job trying to find something I was passionate about; something that really lit me up, but time was standing still. I often felt alone, that I was the only one who wanted to do something more with their life. Looking around me, all I could see were people doing what they were told, stuffing their dreams out of memory.

Was this what my father felt like? Was this why he took his own life? In his own search for meaning and purpose, he simply gave up, and said no to living. I could have easily followed in his footsteps, given up hope, and thrown in the towel. But I refused to let that be my story. I refused to let his story (history) repeat itself and instead I threw myself into finding whatever it was. Saying no was never an option for me.

I continued my search for something more, and after years of looking, a few things began falling into place. New people, situations, and events started appearing in my life. As opportunities appeared, I started saying yes. In November of 2008, I attended a four-day workshop on Internet marketing for my new coaching practice. Investing in myself more than ever before, but trusting that I needed to be there. The last day consisted of a few guest speakers – one of which spoke specifically on Life Purpose (Baeth Davis). For the first time in my life, I was in a room with hundreds of people who were actually living their dream and profiting from it.

My whole being was energized and enthused, and I finally saw that life did have purpose. It *did* have meaning. I wasn't quite sure what it was or how to put my feelings into words, but something was different. I called my sister, elated, and told her what I discovered. I wanted her to know that she could find her purpose, her path, and have the meaning that she'd also lost in her own life. We cried on the phone together – knowing that I had stepped into something beautiful.

I finally realized that living the life that you were meant to live simply meant saying YES. Yes to life, yes to opportunities, yes to opening yourself to new things, the exact opposite of what my father had done – the opposite of that resounding no that will echo throughout eternity.

Despite every story or excuse I could have made for myself over the years, I instead chose to say yes. Choosing to change how my story will end, step out of conformity, and do something different with my life. I have a life of purpose and meaning by contributing to this world, helping others, and giving back. I now have a deep a sense of belonging and community that I lacked for so long.

We all have a choice. We can either take the tragedies that happen to us and continue to relive them and make excuses for the sub-par results we get, or we can make a decision to change our story and to create our own reality.

Andrea Costantine is often known as the Soulful Marketer, working with conscious-minded entrepreneurs to help them creatively and consciously share their gifts and talents with the world through believing in their value and being of service to others. She's passionate about service, self-expression, and personal growth. To find out more about Andrea visit her website and download your free conscious entrepreneur resources at www.andreacostantine.com Personally, Andrea completed her Master's of Science in Counseling Studies in 2009, resides in Denver, Colorado with her two cats, and loves yoga, reading, nature and traveling (sometimes with her mom and step-father in their R.V.).

Knowing My Roots and Planting My Trees

Kelly M. Calton

On a recent visit to the Midwest, I was reminded of my roots. After living in the big city for almost a decade, I have forgotten them from time to time. One short weekend back home, and the doors of memory flew open wide, shedding light on how I got to where I am at today.

Born in a small town of 5,000, I grew up sharing summer evenings with my neighbors, graduating kindergarten and high school with my cousins, and spending every Sunday lunch at my grandparents with the rest of my 30+ member extended family. A quick errand to the grocery store was never quick because I always (yes, always) ran into someone I knew. These things rarely happen in the large metropolis where I now reside. And, when they do, boy, am I surprised!

Corn, soybeans, cattle, and pigs. A day didn't pass without hearing about or seeing at least one of these agriculture staples. They encompass the life of a Midwest resident. Our town revolved around the planting and harvesting seasons. Basketball games, church activities, and parent-teacher conferences were scheduled accordingly. There are no days off for farmers; it isn't unusual for my relatives to see the sunrise and sunset in the same work clothes. These people are the hardest working people that I know. Their drive isn't verbally communicated to one another but instead learned by the morning milkings, hot summer detassling of corn, and late night birthing of pigs, cows, and horses. *Hard Working.* Even though I didn't grow up on the farm, this hard work attitude has deep roots within me. I strive to produce quality work I can be proud of and am internally rewarded with the words and feelings of a job well done.

The small town culture was all I knew for 20 years of my life, and I loved it. I didn't realize until I left that the big, bad world outside was vastly different from the quaint, conservative area of the Midwest. Sure, there were problems, but everyone I knew was generally positive.

Death, fires, accidents, and disease occurred, but were followed by showers of love and encouragement from all of those around. Genuine Support. A hot meal. A drive to the doctor. A fundraiser for a local youth group. An extra hand during harvest. These were everyday occurrences done without questions. My hometown understood and demonstrated genuine support with a clear expectation of nothing in return. This is another strand of my roots. It digs deeper and deeper into my new soil, taking hold of the ground and expanding.

I believe I was raised in a tribal community where everyone looked out for everyone else. I rode my bike around town as a 10 year old without a worry in the mind of my parents. The 9:00 p.m. whistle blow reminded kids of the unwritten curfew and sent them all home to their beds. A mention of my last name brought stories of my grandparents, aunts, uncles, and cousins. Carpools were easily arranged and always utilized. There were countless volunteer teachers, chaperones, and coaches throughout the years that motivated me to reach my dreams. Instinctive Mentoring. The older adults in my life instilled a mentoring root in me that I would sow in the years to follow.

I didn't always feel this way about my childhood roots however. I left the Midwest several times to explore other parts of the world, tossing the roots aside like they were old, outdated, and unusable. By the time I graduated from college, I had traveled more outside the US than I had inside. I studied abroad twice, collecting countless souvenirs from various countries and trying to grow new roots. I wanted something different, something that was my own. The desire was one of both passion and resentment. I moved to the big city because of this reason. I was 22, determined to leave what was familiar in hopes of more adventures and new experiences. I was ready to be transplanted.

I found a job within a month of moving. Hired as a first year staff accountant with a small, local CPA firm in the metro area, I was very excited about my new position. I began the 16th of October, the day after the final tax returns were due. Of course, I didn't realize the importance of the various tax deadlines at that point; I was purely book smart and possessed no actual accounting experience. I learned what I could in the following 75 days and soon enough it was time for tax season. Expected to work long hours from January 1st through April 15th, I went above and beyond, working until 10:00 or 11:00 p.m. many nights and always on the weekend. *Hard Working*. Later I found out that I worked more hours than anyone else in the company and was told that I needed to work smarter, not longer because longer did not necessarily equate to more productive. That conversation would be a lesson that I would try to learn over and over again and still think about today.

I later started my own company offering accounting and bookkeeping services to families and small businesses. I work closely with my clients and play a unique role in their lives. At the base level, I enter checks and deposits. But, there is much more than what meets the eye. I become a resource, a businesswoman who walks alongside, someone to bounce ideas off of. As a small business owner myself, I realize the need for an outside and unbiased opinion. By assisting others with their finances, we work together to determine solutions that will work for them. Genuine Support. This support doesn't come just because I possess a CPA license, but comes out of the organic way that I want to support the local businesses I now serve.

New clients usually come to me when their finances are unmanageable. Too many transactions, too many accounts, too many companies. It doesn't matter what the situation, I immediately move into teaching mode. I explain the different financial statements and why they are important. I model how to do a budget and project their cash flow. We work together to find a good recordkeeping system for them. The focus on teaching and learning allows my clients to gain control of their finances and restores a sense of hope. Instinctive Mentoring. By helping families and small businesses understand their finances, they are equipped to make better financial decisions and to be financially free.

I had visited my hometown regularly after leaving, but it wasn't until four years later I realized something had changed. I saw beauty in the land and kindness in their hearts. I distinctly remember sitting on the airplane wondering why I had bottled up so much bitterness for a place so remarkably sweet. The 1 ½ hour flight back to my new home marked the turning point toward the appreciation of my old home. My roots were waiting just where I had left them. I carefully inspected them, this time knowing why they were mine.

Today, I am clearly witnessing the growth of my small town roots. They are planting my big city trees. I am transplanting my values of Hard Work, Genuine Support, and Instinctive Mentoring into a new terrain. I chose to start my own accounting business so that I would be able to impact those around me. I want to work within the values that touch me to the core. I don't want to represent someone else who doesn't share my same small town roots.

It's no coincidence that I am working with families and small business owners. The small town culture of one-on-one, personal relationships shaped my business. In order to fully enjoy my work, I need to know that I am making a positive difference in the lives of others. I learn my clients' passions, family names, and recent vacations. This doesn't help me with the debits and credits, but it does help me understand why the bottom line is so important to them. In an environment where we hide behind the computer screen, it is nice to connect with someone, learn their goals, and influence their future.

When I work with people, I realize that it takes a huge amount of trust to divulge financial information. Money is emotional, and it affects everyone differently. No matter if I am working with a multi-millionaire or a person filing for bankruptcy, I am honored to be the person they selected to work with. Because our American lifestyle focuses so much on money and what it can or cannot do, the dollars and cents can be overwhelming. If I can help ease the burden, even a little, I have accomplished something. This is worth more than any fee I could charge.

My clients are my clients because we have a similar alignment. I know that it has something to do with the roots. We share values and water each other with encouragement. We want to impact the soil around us. We want to grow into tall trees together – a big city forest starting only because of small town roots.

Kelly has provided accounting, bookkeeping, and Human Resource support for families and companies in the Colorado area since 2002. She is passionate about providing services that become solutions and strives to make asset management less stressful and easier to understand. Kelly is a Certified Public Accountant, is on the Board of Directors for the Credit Union of the Rockies, and serves on the finance team of her church. When she's not working, you can find her outside, tending to her city garden. Visit www.confluencefamilyoffice.com for more information.

The Choice to Break Free

Tammie Limoges

She was 4 years old at her earliest memory. She hid in the closet, peaking out through the horizontal slits of the door and hoping that he wouldn't realize she was there. There, watching his anger grow, his screams getting louder, the curses and threats rolling off of his tongue, she saw the emptiness in his eyes. He felt nothing, and tomorrow, he would remember nothing.

He would awake the next day as if nothing had happened. As if he hadn't hit his wife, and hadn't thrown his older daughter against the wall when she tried to step between him and her mother in a small effort to save her from just one blow. He would remember nothing of the threats of killing all three of them and putting their bodies into the pond on their property. No one would ever know and they wouldn't be missed, he would say. With the revolver pushed to her temple, she stared at her mother and sister and cried out. Cried for help that she knew wasn't coming.

There was no way to reason with this man, who started his day by cracking open a can of beer and finished the day with a bottle of whiskey. This evening was one of many that ended with him finally passing out, and the two little girls helping to clean the blood from their mother's face and clothes before laying down thinking of the next day to come, which was sure to be much like this one. As she lay in bed each night, she thanked God that on this day there were still four beating hearts, broken but still beating. Before closing her eyes, she thought of the duffle bag under her bed which contained two clean outfits, a nightgown and an extra toothbrush. She also thought of her favorite toy, and made a mental note to take it with her if they needed to escape in the night.

Each day presented an opportunity for the story to change, and many times she thought it had. Grabbing the duffle bag and anything else that she could quickly get her hands on before being shoved into the car, she hoped for a better life. Not all families were like this and she always knew it could be better. After escaping for a few days to her grandmother's house, he would always come groveling back. Her mother would forgive him and go back, believing his promises that this time would be different.

At 8 years old, her dream came true. Her mother had been in the hospital for several weeks and had just returned home. He had been horrible to live with during this time and despite their effort to clean their messes, fix dinner, and do their homework, they could never do it good enough. With no one there to protect them from the monster, she and her sister suffered several beatings. Her mother felt that she could no longer suffer through these brutal nights so they packed up, and snuck out for the 3 hour drive to her grandmother's house. Traveling this deserted stretch of highway was always welcome. This was the road to peace, love, stability. No one talked about the episodes, or why they had come to visit grandma. And no one talked about the divorce that was being filed.

Sometime that year, her mother met someone new and before long, life was changing. They soon married and Bo was all that she could hope for in a father. He was kind and caring. He was attentive and affectionate and she loved it when he took her to school each morning in his police car. Much to her glee, he would turn on the siren or lights as they pulled into the parking lot and sometimes, to her delight and that of her friends, he would let them play with his flashlight or handcuffs. They lived in a mobile home in a poor but welcoming town of only a few hundred people in rural Mississippi. They were poor, and being one of only a couple of white families they were different, but life had turned a corner and she was sure that happiness was waiting for them.

The backyard was filled with stickers that poked deep into the soles of your feet and at the far end of the yard was a swing set. The only one they had ever owned. It was rusty and unstable, but gave the young girls hours of laughter. One afternoon, their new stepdad barreled out of the back door leaving it open and swinging. Without a word to them, he left. This was not behavior they had seen before and they rushed into the house to ask their mother what was going on. They found her balled up on the floor in a pool of blood. Her pink and white striped button-down oxford shirt completely soaked in red. She was unrecognizable with teeth missing and most of the bones in her face broken. Without a phone, they ran to the neighbor's house and found no one home. They were afraid to leave her alone for fear that he would come back or that she would simply give up and fall into a never waking sleep. At 8 and 11 years old, it was difficult to lift her battered body and drag her down the street to find someone with a phone, but they knew it was the only way to save her. Several weeks passed, and their grandmother refused to let them go to the hospital to see their mother. The bruising and swelling were too severe and she was undergoing reconstructive surgery to make her look like the woman she had been before. No charges were pressed, no jail time had for this brutality. Months later, they learned that he had gotten mixed up in drugs and the guilt of the incident had prompted him to commit suicide.

To the surprise of the girls and the family, a few months later she packed them up and moved back to the man she had originally fled. She reasoned that it was easier to go back and know what life would be like than to trust someone to love and care for you and have them destroy that with the blow of a fist.

Days turned into weeks, turned into months, turned into years. She always knew that the moment she turned 18 she was getting out. Getting out of this abusive and violent home and not looking back. She would make better choices. There was happiness out there. Her life would be different.

After high school, she moved out to attend college only 20 short miles away. She was on her own but found herself in an unhealthy relationship with a man who began to be abusive. She knew this road was not leading to her destination and on New Year's Eve, she packed up all that she owned into the back of her pickup truck and set out to find her happiness in another community, in another state, in a New Year. The sun came up over Tulsa as she pulled into town on January 1st, the first day of her new life.

Over the next 2 years, she settled into her new surroundings and dreamt of a life that she was not sure she would ever live. However, one day a door opened and she decided to walk through. It wasn't an opportunity to go back to college after dropping out after only three semesters. It wasn't a job with a great salary that would allow her to buy an expensive home or clothes. It was an opportunity to travel around the world for a year, where she would perform in a musical show and perform community service. It was everything that encompassed who she was and what she wanted to experience. She never could have imagined that she would not only have the opportunity to be on stage for thousands of people, or that she would experience helping the homeless one day and reading to the elderly the next, or that her future husband would be there, waiting to experience it all with her.

Thirteen years have passed since the day that a little girl moved on from the life she was dealt to the life she chose. That little girl grew up to be me, a woman who tries to give her children the things that I didn't have. I share my life with a man who inspires and values me. I go to work each day to a nonprofit organization where I support a mission to help the greater good, and I raise my children in a loving and secure home. As a mom, a wife, and a woman, I believe we all have a choice in life to break free from societal or familial expectations to find who we are. When a path didn't present itself in my life, I beat down trees, moved boulders, and cleared my own way to have a life filled with laughter, happiness and security.

Tammie Limoges was born in Mississippi and grew up in south Arkansas. She now lives in Colorado with her husband and 3 children and has a successful career in non-profit management.

Overcoming Impossible Odds

Carole Warga

Baking in the oppressive January heat in Equatorial India, I tried to smile pleasantly and pay attention as the young youth pastor enthusiastically told me not only that I would become a mother, but also the sex and exact date of the birth of my child.

Really loud conflict alarms began to go off in my head as I fought to control my mind. I was telling myself, "This kid is only 18, what does he know about life in America? Doesn't he know I have already been through all of this and it just isn't going to happen? The doctors say I can't ever have children. Is this what Sarah and Hannah felt like?" (Remembering the Biblical women I had studied in my three-year quest to give birth to a living child).

Just weeks before, I had closed my resume' writing business and concluded the final execution of my mother's estate. I went on a mission trip to India in an effort to change the direction of my life and determine what the future would hold for me, and my very broken marriage. I really wanted this to be a time of self-reflection and hopefully open a door in my heart that would allow me to love again.

As this very sincere young man concluded his dialogue, I nodded and silently prayed for a distraction to enter the room and change the course of the conversation. I just wanted it all to be over. I didn't think of myself as one of the matriarchs of Scripture who were told of the birth of her child by means of some divine counsel. I truly felt I was not worthy of any such reward.

Failure seemed to pursue me everywhere, and I could quickly cite numerous events that supported this line of thinking. I had been engaged to nine different men and actually married none of them; I had an abortion before marriage; failed at every job I ever held; and now was resigned to my failure to conceive a child. While I was married to a very forgiving and loving man, all these things had taken a toll on the promise of a bright future together. We had struggled together for eight years by this time and had finally decided to give up on the whole idea of becoming parents. We had even failed at adopting. We were ready to move forward and stop looking at our failure.

Yet here I was sitting with this man who was opening up the door of hope again, and telling me, "You will conceive, you will have a son, and he will be born at the New Year."

Questions started to flood my mind and heart as our conversation concluded. Should I mention this to my husband? No, I decided, that would just open up a wound that was just beginning to heal. I would carry this burden alone, just me (and God), it would be our special secret, and that way if it didn't really happen then no one would be the wiser. And absolutely, I was never going to communicate with this young man after I returned home, I quickly decided, as he handed me his address and asked me to send a picture of the child.

I made a lot of rapid-fire decisions in only a few minutes, all based on error. Error that I was not qualified on so many levels to become a mother. After all, I was a true failure in every sense of the word, or so I thought. But God had a different plan.

I arrived back in the USA about a week later ready to keep my secret and get on with my life. A few days after my arrival, my dear grandfather died and I was consumed with caring for my family through another tragic death scenario. Having no business to run left me with nothing to do all day, so I spent a lot of time reading and processing over the next several months, and pretty soon it was winter again.

I looked at the calendar in November and realized I was not pregnant and breathed a sigh of relief and joy realizing that I would never have to face the pain of childbirth, and the scary scenarios involving raising a child in the difficulties of life today.

My husband and I decided to find a home closer to his job and we ended up moving south about 80 miles. At the end of April 1998, we moved our belongings into a new house and left behind my perfect home for raising kids. The plan was that we would move all the boxes and furniture, he would go on a business trip and I would unpack and organize the house. It seemed like a good plan at the time.

I slept on the couch the whole next week! All the boxes remained unpacked and I thought I was just depressed and exhausted from moving. Then on Saturday morning we were fixing breakfast. Actually, I was still on the couch and my husband was cooking bacon. Suddenly, I needed to run to the bathroom, overcome with nausea. Afterwards, I threw myself on the bed in frustration and cried out, "God, what is wrong with me?" I wept tears of frustration, feeling an overwhelming sense of worthlessness—now I couldn't even keep a simple commitment to unpack boxes!

It was at this point that everything in my life changed forever. I saw a vision of myself standing in my church. My pastor was in front of me and he was holding my hands in his and praying. Then I heard him say, "Daughter, I am restoring that which was stolen from you." While this didn't literally happen, I saw it in a dream-like image during my stricken emotional state. I really thought it was just something I was wishing for.

The next day I told my best friend about it, and she asked me if I was pregnant. I laughed, and she said, "You have all the symptoms." My mind went into rewind and I realized that it had been about 16 months since the young man in India had said I would conceive. I reasoned, "But he said that the baby would be born at the New Year." Then I realized that he never said what year – only at the New Year.

After church my friend and I went to the store and bought one of those convenient home pregnancy tests. We formed a conspiracy, agreeing that I would use it the next morning and call her right away, and for right now, we wouldn't say anything to our husbands. But that was such a hard secret to keep, because all afternoon we were exchanging glances and smiles, and remembering hopeful conversations we had exchanged in years past of what might happen one day for me. The guys knew something was up—and finally by the end of the day we could hold it in no more and blurted out we thought I was pregnant.

The look on their faces said it all. My husband's face turned white as a sheet and I thought he would fall down! Later that evening in the privacy of our home, I quietly shared the story of the experience in India with my husband. He took it in, and neither of us slept much, because all the old dreams and pain returned.

The next morning, the moment of truth had arrived. It was the day after Mother's Day, 1998. The test: POSITIVE. Step one happened—I had conceived. We did some quick calculations and realized that the baby would be due around the 10th of January. I wondered if that was what God meant by the New Year.

For some reason, I vividly remembered every detail of the morning in the hotel lobby in India. Suddenly, I wanted only to contact that young man. But in my haste to deny what he was saying, I had discarded his address and had nothing left except his first name in my memory.

I was happy, and scared, and for the first time I wanted to talk to my mom, but she was gone. There were no women in my life to turn to for advice. So I called a doctor and made an appointment. I tried to explain on the phone that I had experienced an ectopic pregnancy 8 years before and we needed an ultrasound exam right away to determine if I was having another one. They reluctantly made an appointment.

When I went in for the exam the doctor said, "Because of your advanced age, we should probably abort this pregnancy." I remember looking him straight in the eye and saying, "Are you a Christian?" He responded with a cautious, "Yes." Then I asked him, "Have you ever known God to botch a miracle?" He was immediately offended and I left, committing to never return to his office for my prenatal care.

I called the gynecologist in the town I had moved from, and scheduled a 12-week check-up. She also confirmed I was pregnant, and that the baby was due January 6, 1999.

I went through most normal pre-natal experiences I suppose, except one; the day they did the expanded ultrasound examination at 5 months gestation. During this exam we were able to determine the sex of the baby. My husband was present when we clearly could see that I was carrying a boy. I recall my husband being very disappointed as we walked to the car, as he had always hoped for a little girl. I was just trying to peel my banana because I was always hungry, as I casually explained the fullness of what I had been told while in India 20 months before. I explained that I was beginning to think that the young man who spoke those words to me may have been speaking for God after all.

There were no other significant experiences in the months that followed, but near the middle of December my doctor decided to induce my labor on December 30, 1998 because she wanted to go on a skiing trip with her family and was afraid that I would deliver while she was out of town.

So, on December 31, 1998, baby Nathan was born at 4:19 a.m. God's promise was true, I did conceive, I did have a son, and he was born at the New Year.

Now I know all mothers think that their children are special, but the circumstances of this birth are certainly unique. I am sharing this story with you today because I want you to know that even though you may have failed at things you have tried, there is a power beyond yourself that wants you to achieve your purpose in life. My purpose began with the birth of this child, and my passion is helping children around the world who think they cannot overcome their adversities.

Allow me to encourage you to press into the deepest desire of your heart and pursue it, and even if you feel like giving up, or do give up, like I did—your future will pursue you, and perhaps send you half-way around the world so you can get on the path to your future. With God all things are possible!

Carole Warga is a full-time mom on a mission to help disadvantaged and suffering children around the world by giving generously from the proceeds of her business. Married 21 years, her son is now 11. She shares her dreams, passions and experiences to help people develop business skills so they can achieve more prosperity in their lives. She someday hopes to own and fully staff a 747 aircraft to fulfill her passion of helping orphans. This tool would bring medical supplies, school supplies, nutritional supplies, seeds, as well as teachers and medical professionals to third world countries. Available as a speaker, Carole can be reached at carole@goritraining.com. She specializes in topics related to the application of basic business skills and strategies in changing market environments. Visit her website at http://www.achievers-success-center.com.

Role Reversal

Marjorie Webb

The door that opened, throwing me into an entirely different role, swung wide open on October 23, 2003, my 52nd birthday. That was the day I left Colorado with my daughter and three grandchildren to Iowa for a short, spur-of-the moment visit with my elderly mother.

In July, just three months prior to that day, Mom, my older sister, Dianne, and I met in Chicago where we celebrated both of their July birthdays. Although I visited my mother a couple of times every year, it had been three long years since I had seen my sister.

During our visit, we pampered ourselves splurging on such things as high tea in the elaborate lobby of the luxurious Drake hotel, lunch in the Signature Room on the 95th floor of the Hancock building, a harbor cruise, and the fun of ordering pizza delivered to our hotel suite at eleven o'clock at night. The highlight of our Chicago trip was when we enjoyed the formal dinner cruise on Lake Michigan aboard the Odyssey, a fancy yacht. As the dinner-cruise ended, we watched a spectacular fireworks display over the lake without one single clue as to what direction our lives were about to take.

Dianne and I emailed each other nearly every day, and one of us would call the other once or twice a month. We would chat for over an hour at a time. Sometimes we discussed whether or not to intervene and move Mom closer to one of her three daughters. Mostly, however, we talked about our children and grandchildren, our jobs, current events, the latest book we'd read or the latest movie that we'd seen.

During one of our conversations, sometime after our Chicago trip, I mentioned once again my concerns about Mom starting to go downhill. "She's not eating, Dianne. When I asked her what she had for lunch, she told me a half can of soup. So, I asked her what she had for dinner, and she said, the other half-can of soup. I don't think she's taking her medication, either, because she hasn't cashed any of my checks for two months."

"I think we should leave her on her own as long as we can," Dianne suggested. "I've heard that as soon as you move them into a nursing home or an assisted living arrangement, they start to decline very rapidly. And the average life span for them is about two years after they're admitted." At first, I felt relieved that my older sister felt comfortable with Mom living alone. I was happy thinking I didn't need to worry about Mom just yet.

"After all," she reminded me, "Mom still goes to her job every day, and it's good for her to have that outlet. It helps her get out and have something to look forward to each morning, to be useful and feel needed."

For the past couple of years, Mom had been working in the Grandmother's Program, a government program intended for helping senior citizens by keeping them active while they also earned a small salary. The seniors were assigned to an elementary school teacher they assisted in the classroom by reading stories to the children and helping students with their class assignments.

"I can't do this anymore." The anguish in my mother's voice told me she was talking about more than just balancing her checkbook. Her phone call one afternoon in late September seemed more like a cry for help, rather than a remark made in conversation that she couldn't figure out her bank balance. A sudden rush of emotions overwhelmed me: fear, love, concern, and worry, but I didn't know what to do. About a week after Mom's anguished phone call, while I was sitting at my computer at work, my daughter called me.

"Let's go see Grandma during fall break. The kids are out of school the last week in October. We'll get a couple of rooms at the Double Tree, there's a pool, and we can get adjoining rooms so that Grandma can have her own room. We'll take my van and buy her a bunch of groceries at Costco and get her all stocked up with foods that would be easy for her to fix."

"Okay!" I readily agreed thinking ahead of a visit back home to see Mom again. "You go ahead and make our reservation, and I'll arrange to get the time off work. It'll be fun." I felt happy as I hung up the phone thinking that everything was going to be okay.

"I'm going to Iowa to check on Mom." I announced to Dianne when I called her later that week. "Danielle and I are thinking of going shopping for her at Costco and stocking her shelves with canned goods. We think that might make it easier for her to fix her meals. I don't think she is buying food when the senior bus takes them grocery shopping every week. Silence. "Why don't you come with me, Dianne; it might be fun? We can take her out to dinner while we're there, and we can spend some time visiting while we assess the situation."

Dianne sighed. After a long pause she finally asked, "Well, when are you thinking of going?"

"I am planning to go the last weekend in October so that Danielle and the kids can go, too. Will you join us?"

"No, I'm busy that week. Why don't you make it for another weekend? I've signed up for a bird-watching walk on that Saturday."

"Because," I answered, "That's when the kids are out of school and I want Danielle to go with me so that she can help with the driving. Can't you do the bird walk another time?"

"Well, I would just let the bird-watching tour go," she explained, "but I've paid for it, and I don't think I can get a refund on my money. Besides, I've been looking forward to it. You go visit Mom and let me know how things are. You can call me when you're there."

When we first arrived in town, we drove directly to the senior housing where Mom lived. We didn't even need to go inside her building, for she was anxiously waiting downstairs by the door with suitcase in hand. Danielle had made reservations for two adjoining rooms at the Double Tree hotel in Omaha. We planned to get Mom settled into her apartment with all of her groceries from Costco on Sunday afternoon, and then leave for home on Monday morning. The kids could hardly wait to swim in the pool at the hotel.

Later that night, after we'd settled into our hotel suite, we set up the karaoke machine we'd brought with us. Singing along with some of our favorite tunes, we celebrated my birthday and our time together. I always enjoyed being with my mother, she was so full of life and enjoyed any chance for a celebration. Her hearty laugh was contagious and soothing to my soul. We laughed and sang the entire evening until well after midnight. I didn't want to think past that happy evening or worry about anything that might lie ahead of us. I pushed all negative thoughts aside and just enjoyed being with my mother.

On Sunday, we drove to her apartment, as planned. The moment that we opened the door, my life changed forever. My daughter and I stood in disbelief and solemnly turned to each other with a look on our face that said *what do we do now?*

The situation was much worse than any of us had suspected. Mom's apartment was in total disarray. There was food rotting on the counters, dirty dishes in the sink, clutter of books, magazines, newspapers, and piles of junk mail strewn throughout the small one-bedroom apartment. Mom's laundry basket, filled with clean clothes, was sitting in the middle of the living room. Her pots and pans were leaning along the wall surrounding the dining room.

When I went in to use her bathroom, I was horrified to find I could not sit on the toilet seat of my own mother's bathroom. It appeared that Mom had an accident missing the toilet seat when she'd had a bout of diarrhea. Because of her macular degeneration and failing eyesight, however, she surely must not have seen that the toilet seat was smeared and dirty. I felt like crying when I stood looking at the sight before me, yet I also felt panic starting to rise up within me.

"Rachel, please watch Dane so he doesn't try sticking anything into his mouth." Danielle put her oldest daughter in charge of my 14-month old grandson and immediately started cleaning the bathroom. Hearing the sound of her voice brought me back to the task at hand, and I immediately jumped in to help.

"I'll start in the kitchen," I said aloud as I left the filthy bathroom to my daughter. Together we gathered up and emptied the trash, scrubbed the bathroom and washed the dishes, folded and put away the laundry. Later, while we were in the kitchen away from Mom's hearing, Danielle whispered to me, "Mom, you'd better do something. We can't leave her here. We need to take her back home with us."

Slowly, I walked into the living room where Mom was sitting. "Why don't you come out to Colorado with me, Mom? You could just take a look at this place that my friend has suggested; see what you think."

"Well, okay," she agreed. I sensed that she was actually relieved that I was taking her out of her apartment and back home with me, even if just for a visit.

"I'm taking her home with me to Colorado, Dianne. You wouldn't believe her apartment, it's just so heartbreaking!" I called my sister later that night from our hotel room and described the scene we'd found and the terrible sadness that I was feeling, realizing our mother had been living that way for several months.

"Well, I suppose we'll have to get together sooner or later and clean out her apartment." My sister sounded straightforward as she communicated her plans over the phone. She would take time off work and bring her oldest daughter, Jennifer, with her when the time came to sort through all of Mom's things.

"We'll need to decide what's going to Colorado and what to throw out. I'll need to drive the car so I can bring things home with me in my trunk. I can leave work with only one or two day's notice. So, be sure to call me when you make any decisions."

I sat silently clutching the phone wondering why Dianne was already thinking about what she wanted out of Mom's things and not what Mom's future held. I imagined a scene of too many people in Mom's tiny apartment fighting over who gets what. We finished our phone call and I slowly put down the phone.

God help us get through this I thought as tears formed in my eyes. I felt like I'd had the wind knocked out of me, slugged in my stomach with a large invisible fist. My heart was heavy with sadness, and I could hardly swallow because of the huge lump that had formed there. I didn't want to think that far ahead just yet. I couldn't imagine dispersing Mom's things while she sat helplessly watching us tear apart her home.

"Do you mind waiting one more day, Danielle, so I can go to Mom's doctor's appointment with her tomorrow?" I meekly asked my daughter, thinking it was almost too much to ask. I assumed she'd want to get on the road as soon as possible to head for Colorado.

"Sure, we can do that, not a problem." I felt relieved when she readily agreed it was important to hear what Mom's doctor had to say. As it turned out, he confirmed that she's going to need some help. After I told him I had already decided to take Mom home to Colorado with me, he went through the long list of meds that she was supposedly taking. He explained that he couldn't be sure if she had been taking them as prescribed. He didn't think she was keeping track of her blood sugar, so he wasn't sure about the dosage. If the medicine he'd prescribed in the past didn't work, he would add another one or increase the dose. If she started taking them, now, as currently prescribed, it might be too much, and her blood sugar might go too low causing her to lose consciousness. "If that happens," he warned, "Stop giving her Metformin. You'll have to keep track of her blood sugar every day."

Heartbroken that my mother's independence was coming to an end, I was also very scared. I couldn't know how much longer we would have her, for her health was failing. More importantly, I didn't have a clue where to start or what to do as her caregiver.

I raised two daughters, so what could be so difficult? I was afraid of all those prescription meds. Scary thoughts started racing around in my head: *What if I get the meds mixed up? What if I give her too many or not enough? What was it he said about the dosage, and what was it that I am supposed to do if her blood sugar gets too low?*

My thoughts continued racing as I sat alone in the bathroom of our hotel room where we'd stopped for the night. Everyone else was asleep, and I was alone with my anxiety. My mother slept peacefully in her adjoining room. She seemed so fragile and childlike. I knew I would have to be strong for her, she was depending on me.

One step at a time, I answered my own question. *We will take each day as it comes, and no matter what happens, I will handle it*, I told myself, trying to believe it. For now, I needed to get some sleep. Tomorrow we would be home in Colorado. Tomorrow I would figure out what needed to be done, taking care of my mother. My role had completely changed in one short weekend from daughter to caregiver and I was ready to get started.

Marjorie is thoroughly enjoying retirement. She lives with her husband in a rural area about 45 miles south of Denver, Colorado. They enjoy travelling all over the world and scuba diving together. She has been blessed with two daughters and eight beautiful grandchildren and is happy they all live near her. Marjorie has always enjoyed writing and finds it helps her work through anything. She believes the process of writing brings healing. At the time she lost her mother in April, 2005, she felt she would never get through the grief. Writing about it helped her accept the loss and learn from her mother's death. Marjorie can be reached at scubidi@msn.com.

Beginnings and Triumphs

Sharon Ledford

I was born 4th in the line of 6 with three sisters older, one sister my junior, and the youngest, my baby brother. My younger sister and brother would not come to existence for my first five years of life. These five years, being the baby, there was love and trust, thus I was made to feel special and secure. For me, those were my formative years.

We lived initially near my maternal grandmother, in Lafollette, Tennessee, a podunk town on the ridge of the Smoky Mountains. As I recall, life was a struggle and we learned to survive. Life began, born into a poverty-stricken lineage with rampant alcoholism. I was told we moved north shortly after my second birthday, moving near my paternal grandmother's house to another small town of Corning, Ohio, with coal and mining the main economical structure. We were now closer to my father's family, nine brothers and one sister.

Life in the early years was very unsettled, moving from state to state, my father always in search of employment. He was a brick mason by trade and would leave home early in the morning to head off for his temporary day jobs, when one was available. He often was home before noon, staggering amongst us with verbal threats to stay quiet and hidden. Counting the pennies from my father's emptied pocket remains a golden memory for me. I was learning to count and beginning to save. A penny saved is a penny earned. This simple gesture made an impact on my soul.

My personal growth stems from all the stories in my childhood. I remember my mother having to take on meaningless jobs to support the growing family as my father skirted from job to job. She'd bake pies for local truck stops, drive a fork-lift in the local warehouse or waitress late at night to pay the bills. She would remind us all that her graduation from high school was something to be proud of. A diploma meant opportunity. Her message was loud and clear, stay in school and get an education. College was unheard of, beyond reach. Her teen years were limited. She married out of high school beginning life as a mother at 18.

We left Ohio shortly after I started kindergarten, moving north in search of a better life. The south was in a deep depression, but Michigan was thriving, blazing with the booming auto industry. Life seemed pleasant, but my father's drunken state became the norm. Then my sister and brother were added to the already struggling family. Alcohol and the burden of raising a family stripped all the life and hope out from under my father's feet.

Both parents became jobless. My father's alcoholism escalated us into poverty even further. The eldest sisters began to act out, skip school and began to look for love in the wrong places. My mentors, my sisters, each dropped out of school, became pregnant and got married by age 16-18. As I ventured off to elementary school, into junior high, survival was my way of life. Off to school by day hiding the shame that surrounded me at home, I tried to fit in with other school children. I learned quickly that I was shunned and ridiculed by my classmates. I clung to others that were shunned. Easily impressed by others, I found myself being led into the wrong crowd. I became a follower. At the age of 15, I so desperately sought love and acceptance by others that I began to hang out with hippies. Remember, this was the late 60's, early 70's. All around me was sex, drugs and rock 'n roll. Unfortunately, I was easily impressed and seduced by the inevitable. I was impregnated at 15 and a mother at 16.

I felt despair, embarrassment, and shame. Escaping into the world of denial, I was able to hide the truth from my parents, for 6 months. Each and every day I wholeheartedly believed it was not happening. Denial was my only friend at that point in my life. I never told anyone what was happening inside me. My eldest sister was first to uncover my daunting secret. As tears flowed down my cheeks, and the truth was revealed, I understood, in a household of denial and dishonesty, anything could be hidden, even yourself.

Following the footsteps of those before me, I felt doomed. My spirit and strength deep inside me realized my mother's worst nightmare: graduation from high school and opportunity might be stripped away. I could not and would not let that happen. I promised my mother, no matter what, I would graduate from high school. I did not marry my child's father. I lived at home with my parents. They helped me raise my first born, my son, Shane.

I was a high school student by day, mother by night. Having the help of my parents gave me leeway to wander off after school. Struggling to fit in, I once again connected with a malignant crowd. We rallied and marched against the Vietnam War, smoked pot, listened to loud music and experimented with sex. You'd think I'd learned once, but like my sisters, I went "looking for LOVE in the wrong places." I found myself pregnant again at age 17. In the year 1972, I married, graduated from high school, and gave birth to my daughter, Angela. In those days, pregnant girls were separated from the high school and sent off to be schooled with other like girls. These days were the first days of inspiring others. Staying motivated, I managed to graduate from high school. Nine months pregnant, in graduate cap and gown and standing in the ring of fire, I would not shrink away.

Unfortunately, I found myself living my mother's life. I married an alcoholic like my father, and both of us were unemployed with two small children. I had never taken the time to get to know myself or what I wanted. I had to thank my mother for the simple message of staying in school. I made up my mind. I chose to be different. I seized the opportunity to adapt to the circumstance and right my actions. I felt lucky, I understood early on. I was not going to blindly accept my life as it was. I knew if I were to survive in this toxic, stressful, unhealthy world I had to approach things differently. I researched careers that would create stability, longevity and opportunity for growth. I chose nursing, because it offered all the criteria I had listed.

While living in poverty, attending nursing school seemed out of reach. But, I took advantage of a great thing, government sponsored education. I completed my entire associate degree with a government sponsored program. I used the program the way it was designed, to get citizens off welfare. I'm proud to say I beat the odds. Because I launched myself into school, my confidence to reach for a dream and the adventure of life became alive. My husband became threatened and plummeted into further alcoholism. I was not going to be betrayed, shriveled, or close myself away, so I left him. We divorced, but I continued on with nursing school, graduating as a single mom. My children at my side, this was their initiation of persistence with a principle goal in mind.

The storms in our lives build our characters, make us stronger, and cause us to grow in wisdom. At that time in my life, thunderous clouds loomed overhead. I struggled to provide for my children financially and emotionally. Needing someone to share the burden of parenthood, I discovered the law of attraction. With fear as my co-pilot, I was drawn into another unhealthy, dysfunctional relationship. I got married again. Fortunately, we moved to Colorado. It was 1982, the auto industry in Detroit was failing and the oil industry in Denver struggling. Economically, the country was in a recession. For us, the move to Colorado was an incredibly positive decision. The marriage failed after 5 years, but to be true to myself and my children, the fear of not fulfilling my dreams overpowered the act of giving up. We stayed in Colorado.

I remained single for 26 years. Through these years, I obtained my BSN, while raising two children, and worked as a nurse in various positions. We created our home, surrounded by a large circle of friends that supported us in navigating life. The three of us were a united, supportive threesome; taking risks, failing in new adventures, grieving, but did what it took to sustain ourselves without shrinking back. Remembering to accept personal responsibility for my own life is empowering. Understanding that I can become energized by my own visions and that I can let go of life's betrayals, I touch the center of my own sorrow.

As far as my siblings, none went on to graduate from high school. Minimal principles were taught to us as children. Their ability to create a life of quality was aligned with their need to fulfill their basic human need, survival. Throughout the years, I realized the unfortunate circumstances of struggle gave me the courage, determination and the wisdom to envision the possibilities life has to offer. I learned to swim upstream, going against the environment of ingrained habits and scripts of my childhood. I learned to act instead of being acted upon.

After 26 years of being single and my children grown, now with their own families, I decided to remarry in 2007. I'd spent wonderful years of exploration with relationships, employment as a nurse, and travel. My personal vision of success at times is still faltered by the scripts that were handed to me by my family, which has contributed to my capacity to contribute fully. Creating a passion of vision clarifies my purpose, gives me direction, and has empowered me to go beyond expectations.

I've spent the last two years on a personal journey to uncover my unique self. Visions of success run through my head. I've explored new opportunities that led me to creative businesses, network marketing, Landmark Education, Warrior Camp, spiritual camps, dance workshops, and volunteering. I've even experienced working with a Passion Consultant to uncover that I am passionate about self-empowerment, achievement, and unity.

I've been in conflict with my role of new wife, career women, visions of an entrepreneurial lifestyle, and family. I was beginning to feel unbalanced, so I learned to listen to my inner voice to make effective choices.

My career as a Nurse Case Manager in a busy emergency department remains my role to provide financially. I can't say I'm passionate about the role I play, but I've learned it doesn't have to be either/or. It can be and. My marriage becomes stronger every day, as I've restored more balance in the relationship. I've accepted living in a small community where there are plenty of opportunities to create friendship. I add play to my life as a daily ritual along with meditation, exercise, and me time. I use synergy to empower myself and restore balance by making healthy choices AND bring ME to every role I play.

I see life as an adventure. I choose to live by principle-based values. I accept personal responsibility for my life. Feeling confident that I can live in harmony with true quality of life, I learned to live with my inner voice, and follow it. I am continually educated by life's experiences. Life is full of choices. Knowing I have the ability to create anything in my life by the choices I make gives me strength and a feeling of power.

Sharon earned her Bachelors of Science from the University of Colorado Health Science Center. In her nursing positions, she has been placed in leadership roles where she has won several awards. Many years were spent as a single mother and cultivating her nursing career. Although focused in health care and adored care-giver, Sharon has broadened her interests. She is passionate about travel and sailing, including sailing on a private vessel "Epiphany" exploring the Bahamas, and a catamaran around the Greek Isles and down the Northeast Coast of Spain. Sharon is passionate about self-empowerment and achievement. When she is not working as a nurse, she loves to empower others through the opportunities of entrepreneurialism, which includes Send Out Cards www.sendoutcards.com/58326.

Spirituality

That One Thing

Denye Robbins

Speaking my truth has to include a story of crisis, seeking, transformation, and ongoing healing and integration. By the age of 33, I had created a life for myself and my two young daughters. I had managed (with whatever childhood programming, conditions and patterning I had) to attract and marry a very wealthy and powerful man. He was a Greek Orthodox Christian born and raised in the old country, and twice my age. On the outside, our lives seemed to be admirable, affluent, and respectable. On the inside there was pain, suffering, tyranny and control.

The church was a huge part of our personal and professional lives. To be seen and experienced in a certain way was paramount in this patriarchal society, culture, and community. I wasn't raised in any particular religion growing up, and did not have a sense of God, church, tradition, culture, or community. Raised on Naval bases around the world, I experienced many different peoples, races, cultures and religions. Being stationed somewhere new every two to three years, my family wasn't grounded like traditional American families. This set me up for feeling like I was on the outside looking in, like I was just visiting anyway. Like a gypsy, I would soon be on my way to the next new adventure, exploring the world and everything it had to offer.

When I had what I now refer to as a spiritual crisis, and a literal breakdown, I began to search for that one thing, the insight to give me peace, and the understanding about this world and the way it worked.

Shortly after my 33rd birthday, I woke up. Not like from a nap or a long sleep, but in consciousness. It was in an expanded way with insights and awareness I didn't have before. Through reading a book about the Divine Mother, I knew to my core that my entire life and what I created for myself and my daughters was a lie. To the world I had everything: a wealthy husband, a home with a panoramic view of the city, cars, trips, and a bottomless bank account with no accountability for balancing it. I had status, beautiful clothes, extravagant jewels and every material thing one could imagine. I was seen with the right people at the right places. If my children wanted something, it appeared upon request from their proud father, who also had them dressed and presented perfectly for every social occasion. He would be judged by his peers on whatever he had accumulated or created. "Powerful and Powerless" is what I now call the game. Looking back there was nothing real, authentic, or truthful about any of it. I was experiencing complete spiritual bankruptcy, and my soul longed for something more. I knew I would die trying to find that something, yet I committed to finding it.

I had my ex-husband's church, the doctrines, the sacraments, the classes, the Scriptures, the liturgy, and the Holy Day feasts and fasts – which meant nothing to me, as it was all Greek! I just didn't get it. Everything inside of me was saying seek the truth. Not perspective truth, not subjective truth, not conditioned truth of a lineage of peoples who just did and accepted what their ancestors did. I checked into the myths, stories and beliefs of people who had bought into the fears and control of a patriarchal system, holding us all in the subservient roles of a fallen and sinful nature. What is the real truth about each of us? I reeled in the agony and separation of it all. How could this be? How had we all bought into this belief in the Judaic-Christian western half of the world? Was it like this all over the planet or just here? Did the East know something we didn't? What were the other master teachers saying about how awful we all were? Did they have spiritual hoops we have to jump through to get back home, back into grace, back to where I assumed we all came from?

In the church I found no real answers to the questions of my emptiness, or the longing in my heart for that one thing to make it all better; to fix it, to fix me, to fix us. The church had made it clear that we had things to do and be before getting God's forgiveness for our fallen nature. Humans had done something terribly wrong to be kicked out of Eden to begin with. How and why swirled in my head and in my heart for years as I began my search. I was on a path, unlike most seekers with devotions, pujas and prayers. My path included a rebel's yell from the heart of a warrior goddess demanding to know, feel, and understand the truth.

I began to pray, meditate, and read everything I could get my hands on that had to do with enlightenment. I studied current and historical master teachers, connecting the common themes, truth threads, and teachings. I attended lectures, seminars, camps, courses, looking for insights or clues to that one thing to make me feel better about myself, about humanity, and what happens to our consciousness when we are done here on this earth. I studied the after-life, near-death experiences, the Saints, sages and mystics in history. I knew that they too were looking for that one thing. I wanted to know what they knew, to experience what they had in truth.

I began to chant, sing and collect things that might remind me of that one thing. I went to power places, tours and visited relics that had anything to do with that one thing. Like a thirst that could not be satisfied, I searched high and low *outside* of myself for it. I devoured books, tapes, CD's & DVD's on self-development, self-actualization and realization. I found the common theme running through many of the traditional spiritual paths: *The Kingdom of Heaven lies within.*

The Kingdom of Heaven Lies within? What did that mean, really? What was it about this image and likeness thing? What was it about us being pitiful sinners trying to get back into heaven? And what does that mean for those of us who are not part of God's chosen, the one true church? I wondered and asked the universe: "Who am I? What am I here for? Why are there so many different kinds of people, beliefs and paths? Which is the one? Which is the *right* one? Which are the *right* people? What is the truth?" I came to realize if I was going to be on a boat going to heaven, then I was going to be on the **right** one! I had spent enough time, money, and energy on this enlightenment thing already!

I knew with every fiber of my being that my relationship was completely out of alignment with my true self, and my rebel yell turned into warrior goddess action when I left my ex-husband. I had to get myself and my girls out from under that tyranny and patriarchal modeling. I've since created a beautiful home and environment for us, and proceeded to rebuild our lives in a home that was a soft place to land. It was from this space I attracted the beautiful man I am now married to. He cherishes and adores us, is the mature masculine in our lives, and empowers us with his love. He gave me the space and safety to continue exploring who I really am.

I studied duality, and non-duality: right and wrong, good and bad, superior and inferior, powerful and powerless, victim and tyrant, tyrant and rebel, form and formless, loss and gain; and all of the other polarities we experience on this earth. Dualities and opposites seemed to be the only thing to experience here. Where was that one thing? Was there duality in the kingdom? Was there judgment at all? All indicators and admonitions said no. In fact, the concepts of love, tolerance, acceptance and forgiveness were advocated and modeled by the Master teachers from all paths, opposed to what many religious doctrines and human interpretations suggested.

Judgment – that's it! Maybe acceptance was the key on the path of that one thing! I kept myself separate by judging everything. Was I was holding my entire world together with judgment? Things I liked and disliked, things I desired and feared. Some I pull towards me in acceptance, some I push away to reject. My preferences were the parenthesis of my life's experience. Was it smaller and much more limited that it needed to be? Was there free will and choice about this? Did I have the courage to explore the options?

I started to study projection and shadow work. Whether it was a dark shadow or a bright shadow, I took a look at things like: the tyrant, the bum, the arrogant ass. I saw all of the ways I'd usually say "That's not *me*!;" I'm superior, I'm separate from THAT. But, I'm not a beautiful singer, a tycoon, or that heroic contributor either; I'm inferior and separate from THAT. I saw how I held myself separate by not embracing all of the mirrors from that one thing. I realized I'm only living a very small part of myself, while projecting the ***rest of*** THAT onto others.

I understand now that nothing and no one is separate from that one thing. It is only with my preferences, judgments, and perceptions I keep myself from having it; ***allowing what was here all along***. Grace and Truth never left me. I had chosen dualistic thinking which bought into those limiting beliefs. I did have free will, and the grace to see diverse unification instead of the fear based systems of old. My warrior's heart chose, this time without the rebel's yell. Love, forgiveness, and acceptance of self and others gave me the eyes to see the truth about each of us.

Seeking or projecting anything outside of me is futile. The one thing keeps me turning inward, to the very source of myself as image and likeness. I am whole, complete, and perfect; in that one thing nothing is missing. When all of the parts and pieces of me I projected outward are pulled back into the heart, and they are all seen, loved, accepted and forgiven, I remember I am everything, everything is me. Heaven is here and with me now in that one thing. I am THAT, and THAT and THAT. THAT includes the tyrants in my life. I've learned to love and forgive THAT which was the catalyst for expanding my awareness. I have the courage now, to own even the ugliest parts of the projected me.

Heaven also may very well be a place that we experience after our consciousness leaves our body. I however, am committed to experiencing and creating it right here, right now, on this earth that is too a part of that one thing.

Currently Denye is the Chief Creative Officer and Co-Creator of Bridge2Bliss, Hostess and Creator of Conscious Conversations and Contemplations, and Master Coach of Higher Ground Professional Coaching. She inspires human potential by empowering clarity and confidence to find one's purpose and communicate authentically. Her camps, courses and events are interesting, heart-felt, and high-impact; creating enduring transformation. Each event, camp or course mirrors real life, as participants (individuals, professionals, teams and families) learn to break through obstacles, banish fear and separation, to emerge with the tools to lead more courageous, passionate and fulfilling lives. Her personal mission is to see everyone on the planet self-actualized and living in their hearts. She can be reached at: www.bridge-2bliss.com, www.ourconsciousconversations.com, www.higherground-coaching.com, or 720-219-3024.

Synchronicity, Healing and Light

Paula Robbins

I've heard it said that the abuse, the alcoholism, the deepest, darkest part of my history, make up my credentials. Those who have walked a similar path are the ones I trust, rely upon and respect the most, yet I have often hesitated to share my own background too readily. Often wondering, "Would people see me differently if they knew what my past was really like?"

The life I live today is one of leadership, in a position of trust as a Hypnotherapist, Spiritual Counselor and mentor to several other women including my two daughters. I previously had a successful career in Corporate America in which I was a solid producer in sales, a trainer and a manager, which sustained me and my two daughters for more than 14 years as a single mother. While I may not have shared my background too quickly, I am clear that it is what has propelled me to strive for a more meaningful and fulfilling experience in this adventure of life.

My childhood was at best, challenging. I was raised in Colorado, born the second child to a woman that was 20 years old, in her second failed marriage, and my birth father was not her husband at the time. He was a married man with two sons and a pregnant wife of his own. Upon learning I was coming, he promptly moved his family to another state, never even learning my name. A few years later, my mother met and married her third husband, who abused me physically, sexually and emotionally from the ages of three to eleven. Most of my adult family members struggled with drinking problems, failed relationships and lack of direction or purpose. Due to many moves, I attended more than thirteen schools from kindergarten through my junior year in high school. At 17, I dropped out, declaring I'd rather get my GED than move again. In my teen years, I turned to drugs and alcohol as a means of coping and had a significant substance abuse problem by the time I had turned 18. I had no idea how to change my path, but was very clear that I wanted and needed to.

In looking back at my years as a child and adolescent from this summarized viewpoint, I am often in gratitude and awe of just how amazingly graced I am that my life has flourished as well as it has, and I am happy to share that even though growing up had so much difficulty and dysfunction, I was lucky and blessed to have one particular adult in my life that taught me a few very simple principles and values that I believe were offered as gifts to me as a child and serve me still today.

My grandmother, though a small woman physically, had a large presence in my life. She took us in or moved in with us several times through my childhood and teen years. During the times we lived together, she cooked, helped with homework, talked and offered her words of wisdom and love. She knew that her seven children were not perfect, but she loved them all anyway and I respected that. She knew I was a confused, hurt and searching soul that wanted a better life. I remember she had this way of saying things so simply that I to this day can hear her voice saying them, "Never give up" or "God loves you no matter what." They are words I repeat to my own children and many others, smiling when I hear them come out of my mouth. They are words within the principles of love and faith.

At 18, I was given the opportunity to go to a vocational school and obtain my diploma, as well as learn a vocation. I spent 18 months in Clearfield, Utah, in a program created by the US Department of Labor called Job Corps. I graduated with honors just before my 20th birthday, even though during the entire program I struggled with my substance abuse problem. I was determined to succeed and regardless of the many oblivious weekends and evenings out of class, I did. It was like night and day. In class I was focused, present, excelling, and in the off hours I was drinking, drugging and unable to control myself. I felt like two different people and wanted to figure out how to hold on to the part that had it together.

On my twentieth birthday, I ventured to California with hopes of a bright future as an adult. I started off in the same out of control behaviors that I was trying to steer away from and yet each and every day I would wake up, dust myself off and keep thinking of those three words "Never give up." I had become a serious black out alcoholic with tendencies to get violent and struggled to accept that. I knew what alcoholism looked like based on my childhood, but so fiercely sought to break the chain. My denial was significant, yet I was drinking daily. It's easy to deny alcoholism when you are not even of legal age to drink.

It's a pleasure to look back at this part of my life now, knowing how certain synchronicities and divine interventions played into my becoming who I am today. You see, at twenty years old, I was simply a mess. I wanted to be a better person, but had no idea how to get there. I knew I was in trouble and on a terrible path of destruction if I didn't change soon.

One morning I was standing outside on my apartment balcony, full of shame and humiliation at how I was living and thinking of that very tiny woman that used to tell me "God loves you no matter what." Prayer or religion was not a part of my life as a child, but I knew I had to do something. So, I bowed my head, empty, ashamed and completely unsure of what to say and prayed out loud, "God, if you are real, I need help." I remember it like it was five minutes ago, because it is a moment that changed my life forever.

Shortly after this, I was picked up hitchhiking by a man who was a member of a twelve-step program. He introduced me to an entirely new way of living. He said alcoholism is not selective as to who it affects, that many of those suffering from alcoholism and drug addiction, suffered as teens too, but sobered up much later. I learned about the value of my background and how there were a lot of people like me. If I began to walk differently, my history could help others. I learned how to live substance free and the spiritual principles that can keep me that way as long as I live.

Now, of course, I did not realize that my simple prayer would offer so much when I made it. In fact, it was years later that I realized that being picked up hitchhiking was an answer to that prayer. It was years later that I would hear the voice of one of my early mentors in my sobriety telling me, "If you stay clean and sober, one day a young lady that has a story just like yours will walk in and you will be able to tell her what getting sober this young is like." It was also years later when that young lady did walk in and, in fact, had a story very, very similar to my own. The synchronicities are a joy to reflect upon, as there is so much from those early years of my spiritual awakening that I see divinity in.

At twenty, I began living a life of greater meaning. I learned about spirituality and how to apply the principles of honesty, perseverance, faith and service. They made my life more fulfilling than anything I could have imagined in years prior. As I began to learn, practice and teach of the principles, they affected my life in such a way that my heart and soul began to heal from all of the dysfunction and damage from my childhood and teen years. I saw others heal and shift to such amazing degrees that I truly believed I was witnessing miracles.

I experienced love at first sight, got married and had my first child all at the age of 22. Through other synchronicities I started a career in staffing and recruiting at age 25, had my second child at 27 and by the age of 28 had become a single mother through my choice to leave my husband and his drug addiction, which is another story for another time...

Through my divorce, the company I worked for was able to transfer my daughters and I back home to Denver. I was still living sober and was gainfully and gratefully employed. My love of people and ability to understand them led me through a very successful career in the recruiting industry. I understood the various cultures and dynamics of the organizations I served, as well as the internal dynamics of what made a successful recruiting firm. In 2003, I was promoted to manager/trainer over the state of Colorado for the financial arm of one of the largest recruiting organizations in the world.

Initially, I felt like I'd really made it; this was a solid path into retirement for me. I also loved how my career allowed me to assist so many people with one of the most important aspects of their lives, their financial livelihood. My many years of involvement in the 12-step programs had afforded me an opportunity to volunteer one-on-one with many people as a spiritual advisor. It seemed these two primary roles were a perfect compliment to one another. My spiritual expansion and awareness was my primary foundation during my entire professional adult life and moving into a higher level of achievement by my promotion seemed like a gift. However, by my third year in management, I had a greater view of the dynamics of large corporate politics and bureaucracy. While I gained an ability to understand and work within them, I also understood that my primary priority to grow spiritually was being compromised as I could not align with the politics and bureaucracy.

It was a natural response by now, in times of question or challenge, to turn to my spirituality. I prayed for a new career direction. Familiar with how the Divine would offer signs to me, I had a great deal of faith that I would know when they came. I also knew the path that would be revealed would be one of service. I went to see a hypnotherapist on a spontaneous whim that had nothing to do with my career concerns. In the initial consultation conversation, I was crystal clear this was to be my new career. I walked out of her office, before even doing my first hypnosis work, called my best friend and shared that I had found it. The elation and solidity in the decision were at a very deep level and the knowing was profound.

So much has happened, with more synchronicities than I can even put into words. To this day I cannot account for where the money came from that not only paid for my schooling, but my transition leaving my corporate position and into my role as a small business owner. I have experienced deeper layers of healing through my own hypnotherapy sessions and learned that the onion really is pretty big. The healing journey, when spirituality is incorporated, is one of beauty and expansion far beyond what I could have imagined. I live my life with a freedom to be more authentic than I have ever been. I cannot begin to tell you how much better I breathe, sleep, think and feel. There are struggles still, as life isn't perfect, but I embrace them in a way that is more fluid and rewarding because through all of this, I know that life is rich when we live from the inside out. I am gifted to facilitate and take part in the healing work of clients that are often quite similar in their background. It is beautiful to look them in the eye and tell them, "Yes, you can heal."

I still have reservations about sharing of my past too freely, but I am clear that this history continues to bring me to places of joy and gifts beyond my wildest dreams. I relate my life to a quote by Richard Bach, "What the caterpillar calls the end of the world, the Master calls a butterfly." When I consider the path I could have walked and where I am today, the contrast is quite stark. I know what my life could be like today, if the Divine interventions and synchronicities had not crossed my path. I don't take it for granted even for a moment. My heart is full and shining; I make strides to continue growing and expanding, regardless of what fears or obstacles are in the way. If I share my truth, of my past, my present or my future; someone may receive the same gifts that I have. I hope to meet you here in this moment, putting one word in front of the other and say thank you for sharing in my journey. May light shine upon you as it has upon me.

Paula Robbins, CCHt a Certified Counseling Hypnotherapist who specializes in the healing works of transpersonal hypnosis and spiritual transformation. Her desire to help people change their lives for the better is a natural way of being. She is committed to supporting the efforts of all who wish to live a life of Higher Purpose through healing within, spiritual expansion and maintaining states of peace through any circumstance. For more information visit www.SunriseHypnotherapy.com or contact Paula directly at (303)921-1473 or by email at Paula@SunriseHypnotherapy.com

Hold On Loosely

Susan Reardon

This morning, sitting with my cup of tea, I quietly breathe. I watch how my breath changes over time simply because it feels seen. It becomes deeper, slower, more regular, and more balanced. My body opens. This phenomenon is not new to me. It is a practice that I have followed every day for the past 10 years or so. Most recently I have utilized it to inspire my writing. As I intentionally watch my breath, I witness my thoughts. Today, I notice thoughts coming up around a recent experience. Usually, I would just notice the thought and release it, refraining from telling myself a story about it. But today I will tell you my story.

It was the evening that Haiti shook vigorously. I remember exactly where I was, sitting on the love seat in my living room watching Oprah. I remember the uncomfortable sensations in my body, my entire system felt like it was vibrating vigorously inside, incredible trembling but nothing that could be seen by the eye. When Oprah was over, I decided to read. My house was perfect for that, warm, cozy and often quiet, I was home alone. Around 5 pm, I relaxed on my big couch propping my feet up with some pillows. I was aware of breath and body, except on this late afternoon there seemed to be something exceptional going on with me, it was distracting. The feelings of vibrating and shaky energy transformed into racing and pounding in my heart; my body felt tense and surges of adrenaline shot through me as if I was running for my life. I sat quietly on the couch with my book and watched, detached from it all, as these kinds of experiences are familiar to me. At times like this, I rely on my trust in the life process and relax into the knowing that if I am meant to know more I will. As I experienced these events, I told myself no story about what was happening, it remained part of my world of sensation – nothing more, nothing less.

This feeling of heart racing, adrenaline pumping continued for quite a while, an hour or more. In my mind, I connected with family members and those I feel closest to, and asked, "Are you okay?" Each time I did that, I got the feeling that they were fine and so was I. The feelings, while respected, acknowledged and breathed through, remained a mystery. Eventually, the significant vibrations and the adrenaline rush quieted down, either that or I just got used to it and unable to make further connections, I went on with my life. That is until I turned the 6 o'clock news on the following morning. Then I connected the faces with my experience from the night before. The vibrations were my experience of the earthquake, the adrenaline rush my experience of the Haitian people running for their lives. My heart sank; I cried watching, as I *knew* energetically what they had been through. Connecting with the individual faces, I easily connected to sadness, this time, it took me a while, a few hours or more, to cross the bridge from sadness to love and what we commonly call compassion.

Yes, I am an empath. I feel the overwhelming feelings of others, including Gaia, Mother Earth. That day my Spirit was with Gaia and with the survivors, supporting them through their ordeal. My body acts as a mirror and through my ability to detach from experience as personal, I am able to help others heal. As part of my experience, I have often acted as a medical intuitive helping people identify the root cause of their disease. Through my emotionally intimate interactions with others, I have learned that much of physical disease/discomfort has some connection to unresolved emotion. Through empathy and compassion, I lead others into healing.

Another sip of tea, again watching my breath, not knowing now where this story will go next, I hear the words "**Hold On Loosely.**" Immediately, this feels like Higher Guidance, guidance that is meant for you and ultimately the reason why I share my story. The guidance continues:

"Hold On Loosely" to your beliefs always leaving room for a new idea, a new experience, and a new perspective to touch you deeply.
"Hold On Loosely" for if you hold on too tightly you will crush your chances for heart expanding experiences and miss out on the true purpose of life.
"Hold on Loosely" so you can know through experience deep in your bones, for once you know it there in your body, there will be no reason for "belief."
Belief systems are constructs of the mind not necessarily based in experience or truth. They keep your egos safe but keep your Spirits small.
"Hold On Loosely" to everything, allowing the Truth of an experience to rise up and meet you, to form the moment and then fade back to whence it came.
The more you can let go, the freer you are to receive life as it is truly meant to be, Moment to Moment in the Now, with Freedom and Soul Purpose.

Letting go is where my spiritual story begins. For years as a young person, I lived in pain. At times there was physical pain as well as strange and unusual physical symptoms. Often, I felt overwhelmed emotionally without reasons that my family or I could understand. Mentally, I felt tortured as I tried to explain to myself and others why I felt the way I did. For years, I blamed my family, an over-controlling mother and a father who did not protect me enough. I saw things differently than others around me, often with clarity well beyond my years and my family denied the validity of my perspective. As a child, I moved in and out of spiritual grace as I shifted from the freedom of breath and body that gymnastics and dance offered back into a world of pain and misunderstanding, a world I eventually got stuck and felt crazy in. By the time I was a young adult, I had little confidence and was confused about who I was and the way I experienced the world. The only thing I knew for sure was that I needed help. With the help of a good therapist, my story began to unravel and I came to see I held a significant amount of trapped emotions within the cells of my body. As an adult, they manifested themselves mostly as symptoms of what many call fibromyalgia and generalized anxiety disorder. My body was always on high alert, ready to shut down any time an intense experience was on my radar.

This experience of opening and closing just became too painful and eventually I began to spend most of my time shut down (in other words, out of my body). After some time in therapy, I began to feel a little bit of safety around my emotional experience and I came to realize just how sensitive I was. Through group therapy my empathic experiences became validated. I realized much of my childhood experience was the experience of others' overwhelming emotions that they felt no control over or awareness of. I began to view myself as a radio that picked up emotional frequency, and I finally began to discern both past and present experiences. Through my process of healing, I reconnected with the medium of breath and body similar to childhood, except this time instead of gymnastics and dance it was yoga.

The addition of breath and body to my healing process again helped me to reconnect with and re-enter my body. Embodiment made me feel spiritual and supported letting go at a cellular level. Being in my body again was like coming home, being relaxed in it supported "holding on loosely." I was reminded of that childhood place with clear sight, except for this time I had the ability to understand and discern my experiences. Grace, again, began to unfold for me. Breath and body…breath and body…this has been the spiritual process that has allowed me to let go of the past and live in the moment. Eventually, I came to see my nemesis as my gift and took leaps of faith great and small to reshape my life, utilizing the way I experience life to help others. In looking back, I see my life today is similar to childhood, but as a child, without wisdom and understanding it was torture. Experience plus wisdom has become my circle of grace.

Wisdom has taught me to let go of the idea that what I feel is personal. Each day, wisdom reminds me to hold on loosely when I feel something in my body, knowing it is a signal or a symptom of a greater kind of communication. Wisdom supports me in holding on loosely to feelings, emotions, beliefs, ideas, and experiences so I can utilize them for as long as they are useful in supporting healing (myself, others, or both) in the moment. Then, when they are no longer useful, they go, along with my breath and freely I move on into the next moment. Since wisdom has brought me to this place of connectedness, it is no longer a concept in my mind or a thought that there is evidence of connection out there. Instead, connectedness has become a daily inner experience through feeling, empathy, and direct knowing. This is my spirituality, a process of letting go and holding on loosely so that all I am left with is what I am becoming in the space that stands right before me.

It has been my soul's journey to utilize empathy as a way of leading others into their bodies and their truth, supporting the integration of their experience so that they can experience connection and oneness. I have come to know and to teach that we are all connected. Your pain is my pain; your healing is my healing. To me these words are not just a saying, but a reality. I need not be physically present to support your healing, nor do you need to be physically present to support mine. Each of us just need be spiritually willing to experience life, breathe, feel deeply, not personally, to let go and hold on loosely. When we utilize our everyday experiences and the resultant feelings, emotions, ideas and beliefs that arise within us for our healing, with the intention of making peace with what is, we become healers on this planet and enter the Circle of Grace.

Susan Reardon, M.A. is an innovator, educator, and transformational guide in the field of health, fitness, and natural healing. She works as a Licensed Minister in the State of New York. Also trained as an Exercise Physiologist, Reiki Master/ Teacher and Phoenix Rising Yoga Therapist, she considers herself a Spirit Guide in human form with the mission to expand the Circle of Grace one soul at a time. Utilizing her Higher Guidance, Spiritual Principles/Wisdom and Yoga Therapy/ Breathing Techniques, she supports her client's spiritual growth. She creates a safe space for individuals to experience themselves, shifting from fear, anger, and despair into acknowledgement, acceptance, and integration. Visit her website at http://www. sixthsensejourneys.com and learn about the 501(c)3 "…Be The Example" by visiting: http://www.betheexample.org

Peace Reaper

Jacqueline Empson

This journey of over 9000 miles began with a single step… one that would change the direction of the rest of my life. It was a decision to move from a state of despair and dependence to one of joy and peace. I will never again be the same, for I have found a sense of oneness. As if my future was laid before me, my path was unmistakably clear.

I began this pilgrimage into healing my life, my identity, in the fall of 2009. It was a process that involved leaving behind my home, my husband, my son, and my office. It was a search for direction. I was looking for that beacon, like a lighthouse shining its light through a dense fog. My heart felt as though it was being ripped from my chest… and my spirit suppressed.

They say that time heals all wounds. I believe this to be so, if the mind is willing. To transcend the darkest memories, to rise above with the desire to overcome adversity is a gift you give yourself. Through those experiences, we are able to offer knowledge to help others to find the strength to move forward.

This is how my awakening began. I was sitting on a patio in Wisconsin with good friends. The summer evening was warm with a light breeze. We enjoyed sharing good food, each other's company, and thoughts about living our best life. We inspired one another weekly by sharing a focus point, and this week was to state your dream. What is it you want to attract in your life? Mine was short, sweet, and utilized all of my senses. By invoking the use of tasting, seeing, hearing, smelling and touching - I became that experience. It felt as though it was a part of my being.

"I sit on my balcony and watch the majestic rising of the sun over the ocean. I taste the mix of the salt in the breeze, and the refreshing flavor of my warm lemon water on my lips. I hear the beautiful music of the ocean, as her waves splash against the rocky shoreline. She is calling to me. I walk down on the beach, and feel the sand between my toes. It is soft and inviting. The smell of the fresh ocean breeze awakens my mind and I feel blessed."

It is amazing how life changes. For many years you imagine growing old with the same person and look forward to your golden years. The moment came when I realized we no longer had anything in common, and the person lying beside me was a stranger. And worse yet, I no longer knew who I was. Spending nearly 20 years being a wife and mother was my identity. When that went away, I was left with a huge canyon that seemed like an impossible void to fill.

Even our son Dillon could sense the incompatibility that grew between Craig and me. His course of action was to focus on his education and requested we allow him to attend boarding school. I had this deep inner knowing that I had taught him everything he was willing to learn from me. We made Dillon's final school preparations... as I quietly pondered what I needed to do about my marriage.

This year has been filled with many changes. It was with a very tender heart that I have allowed us both to embrace this opportunity, so Dillon and I could discover our individuality. I hope one day he will understand how much love and faith it took to leave behind everything that I had ever known. I consider him one of my most valued and appreciated teachers. There came a point where I needed to raise the white flag... where it felt as though I needed to surrender or die.

Two weeks before his first day of school, our cocker spaniel passed away. Chewie had been our faithful companion for nearly 17 years. He was my friend when I felt alone, which was often these days. He had been my one source of unconditional love and affection.

Craig and I had talked about me going away for a little while to get myself together. I told him I had already made some plans to go see my brother, Roger, in California and then go on to Colorado to attend some classes.

Our distance within our marriage began when my husband started filling a void he felt (from my work related trainings that had me often out of town) with friendships that included other women. As his friendships grew, so did the exclusion of me in his life – which was devastating. He told me often how our neighbor, Karen was his best friend. It felt as though my relationship with my husband was being replaced. That sense of feeling important and loved strongly diminishing.

Craig took a job that required him to spend 5 or 6 nights a week out of town. He declined my offers to visit him. I have always loved cooking meals for him and Dillon. I had wanted to bring my electric frying pan to the hotel and cook him a nice home cooked meal. He had zero interest in a meal, sex, a warm cuddle, or an overnight with me.

He took up insomnia as a nighttime sport. I took up surveillance as I began noticing long late night phone calls and numerous texts on our mobile phone bill. My mind began to think the worst. On weekends he began receiving phone calls and texts in the middle of the night. As I monitored his forbidden cell phone after he fell asleep on weekends, I would read the messages. There was reference to being at his hotel room with one of his new female friends. With this new knowledge, I became obsessed and began GPS surveillance.

Craig would always talk his way out of the situation by manipulating my words and professing his innocence. How it looked bad, but they were all just friends. Through his words and actions I realized where I stood on several occasions. Infidelity, whether emotional or sexual, was not the ultimate deal breaker – like I had once thought. It was dishonesty and not being able to admit with remorse for the pain inflicted on others.

Two days after Dillon's departure to school, I left a note in Craig's work truck explaining how he had broken our vows – to love, honor, cherish and respect one another. I could not allow my heart to be trampled on any longer. It was time for change. I left information about a marriage retreat, along with phone numbers for him to call for others who went through the program. During the next seven weeks, while I was away, he made no attempt to contact anyone with regard to counseling or a retreat. He was continuing to dance with his alcoholic tendencies. We stopped talking.

This was the beginning of my spiritual pilgrimage. A clairvoyant friend, Mark, had advised me that the Airport Vortex in Sedona was going to be significant in my journey of healing. As I pulled up to this Vortex site, the rubber molding under my car had come loose and was dragging. My emotions were stressed, and I started to cry. My venture outside of my car lasted about 1 minute, before a nearly complete breakdown.

I bought a roll of duct tape and fixed the car as best I could, continuing on to California. Spending the next couple weeks with my brother, Roger, we went to Mount Shasta and Ashland, OR, for 09/09/09. It was a time of learning how to release my spirit, to surrender my marriage, and place it in the hands of God. This was a very difficult process. Together we returned to Sedona. The solitude in the 4 mile hike around the Airport Vortex was a symbolic blessing. With every step – I imagined the negative energies that were holding my heart hostage dissipating.

After leaving my brother in California, I decided to stop one last time in Sedona, planning to watch the sunset from the Airport Vortex. I had stopped in Phoenix to say hello to Craig's mom and brother, and a few other friends. I was disappointed as I noticed the sun begin to set with 20 miles still ahead of me. I knew in my heart it was okay. Whatever time God wanted me there was the right time for my arrival.

Pulling into the parking area at the Airport Vortex, I quickly jumped out of my car and started to climb. I was wearing a pair of sandals that had no tread on the bottom. When I started to slide, I quickly pulled them off and climbed barefoot. It was a time of prayer, a time of surrender. Feeling that I had no control over anything, I handed my marriage to God.

My mentor and dear friend, Charlene, had been an amazing part of my life.

She was a true blessing. I asked on this evening for Archangel Michael to be with her to bring her comfort and peace as she neared the end of her battle with cancer. I prayed for my marriage, my son, my husband, and I prayed for me – that the feeling of being divinely led continue. During this pilgrimage, I did not feel alone.

After my prayers and meditation, I opened my eyes to realize the sky was pitch black. The new moon offered no light to guide my passage down the rough red rocks and safely beyond the cactus plants. As I slowly made my descent I thought about how timing is always perfect. What is God trying to tell me, I wondered? His presence surrounded me and the words were loud and clear: "Sometimes you feel alone and are surrounded by darkness; it is then that you need to trust in a power much greater than yourself to guide you and show you the way."

As I drove on, the phone call came from a mutual friend – Charlene had passed earlier in the day. She shared with me that she had spent Psalm Sunday in Sedona, with Charlene, for her 72nd birthday. Charlene had climbed each of 5 vortexes, and when she arrived at the top of each, she took off her shoes to absorb the energy. We both got chills as we discussed the similarities and our love for this beautiful fun loving friend.

Arriving in Colorado, I attended a refresher course in Biofeedback. Kind of ironic isn't it? My specialty is in helping others to reduce their stress. I had taken a sort of hiatus during this period as it seemed impossible to help others when my own world was falling apart. It felt wonderful to be among like minded practitioners over this week. Then I continued on to another course, Spiritual Healer Coach, taught by a remarkable husband and wife team at Sunrise Ranch. The insight I gained made this a weekend of great transformation. I quickly realized that each of us cannot judge another's behavior as right or wrong. We can only determine what is right or wrong for ourselves, and then decide what we will tolerate in our lives.

I had come to view Craig's behavior as an opportunity for me to grow, and for him to learn whatever lesson that was his to experience. I fully understood that there was no turning back, it was a time of moving forward. Our instructor, Erina shared some special prayers with me. I walked the Labyrinth in the courtyard of the retreat center. As I lay on a hammock hidden within the permaculture garden, another class member had come down. He walked the labyrinth and proceeded to sing, which brought a sense of joy into my heart.

Back in the classroom, we experienced the sharing of a Oneness Blessing. By chance I had gotten paired up with Juan, the man with the beautiful voice, who is from the Canary Islands of Spain. This left me feeling very nervous, and I found it difficult to catch my breath. Later in the day, I heard him speaking to Erina's husband, Dave. He was seeking relief from a headache. This left me wondering if my anxiety during the blessing might have caused his headache.

I approached and explained to him my aversion to having friendships with men and how I had been nervous during the Oneness Blessing, and asked him if I had caused his headache. He laughed at me, and said no. We continued to have a nice visit. Another participant had invited everyone to a class on Shamanism in New Mexico. Because we both had been intrigued, and had a break in our schedules, I offered to drive.

We spent the next two weeks exploring New Mexico and Colorado, attending lectures and classes together, and rekindling the fire that had been extinguished in my heart. Ours was a passion that made me feel alive and desirable again. We had no expectations for an outcome. We were living in the moment and enjoying everything that we had to offer one another.

I had been happy to share my life with someone who held the same interests. He was amazing. His eyes would smile when he looked at me and every time it would light up my heart. He would call me "Princesa," and tell me "Beauty is in Your Eyes." We were blessed to share our paths with one another.

The drive back to Wisconsin allowed me time to sink back to reality. I knew it was time to file for divorce, and face my future however it was to unfold. It was time to take a leap of faith, the biggest leap I had ever taken. I told my husband and son of my relationship with Juan and that I had been invited to go to Spain. They both were very supportive of my leaving and said that if that was what I wanted, they would not stand in my way.

My path led me to the beautiful island of Gran Canaria, and I tasted the salt in the air, listened to and rejoiced in the beauty of the ocean. The dawn of a new beginning was warm and challenged me with more opportunities to learn and to grow every day. I will continue to embrace these as they are offered to me, as this is only the end to one chapter.

With great determination to honor and respect my spirit, I returned to the U.S. after three months in paradise. My acceptance in a spiritual growth program has brought me to Colorado. It is here that I am finding my voice, my sense of self respect, and desire to claim my identity in the spirit of love. Love for myself, love for humanity, and love for our Earth.

Jacqueline Empson inspires us with the writing of her first book Peace Reaper. She is a stress reduction specialist who works in the field of spiritual coaching, biofeedback and reflexology. As a young child she recalls having a sense of being destined to do something great. Life is the greatest teacher – with the sharing of insight from her experiences, she will help you to see the synchronicities within life's journey. Originally from the Midwest, Jacqueline now resides at Sunrise Ranch, a spiritual retreat center and sustainable farm community located in Loveland, Colorado.

Claim Your Thunder

Linda Van Haver

I wasted many years of my life trying to create a sense of family with an emotionally abusive, alcoholic man. I thought if I lavished enough love on him, he would turn back into the attentive person he was during the heady days of courtship. I gave and gave until there was nothing left – no enjoyment, no money, no friends, and no energy to work or go through the prolonged fight it would take to get away from him. I looked in the mirror and no one was there. I had handed my self esteem away until there was no self remaining.

Feeling more depressed than I had ever been, I crawled into bed one afternoon and as I pulled the covers over my head to escape the world, I pondered how I got to this point. Not only had I lived without a kind word or gesture from him for years, but I was berated and treated badly. My friends and family were disturbed by his behavior and mine because I stayed with him. Feeling trapped and without hope, I fell deeply asleep. But the most wonderful and amazing thing happened to me during my slumber. Someone came and wrapped his arms around me, and I immediately felt loved, safe, nurtured, even revered. He felt so comfortable like a big brother or father who had come to protect me and take me out of there. We spent hours together traveling through time and space, and I felt a kindness, tenderness, and compassion I had never known. Even though I hadn't met him before, he seemed to know me well, and I could feel he loved me completely. I had no clue who he was, only that I felt loved down to my individual cells and elated when I was with him. I asked his name and the answer I received was Yeshua. I had never heard that name before but it resonated a feeling of peace within me as I repeated it.

Filled with such joy, when I awoke the next morning, I was a changed person. I was happy and knew right down to my core I was saved from my life of despair. My lethargy was gone, and I was filled with a brand new vitality. The bleak days of feeling trapped and helpless were over. I rented a car and drove two hours north where I knew no one and contracted to buy a home even though I had no money at the time. I had unwavering faith that everything I needed to escape my miserable way of life would easily unfold before me. When I returned home, I put a For Sale sign in front of my house and it sold within a week for a substantially larger sum than my neighborhood had previously drawn. There were enough funds after paying off the mortgage to give my soon-to-be-ex and me the needed cash to start over separately. Everything that I needed for changing my life was dropped into my lap with ease. I thought of Yeshua often and how meeting him had profoundly changed me.

After my move, I started attending a spiritual center where I learned about unconditional love. This was so different from my upbringing where I was criticized and punished often just for being me. As I look back, I see how the emotional and physical abuse I endured during childhood set me up for attracting abusive men into my life. Even the messages I received in my mother's church were that I was unworthy and filled with sin. During one of the workshops at the spiritual center, the presenter asked us to close our eyes and imagine that whoever represents the divinity for us was standing next to her on the platform. I didn't know who that would be for me but when I closed my eyes, I immediately saw my friend Yeshua who had come to me before. Suddenly I felt myself being drawn out of my seat towards him, by my heart. Next the presenter asked us to check if we loved ourselves as much as we loved whoever represented the divinity. When she said that, I felt myself slam back into my chair and knew that there was work to be done on loving and forgiving myself and the people who had hurt me during childhood. When I discovered that Yeshua was the Aramaic name for Jesus I was stunned and shaken. No wonder his visit had been so life altering!

I've learned that attracting abusive people into my life and acting out in a destructive manner started because of the negative messages I received from an overly critical mother. These messages, that I was severely flawed and not as good as other people, were installed into my subconscious when I was young. Their imprint limited me and held me back from the life I was meant to live.

Like all of us, when I first came onto this earth, I had no thoughts of limitations or boundaries. I crawled around and then dragged myself to a standing position on wobbly legs, feeling courageous and strong. I learned to talk and made known my likes and dislikes. As I learned language, I also learned that not everyone supported me happily on my journey. My mother acted as if children were born a blank slate and could be programmed to her exacting specifications. There was no room for my growing individuality.

Other people I encountered during my trip to young adulthood told me things about myself that turned out not to be true. These people were in positions of authority such as teachers and clergy and since I was groomed to fit in rather than stand out, I accepted the messages that somehow I was not ok. I was told "children should be seen and not heard" and "you always have to have the last word." I felt it stab my heart when disapproving names were screamed at me or when I was punished physically. The ones who called me derogatory names or beat me were actually responding to their own sense of unworthiness and frustration, but it was very damaging to me as I thought I was a good kid who was inquisitive about everything. How are you supposed to feel loved, worthy, valuable, beautiful and talented when someone is hitting you and telling you that you should be like everyone else?

The real truth about me and about you too is that we are each uniquely beautiful, stronger than we know, more capable than we realize, and loved more than we could ever imagine. We try so hard to fit in when we were born to stand out. There is no one exactly like each of us in this whole world.

I've worked hard to dissolve the iron grasp of the negativity I absorbed. My years of soul searching, counseling, attending countless self improvement workshops, and hypnotherapy schools have finally cleared the way for me to be ME. You too can remove the blocks and step into who you really are. It's time to **Claim Your Thunder**. Following the steps below will shift your life in dramatically significant and positive ways.

C – Change what doesn't honor you. Create your life according to your dreams and talents.

L – Lavish love, patience and kindness on your inner child. She is in dire need of it.

AIM – Aim high. You are so used to settling just to keep the peace. Go after what you really want.

Y – Yes! Say yes where you used to say no. It's time to shake things up. Push back your boundaries. Step out of your safe place and soar!

O- Organize your surroundings. Clean out your car, home, and office. Getting rid of clutter will open space for the good to come into your life.

UR – UR important, valuable, worthy of receiving all of the wonderful things life has to offer.

T- Treat yourself kindly. Treasure your unique talents.

H – Halt the bad habits that don't serve your best interest. Hypnosis works!

U – Use your talents. The world is ready to accept your gifts.

N – No name calling of yourself or others.

D – Dare yourself to push back your boundaries. Delight in the many aspects of you.

E – Each day is a new opportunity to recreate your life.

R – Reclaim the power within you. Rumble, ROAR, revel in being YOU!

Like thunder, let your power vibrate over the world. Be loud and clear about who you are. Speak up for what you want and speak out for what you feel is right. Don't let your voice be silenced to make nice or to fit in.

I have come a very long way from that person who felt trapped and depressed and now make my living as an empowerment expert helping people dissolve the negative messages they installed during childhood. I love helping them step fully into who they really are so that their light can shine and their thunder can be heard. Thank you, Yeshua, thank you.

Helping people release the effects of a turbulent childhood and step into their greatness is what Linda Van Haver feels called to do. Through behavior modification and empowerment techniques, she works with people by phone, in workshops, and in private sessions to assist them in creating an excellent quality of life. She is a Hypnotherapist, Energy Psychology Practitioner, Co-Author of One Page Wisdom, and Creator of Reclaim the Power Within™ and Claim Your Thunder™ workshops. www.selfempowermentsolutions.com www.lindavanhaver.com 772 770-MIND (6463) Email: mindcoach@lindavanhaver.com

My Life without Instruction

Sally Hesson

Where shall I begin on this strange journey that most people today would call insane and foolish and I would call liberating?. I was a single mom who bucked the trend and proved the statistics wrong. I had everything: a beautiful, smart son who always made me proud, a strong faith life (or so I thought), a supportive family, a nice house, nice car, high-paying job, the respect of my colleagues, and numerous awards at work. Money was no object; it seemed to flow to me as I needed it. I had reached a point in my life where I did not desire things but things that I needed were always available to me. Yet, somewhere along the line, the dream started to lose its luster; something about what I was doing at work had become unfulfilling and empty.

I wondered why I was doing what I was doing but I was in a state of lethargy, content to take the paycheck and just show up. All around me, people who didn't care seemed to succeed in spite of their lethargy – could I do the same? Things were done for obtaining advantage and making yourself look good at the expense of others; not because it was the right thing to do, but because it was the way to survive. Was I becoming a corporate-zombie – one of the living who does not realize they are dead?

Looking back, the path of least resistance had been my game plan in life. There always seemed to be an obvious course or clear direction that I should take. In spite of my failed marriage, I was successful, according to the world, without even really trying. I was always in the right place at the right time. But all the while, God was knocking at the door trying to get my attention. By having everything, I had grown comfortable in my life, faith and career without realizing I had stepped over into the soul-numbing stronghold of lukewarmness. I was dead because I stopped growing and had lost sight of the ultimate goal in life. I had achieved everything and overcome all obstacles by worldly standards. What else was left?

When I was younger, I was in an abusive marriage which ended in a painful divorce. Up to this point, I focused on what I should be – outwardly caring and considerate – doing a good job without understanding why this was important; praying but with no real depth. I suffered from a lack of self esteem and had no self confidence, so I compensated in doing what pleased others. Their thanks and praise made me feel good about myself and sure I was important. But inwardly, I did not feel I deserved to be loved.

My pregnancy began to jar me out of the self-induced coma I seemed to be living in. Suddenly, it was not all about me – another human being was now totally dependent on my decisions and actions. I knew I could not raise my son in an environment of abuse where mutual love did not exist.

I had to change and take care of this sweet little helpless human being. With that, I become a dreaded statistic – a single mom. I moved to New York and lived with my family, found a job and gave birth to a beautiful baby boy named James – the little light of my life – one of God's beacons in my darkness. I lived with my ever supportive parents and they took care of James during the day while I worked and I began the journey to learn how to truly love someone else and myself. I was successful at my job and was asked to move to Colorado for a promotion. This was a great opportunity but also heart breaking for me and my son, then age 5. We had to leave family and friends far behind. James was very attached to his cousins and grandparents. For the next several years, James cried inconsolably every time we returned to Colorado after a visit. In spite of the difficulties involved in moving, I was optimistic and the future seemed bright. I had a new career, more money, and could afford my own house. I was independent and did not fit the single-mom statistic, so my son adjusted and things settled into an easy routine.

After moving to Colorado, my success at work continued – I was blessed with great bosses so I could attend events for my son in school, go on field trips and adjust my hours to be home with him after school. My life was all about raising my son and working. But as things became easier, money more available, I got closer to 40 and my son started to grow more independent; I realized something was missing. I turned to God, wondering what my life meant or what else I should be doing. I felt called to something deeper. I wanted to know God and my purpose but didn't know how to proceed.

I started to pray more, volunteered, joined a contemplative order, and studied my faith. Bit by bit, all of the promises of the world were exposed for what they were – empty and shallow – but the promises of God turned out to be true and reliable. I learned that God never leaves you where you are because He is the ultimate life-coach. He always draws you closer to Him and pushes and nags you to drink more deeply of life – His life. I realized I had been trying to control my whole life. I was task-oriented so I wanted to do things to cross items off my list; but when I started looking at the list I was keeping, I realized there were some very important things missing.

In my continuing discernment, I felt constantly challenged to something more. I reached a point of no return when I realized I had to completely surrender to God. I had to say the words and put myself in His hands, giving Him permission to do with me what He wanted. All this is difficult for someone who wants to be in control and have a clear map in life. Love is, after all, ultimately about complete trust and total surrender to the beloved. This is the scariest part of life and love especially when God is involved – you must pour yourself out into your beloved. God always gives much more than he takes. As the ultimate life coach, He will always lead, push, cajole, and nudge us in the direction that is best for us but not necessarily in the direction we want to go.

Of course, through all of this, I had not made any changes in the one thing that consumed most of my time and my life – my job. I was floating around the fringes and avoiding the heart of my life. Then, a new twist came into my life; a familiar story really. A new boss came in and I was no longer valued. I had been blessed with bosses who appreciated honesty and realistic answers. Now, I was faced with having to simply say what everyone wanted to hear, even if it made no sense and pretending to do things and make things up so they sounded better, even if it was not entirely true. I wasn't good at pretending and being dishonest, so this was difficult for me.

I was offered a generous package to just go away. Suddenly, choices loomed before me that I hoped to never face. When all of this happened, I did get one very pleasant surprise. I found out that I really did have an impact on people's lives. I got so many calls and well wishes from people thanking me and telling me how much they admired and respected me as a leader and a person, I was brought to tears. I even won an award as I was being pushed out of the door, the irony of large corporations. I was not a failure and someone had noticed. Who I was had more of an impact on people than the title I held. What I did and said was watched and observed.

The economy had crashed, jobs were scarce and employer attitudes were shifting to the just be thankful you have a job mentality. While I waited for the final cards to fall, I prayed even more to a God who had now become my confidant and friend. I begged Him to lead me not to what was easy but to what was best. Gradually, I came to see more through His eyes and realized that leaving, though insane in worldly terms, was the right thing to do. The timing seemed terrible, my son was just starting college and I needed money. But somehow, I kept getting the answer in silence – God had something planned and I would know it when I saw it. This gave me hope, so I accepted the package and suddenly felt free and at peace with my decision.

Nothing happens by chance; everything that comes into your life and everyone is there for a reason. The people that I left at work were jealous of my decision. I found this odd since they had the jobs and I was stepping into the unknown. I should have been scared, but I was not. I was inspired and amazed that whenever I felt I should be scared, I always heard a small voice whispering "have no fear –

all will be well." I was finally learning to let God drive and do all the worrying; it was liberating.

I started looking for another corporate job and then one day, at a networking event, I got an inspiration to pay very close attention to what one particular person would say at this meeting. I went and there was a lady who sold franchises. When she spoke, her words hit me. She was the one I should listen to. I began a three month evaluation process to find a business where I could help others. Finally, I settled on a tutoring franchise. The start-up costs were low and I could work from home, helping others while feeling good about what I was doing. I took the plunge and brought the franchise.

Somewhere at the back of my mind, I still had a suspicion that God was not done; this was simply one stop on the journey. I went to training and started off with a fizzle. I got some clients but struggled with what to do each day and how to plan things out. I kept returning to trust and continued to pray, finding strength and consolation. I knew in the depths of my heart that God is faithful, he had always been faithful and would not abandon me but I needed to know now, because I was impatient and worried about money and survival long-term.

Amazingly, every time I implored Him for guidance, the phone would ring or someone would send me information to move me on my way with a tip, opportunity or helpful suggestion out of the blue. God was telling me He heard me and He kept pushing and leaving bread crumbs; I just had to listen. I made this a daily routine: asking God what He wanted and also for the grace to hear, be faithful and trust.

Once I started doing this, I was no longer fearful. No matter which client got upset about what tutor or what happened with my business, I knew it was going to be ok. I just had to constantly remind myself of this, continue to discern and move forward. I knew, based on reading every life of every saint, that God perfects us in challenges and trials. Anyone who is trying to achieve anything has to work hard and struggle. I didn't mind the thought of suffering but I wanted it on my terms. I had in fact asked God to take over my life. Though surrendered to Him, I still worried that my life would suddenly fall apart. I learned that God will always give you what you need to face the trials He has prepared for you. He never leaves you alone, even when you feel lonely, He is always with you. I had to learn this by going through self-doubt, worry and being forced to truly surrender to God; not a pretend surrender but a true surrender. I was content to surrender before because I had all things in the world.

As I am writing this story, I still wonder what God has planned. I feel very certain He has a plan and it is unfolding according to His Will, not mine. He is teaching me patience and trust. Sometimes you have to fall back into the arms of God and trust that He will catch you. There is no one who loves me as much as He does. This is daunting in itself. But as with the loaves and fishes, God can make a feast with whatever is offered and there will be always more to spare. Life is a treasure hunt and we gather bits of the treasure as we go through life. The treasure is not things or awards or possessions or money, but love. We are ultimately defined by how we love and we are all lovable because we are all loved by God. I fell back into the arms of God and found that I was always on an adventure; I had simply chosen to sleep through most of it instead of living it. I realize I am the luckiest person in the world; I have no real problems because I have faith. I am never alone or lonely. There is one who loves me more than any other so what is there to worry about? Each day is an unexpected joy.

Sally lives in Colorado with her son and is a true fan of that beautiful state. For the past 20 years, she has worked in the field of Information Technology and Management earning numerous awards and taking on more leadership responsibility throughout her career. Sally is a single mom who understands the challenges of working and parenting in today's fast-paced world. She is an ongoing supporter of Denver Kid's Inc. and Bridgeway and is very focused on helping people rise above their life challenges. Sally is a strong believer in life-long learning, has taught religious education at her local church and actively volunteers in the community.

The Journey to Your Inner Light House, From the Pavement You Shall Rise

Galit Lazar

It was heavily snowing the day I started my self-discovery journey in a little town called Three Rivers in Quebec, Canada. It was 4 p.m. in the afternoon. My heart felt heavy. I was sad and depressed. After having gone through a difficult time in my life I was trying to find new meaning because I was tired of feeling the way I felt. I was trying to figure out my life's passion and what I wanted to do with the rest of my life.

I love the Oprah show and have watched it almost every day for the past 15 years or so. I decided to turn on the TV and watch her show as I usually would. On that particular day it was about The Secret and she hosted all the greatest teachers that day including Rhonda Byrne, Lisa Nichols, and many more. When I turned on the TV, I didn't expect the effect that this show would have on my life. While they spoke about The Secret, I had tears in my eyes because they made me realize that there is a different way to live my life. I also knew that from this day on my life would be transformed forever. You see, at that moment I was at the end of my rope. I had no life purpose and I felt that almost every single aspect of my life was a complete failure, both professionally and personally. As a result, I started thinking and believing that I was no good at anything. I felt like a handicapped person, completely powerless.

I didn't know how to succeed and I wanted so desperately to be a success like everyone else in my environment, but no matter how much I tried I could not seem to succeed. That episode of Oprah gave me the breath of life. It was like I was taken out of the dark tomb I was in, into the rainbow and the sun. My whole face lit up. I felt a sense of relief and I knew without a reasonable doubt that if I followed these directions I would have the power to transform my life and create what I really wanted; to feel the way I wanted.

Prior to this awakening, I didn't know what I wanted to do for a career. I listened to what other people told me to do. I tried many things, but the one that had defined my life the most was my teaching program. My father suggested I should become a teacher. To be honest, this kind of career didn't appeal to me very much. What really appealed to me at that particular time was to be in the Arts field. I was very attracted to the media environment. At that time I was in what I thought was a realistic perspective. I thought that wanting to do something in the Arts field was impossible to achieve. I never spoke to anyone about my true desire for fear of being judged. So I did what other people expected me to do; I took the 'realistic' path.

I enrolled in the Teaching English as a Second Language program. Getting into the program took me two years of hard work and a series of struggles. Eventually, I succeeded. I didn't quite know how I could do it and if I could do it. I didn't exactly know what to do. At that time I didn't even stop to ask myself if I really wanted it.

After eight years of University studies, I got my Bachelor degree, but was still without a teaching permit. I missed graduating by less than one point. I was tired and had enough of school so I decided to move in a new direction. After this sad incident, I worked as a substitute teacher as well as doing other kinds of jobs. I was miserable. When I came home at the end of the day, I felt very dissatisfied and depressed. I could barely take care of my children. I submersed myself in work, hoping I would succeed if I worked very hard. No matter how hard I tried and how hard I worked, failure stuck to me like glue. I completely lost my confidence.

At some point, my husband received a new job in a different city called Three Rivers where we moved from Montreal. At the time, I just decided to stay at home. I had tried many times to succeed, but in vain. No matter what I did, how much I tried, I couldn't seem to succeed. I asked myself over and over why? There must be something I am good at, but at this moment I just gave up. I felt lonely and completely incompetent. At that time, not only my professional life was a failure but also my personal life.

This is where my journey towards what I call my "Light House" began. After I saw the Oprah show, I started to spend more time taking care of myself for the first time. I started reading books, applying the principles and techniques into my life. Every day I felt better and better. I began to gain more and more awareness and accept aspects of myself.

As my journey began I knew I had to find what I wanted to do because I needed to find a meaning for my life. I knew for sure that I wanted a job where I could work at home. But before I could do all that I had decided to learn to love myself.

When I found out who I was it became clear to me what I wanted in my life and that was when my life became more meaningful. When I started to focus on myself I was able to love myself as I am. It was when I found my life purpose that I got clearer on the things I wanted in my life. It was then that I discovered what the missing element had been in my life for all those years…passion. Changing one's thoughts, increasing one's awareness and transforming a negative perspective into a positive one is a process. Our minds, in the beginning, need time to adjust. At the beginning I thought it was easy, but I quickly realized that it is a long process, a lifetime process.

When I worked on myself, I had to change a whole value and belief system. I had to find my real belief system, what I wanted to believe in. When I did I find my authentic self...I found the Artist.

What was missing most in my life was doing something that I loved that would give me more meaning. In the beginning I had many ideas, but I didn't know what I really wanted. It took me several months to discover what it was, which surprisingly, was life coaching. By coaching myself, I developed a passion and became more confident about my abilities. In order to find this passion, I made a list of my interests, hobbies, strengths and skills and then I came up with all the things that I could use to make a career. I asked myself what it was that I love to do and never get tired of doing and the answer was talk. This led me to ask myself what subject I was most knowledgeable about and loved talking about, which was self-development.

As I evolved in my research, I realized that coaching was for me because as a coach you are not only a coach, you are an author, a speaker and a teacher as well as a coach. You can do more things with it than just coach, which is what attracted me so much because I love to do all that and more. I am able to use the analytical skills I learned in University as well as speaking in public, writing (which I absolutely love doing) and inspiring people to have a better life, which is my newly-found life purpose. I also knew that I wanted to work from home, be my own boss and have flexible hours where I could have more family time and give more quality care to my kids. Coaching is giving me all that.

As I journeyed into coaching, I began to think about my definition of success and realized that I had always been very future focused. I had never looked to see what kind of successes were already in my life. When I really took the time to think about it, I realized I had to redefine what success meant to me. Now, success for me is the little things. It is all the little things that, believe it or not, can make someone feel happier and fulfilled, which is why they are a success. Most of the time we tend to look at the big picture and forget all the small steps and small things that are meaningful; those things that bring us to the place we want to be.

Gradually, when I started to focus and write about what I wanted, I started attracting more of what I wanted in my life. As I came to this realization I learned that, in the past, I was aiming at things that were not related to my strengths and passions, but rather what I thought society and people dictated that I should be and do. The day I realized this concept is the day my life gradually started, step by step, to shift around for me. I started gaining more clarity, changed some of my perspectives, became more positive and enjoyed life more than I did before. At this moment I had passed to another level where I saw life from a new fresh angle.

At least that is what I thought, until I realized a new lesson during the process of writing this chapter.

It wasn't until recently that I noticed that all my life I had chased success because I was trying to feel competent, until I stopped and asked myself why I desired so much to be competent. The answer came to me — because I strive for love and appreciation. My point here is that we often chase success because we want something that is missing deep inside of us — and what is really missing is ourselves. Everything that we do, everything that happens to us, is about what we have to heal about ourselves. The love and appreciation I am constantly looking for has to come from me. I have to give myself more love and appreciation, without expecting other people to. This is the true meaning of success: Love — Self-love!

We all have an inner Light House. We only have to find what leads us to the Light House and what makes us happy. As you can see, the best place to start your journey is with yourself. I cannot stress enough how important it is because it is the key to having balance, joy and success in your life. Oprah always says that it all comes from within and it comes from within you. It is like a tree; in order for it to grow, become beautiful and give fruit, you have to take care of it, water it and give it love and light. If you abandon that tree, it will dry and die. Your Light House is here. It is waiting for you to come and live in it. It is up to you to take the next step and enter it. Remember that it is a journey, a lifetime. But don't count the time; instead, see what you can learn along the way and learn to be a better, joyful, compassionate person — the kind of person you always wanted to be.

Galit Lazar is currently a life-coach, an author and a mom to 2 beautiful children. Galit is also the founder and owner of Galit's C.A.M.P. Coaching. She helps women in the entertainment business to outperform their achievements, stress free and consistently. Galit currently lives in beautiful Montreal, Canada. To learn more about Galit, you can go to: http://galitscampcoaching.com/home. You can also read more on her blog: http://www.galitscampcoaching.blogspot.com

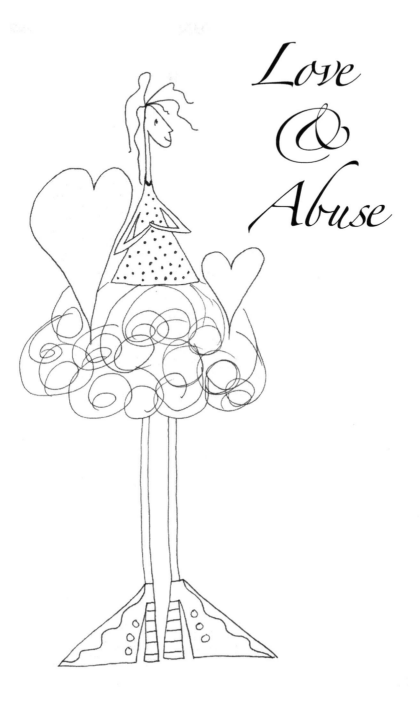

Love
&
Abuse

Standing Strong

Lisa Shultz

Growing up, I was a self motivated kid, driven to do well in school and beyond. I got a college degree, supported myself financially, and paid my bills diligently. When I got married at age 25, I had been living in my own apartment and had a steady career and income. My new husband had college debt and several years of no income as he learned the real estate business. I was the breadwinner for us supplying the cars, new home, food, and paying the bills.

As my husband began to catch up with income, pay off his debts and contribute financially to the household, our lifestyle improved. We moved into a bigger house, gradually upgraded our cars, and enjoyed more luxuries. These first three years of marriage were enjoyable and peaceful as we worked to get ahead financially. Eventually after several years, the scales were tipped, and he made considerably more income than I did. It appeared that we had an ideal life to the outside world, but the inside world started to erode.

Something happened when my husband became successful. He began to get angry at little things. His anger first erupted at a trivial incident of our new dog chewing a door mat. He exploded into uncontrollable rage against her, requiring me to pull him off physically, screaming for him to stop. The episode was so intense and out of control against an innocent, loving dog that it frightened me. I was in shock and could hardly speak for several days. When I did begin to talk about it, it was quickly minimized by my husband. Mentally, I tried to forget or deny the magnitude and hoped I wouldn't see anything like it again.

For awhile the anger didn't come very often and we started a family. We had two daughters close together in age, and I stopped working, focusing on home and family. But I saw the anger again. It was like a cork popped out of a bottle, little by little, he exploded over small things without warning. He became intensely angry above and beyond what the situation merited, and sometimes the situation didn't even merit anger at all.

It was just a matter of time before these moments of rage turned to me. The episodes became more frequent and hurtful. I became his easiest target, as I was around him most. The once strong and independent woman began to erode; the yelling and criticisms of my appearance took a toll on my self-confidence. I remember the day I came home from a hair salon. He disliked my haircut so much that he almost drove to the salon to yell at the stylist, after he finished yelling at me (I somehow prevented him from leaving the house). He began to pick apart my clothes and how I wore them, my weight, and other physical characteristics. My once loving husband now only showered me with words that were unkind and stung deeply.

He progressed to how I did things, such as scolding me for not making pancakes perfectly round. Later, he said I wasn't a good mother, lover, wife. The language and words intensified. The anger episodes became more frightening than before. Each day I grew in fear for what my life had become and where it was going in the future.

These outbursts usually happened in private, but sometimes family or friends witnessed his poor treatment of me. They felt sick and helpless to watch. I was embarrassed and did my best to cover it up. I remember the day my friend told me she could no longer see me because she couldn't bear to witness it any longer. I was scared and heartbroken as I saw my world crumbling around me.

The magnitude of his rage grew. Sometimes he yelled so loud and intensely that he foamed around the mouth. He was about six inches taller and about 75 pounds heavier than me. Occasionally he'd pound the wall or table with his fist for emphasis, and I worried that he would turn his fists on me next. I told no one what was happening; keeping all of the pain, sadness, hurt, and loneliness to myself. I hoped circumstances would improve, returning to a familiar life and the man I once loved. We went to marriage counseling a few times. He said he was coming along to assist the therapist in fixing all my problems!

I began to despair. Years of verbal abuse started to work into my being. I felt as though my soul was being murdered. I tiptoed around everything I did, because I never knew what would set him off. He was unpredictable, and I could never relax or let my guard down. I remember I stopped laughing. I think many years went by without laughing at anything.

Then one day after 10 years of marriage, about 7 years of which I lived with this decline in our relationship, I was given a gift. I didn't see it as one at the time, but I recognize it now as a gift. My husband said he had been seeing someone else, was in love with her, and was getting a divorce from me to marry her. All of which happened.

Despite the abusive nature of our marriage in the later years, the divorce was devastating to me. I didn't realize it was my ticket to regaining my self esteem and my happiness. Through a therapist I saw after the divorce, I began to heal, regain my self-worth and understand my husband was a narcissist. When I studied narcissism, I learned why he behaved as he did. Rage goes with narcissism, so I understood why he was so angry all the time. But the biggest thing I learned was that a narcissist looks for a strong woman and then beats her down. Beating her down feeds his sickness, like feeding a hungry animal. He took me from a beautiful, intelligent, talented, and strong person to a weak and defeated woman. So weak that I am not sure I would have ever had the strength to leave myself. This is why I know it was a gift in disguise when he left me!

Step by step, day by day I moved forward to regain my self-esteem and create a full and amazing life. I spent about a month wallowing in my bed crying and feeling sorry for myself. Then I took action. I read book after book on recovering from divorce, books on how to have good relationships, and books on narcissism. I sought the help of therapists, friends, and support groups. Slowly, I began to feel my soul come to life again.

The underlying reason that I simply had to regain my lost self and succeed in life was that my daughters were watching. What I did or did not do would be internalized and perhaps modeled later in their own lives. Each choice I made mattered. I was not perfect in my decisions and made many mistakes, but overall, I made more good choices than bad.

My daughters were my motivation to improve my life, but I also wanted to prove to myself that I was the opposite of all the negative things I had been told by my husband. One by one, I worked on all aspects of myself. Even when I did not achieve perfection (my pancakes are still not perfectly round), I received compliments on how good they tasted.

I was once told that sometimes our purpose in life is to teach or help others overcome a challenge that we can relate to from our deepest pain. I resisted this notion at first because I wanted to distance myself as far as possible from that pain in any way. I didn't want to remember it. Two books helped me to understand narcissism. I recommend those books for those who suspect they are in a narcissist relationship and need to understand that illness. Those two books are *Men Who Hate Women & The Women Who Love Them* by Dr. Susan Forward and Joan Torres as well as *Why is it Always About You?* by Sandy Hotchkiss, LCSW.

After understanding narcissism, I began reading uplifting, inspiring books and stories. It is still a habit I enjoy today.

I also had the opportunity to have new relationships that were healthy. My ex-husband had been my only serious relationship. I didn't believe all men were like him; I began dating and testing how to stand up for myself. I learned to express my wants, needs, and boundaries. I found the beauty inside and out that I knew had always been there, despite the words I had been told. If a relationship was not working for me, I was able to exit from it. I made decisions from a place of strength. I made decisions that protected and honored me. I even found compassion for my ex-husband. Narcissism is a vicious trap that is hard to get out of.

It damages all the important relationships of your life and leaves you with few friends and poor relations with family members. At this point of my life, I wish for his healing too. Our daughters will benefit most from seeing both parents recover, heal, and grow.

I now live a wonderful life. I enjoy running a business that I am passionate about. My daughters have grown into fabulous young ladies who inspire me. Although my marriage and divorce were difficult, I have created a life I love. I am very grateful for all I have learned and embrace my life with enthusiasm and a positive outlook. My experiences have given me empathy and compassion for those who have been through challenging times and have emerged to the other side.

Lisa Shultz is the owner and founder of Women, Wine & Wellness, a networking organization focused on connecting and empowering women. She is a networking expert and enjoys speaking, writing, mentoring and teaching about the art of networking and business success strategies. She loves supporting her two daughter's passions and talents. She enjoys swimming, skiing, ballet, gardening and travel. Lisa resides in Denver, Colorado and she can be reached at www.LisaJShultz.com.

The Boat Man

Kris Jordan

Alcoholics Anonymous meetings are rarely hard to find, if you know where to look. Since I just moved to my new college town and was without my car, I searched along a bus route and found one at a clubhouse not too far away. A.A. clubhouses are designed exclusively for holding meetings, sometimes more than one at a time.

The people littering the wrap-around porch of a white refurbished two-story gave this clubhouse away immediately. I hopped off the bus and crossed the street to join one of the meetings. As I climbed the wooden steps, cigarette smoke swirled around me and blended with the testimonials and laughter dancing in the air. Every single space in the house seemed occupied. I followed the signs which read Open A.A. and they led me to a room bursting with tables, folding chairs, and nearly 40 people, of various ages, genders and walks of life. I didn't share tonight. I just listened to the stories, the burdens.

After the meeting, I waited on the porch smoking a cigarette and hoping that if I glared at the bus stop across the road, the rain would stop. I finished my cigarette and deciding not to risk missing the critical transportation, started through the downpour.

I kicked myself for not checking the forecast. It looked beautiful when I left my dorm. A tan pick-up truck pulled up beside me as I stood waiting pathetically for my bus. The man inside rolled down the passenger side window and called out to me, "Do you need a ride?"

I recognized his blonde dreadlocks instantly from the meeting we had both just attended, "Sure. Thanks."

"Where am I taking you?"

"I live at the college. A straight shot that way." I pointed.

We both smiled, I jumped into the truck and he headed west. He introduced himself and told me that he was an artist. He spoke with a wandering mind, one thought to the next, disconnected. I watched the creases at the corners of his eyes contract as he spoke.

He may have been in his mid to late-thirties, but his dry, dull skin could have deceived me. I'd never seen dreadlocks up close before. His were sandy blonde matted clumps intertwined with random silky strands, especially at his forehead. I didn't notice the color of his eyes in the dark of the Toyota's cab. The tassels on his faded leather jacket brushed his thighs as he shifted gears.

We pulled up to my dorm, and I sat for a moment out of politeness as he finished his current rambling about a boat he had. I was more interested in the thump, whoosh sound of the windshield wipers gliding back and forth across the windshield. I thanked him for the ride, but when I reached for the door handle, he took off, driving away from my home.

I replayed his last sentence in my head. He wanted me to see his boat. Had I agreed? I didn't think so. He eased to a stop at the sign to exit the parking lot. My hand was still on the door latch. The rational part of me choked back my desire to jump out of the truck and run like hell.

I'd fallen off my bike going down the hill by my house when I was twelve. I could almost feel the road rash as I contemplated a tuck and roll maneuver, but also fearfully considered being pursued by chrome and rubber driven by a mad-man. I felt my conscience scream at me telling me to not be foolish, yet I was trying to look grown up and mature, in control. Looking put together was impor-tant, wasn't it? Jumping out now, he would think I was a lunatic, a fool, or worse, a victim. Where would I hide from him anyway?

My insecurity crept in like a ghost and dropped into my head with the weight of an elephant. What if he wasn't a lunatic but I was? If I jumped out of the car, would he look at me dumbfounded as I stood on the curb? Would he stare at me like I was a shameful idiot the way my mom did?

I knew if I asked him, he would turn around and take me right back to my dorm. But I had already asked him and he kept talking. Talking, talking, talking. Invading the space between us with suffocating noise.

I could do this. I could see his boat. There was nothing wrong with that. I would be smart. I was smart. I watched the street signs and tried to memorize them. Templeton, Jones. Templeton, Jones, Linden. Templeton, Jones, Linden, Vassar. I squinted at the next street sign through the water-blurred window. He suddenly went silent. Light off of a street lamp jumped onto his face and revealed his pale green eyes on me. He knew my plan. He took several quick stair step-like turns. I didn't see the street names and they were too numerous anyway. I gave up.

I lied by telling him that my roommate was expecting me. She would be wor-ried and call the police. I wanted it to be true as badly as I had the time I lay half dead from alcohol poisoning in a stranger's bathroom, when I cried as I wondered who might care that I was dying. I wanted desperately for someone to miss me when I was gone. The hole of emptiness returned to my stomach and my soul. Everything in me seemed to liquefy.

My body bounced and shivered as he pulled off the road into a pit of shadows. He parked, turned off the engine, and got out of the truck. I stayed seated. He came around to open the door and asked me to get out. The ground under my feet was grassy and sandy. I stood on the shore of a river, looking at the black, trembling waters. Goosebumps ran up my arms, so I pulled my jacket closer to my body. It didn't help.

The man pointed to his boat. It wasn't docked, as I had expected it to be, but rather it was a small houseboat bobbing halfway across the river. I nodded with a fake smile then reminded him I was cold and wanted to go home. He reminded me that he wanted me to see his boat.

He pulled a yellow canoe out from behind the shrubbery bordering the river, and invited me to get in. Normally it would have been a lie to say that I was afraid of water and canoes, but tonight I was terrified. The water reminded me of death, of icy infinite obscurity. I told him I needed to get home, but he took my arm and escorted me into the tiny canoe, rowing us to the houseboat.

Across the shore, but high up, I saw a house with its warm yellow lights on. How steep was the cliff that that house sat on? Could I climb it? Would anyone be home? Would anyone answer the door this late? How late was it? How cold was the Minnesota water now, in the fall?

"I really need to get back. I'm freezing. I don't like this. I don't like the water. Can we go?"

"No. Not yet," he responded flatly.

He took my hands and helped me up onto the deck of the houseboat.

The door opened to a blackness that ran like roaches into corners and lingered like fog once the light switch clicked. A round gray and white Formica table with two mismatched chairs sat directly in front of us.

"Sit down," he requested, pulling the scarf off of my neck, "take off your coat."

"I'm too cold. I'll leave it on." I wondered if he noticed my shivering or heard my chattering teeth.

He made his way to a small wood stove and threw in a few logs that soon ignited. He approached me again.

"That should help. Take off your jacket," he whispered while lowering it off my shoulders.

I felt frozen, petrified, immovable. He stood behind me, over me, and began massaging my shoulders. He rambled again, but his voice wasn't as frantic as before. He slid his fingers under the collar of my shirt, informing me of his skill in massage. He had to feel the tightness, the stress in my shoulders.

"Come lay down." He instructed, tugging me and signaling towards the other side of the boathouse.

"No, that's not a good idea. I need to go home." My cheeks were on fire, my fingers arctic.

He again took my arm and guided me in front of the stove. He unrolled a futon mattress leaned up against the wall. I stood defiantly, though I accepted my fate. If I went along, maybe he wouldn't hurt me, or at least not as bad. It didn't have to be tragic. It didn't have to be bad, if I cooperated.

I lay down on my side on the mattress, my arm tucked under my head, as if to take a nap. He sat beside me, shifted my body so I was on my stomach, and continued to massage my shoulders and down my spine. As his fingers reached my lower back, he tucked them under my shirt and shoved his thumbs under the waistband of my jeans.

I wondered if his dehydrated hands had noticed the smooth scar lying like butter cream piping along my vertebrae. The two-foot scar, along with the two metal rods running along each side of and fused through my spine, was hard to miss. The rods had been placed there two years ago to correct my severe scoliosis. Today my reinforced backbone was a hindrance rather than the salvation from deformation. Boat man made no comment and asked no questions, just persistently rubbed me with vigorous circles.

He reached his hands under my belly and unbuttoned my pants. I took a long, deep breath to stop my anxiety, but instead it was a choppy exhale, pushing out air and tears. I wasn't strong enough. I couldn't deal.

He lowered my pants a few inches but continued massaging my lower back. Boat man shifted and straddled me, sitting on my legs, slightly below my behind. The pressure in my legs made me feel trapped. It was more than I felt like cooperating with, but in this position, I had no strength. Because of my back surgery, I couldn't twist or raise my body. His knees were pressed into the back of my knees, immobilizing my legs. I wailed in my head. The back of my throat ached. My ears filled with pressure.

I kept my face in the pillow as my head pounded with fear. This would be painful. It wasn't pretend, and I couldn't make it be. The reality of the moment hit. My vulnerability, my frailty, my illusions, all those things I tried so hard to protect, came into focus.

I screamed at God within the confines of my mind. I didn't know where the words or tears came from. My entire body shook as they poured out of me. Everything I had ever wanted to talk to God about came through my head. Was He real? Did He care? Why was I here? Was He kind or demented? "No!" I lamented to God.

My thoughts turned to the part I played in this world, and I talked to God about how crappy I was, what a phony hypocrite I was. I told Him how I had needs still unmet, longings still unfulfilled. I thought about ownership. Maybe I was responsible for my actions. Maybe my thinking had something to do with the outcomes in my life.

My nose ran and the mucus joined the tears on my face. Boat man moaned as he lay down on me, extending his body fully over mine. My lungs compressed against the dusty, cushiony mattress. He wrapped his arms around me, shifting my body with his. In this awkward, uncomfortable embrace, Boat man let out a sigh.

I knew what was coming next, but I had acceptance. I was a piece of crap, and now God knew, and I knew He knew. It was out in the open, and I was ready for my punishment. Holding my breath, I waited for Boat man's hands to move the few last inches up to my breasts, for the feeling of his genitals hard against me, but I felt neither. His entire body was limp. I let out all my breath and sobbed, audibly now. God must have heard me. God believed me. God saved me. Boat man was asleep.

Too afraid to move and risk waking him up, I lay there, talking to God. I wasn't thinking about the future or the past at that time. I simply talked to my Maker. I told Him that I didn't think I really knew Him. I apologized for changing Him into what I wanted Him to be or what was cool. I apologized for treating Him so small, like a feeling I had instead of like a God who could make mountains and rivers and rain. He must be more than a God of my understanding, as A.A. taught, because here I was, and here God was. Yet I was so far from understanding Him.

I listened to the rain hit the roof for hours, as my mind finally fell silent. The peaceful repetition swayed me yet kept me awake. The weight of Boat man rested on my back. He moaned and rolled to my side, still pressed up against me. I contemplated an escape, but the darkness, the rain, the cold, the unfamiliar, kept me tight against my kidnapper.

When he awoke, the sky was still murky. He looked at the smoldering fire, then at me. Standing slowly and yawning, he went for our jackets. I don't remember the trip home, only the empty room I returned to, the digital clock reading 4:00 a.m., the burning shower I fell asleep in.

I came to realize that at some point that night, all human will was relinquished for that of God's will. I don't fully know what Boat man's intentions were. The A.A. clubhouse where we met wasn't able to identify him and I never went back.

I was taken against my will, not into Boat man's hands, but into His hands. God was there and always had been. Yet I was unaware. God was there that dreary night on a houseboat in the middle of some unknown river in a place I had never been before. He was there, rocking me in my fear, waiting for me to call to Him so He could answer. God still exists outside of my understanding, but now I know that He is this close.

Many years later, when I chose to tell this story and share it with others, I was criticized for my choices. I was angry at myself as well, wondering why I would allow myself to be put into such a dangerous situation. A friend told me that if something happens once, it's a fluke; twice a coincidence; three times, a pattern. I had to look at my pattern of victimization. I grew deeply in my spirituality and with God's help began to sift through the great denials in my life that had protected me, but were no longer serving me, in fact, I found myself locked into a victim mentality and thus creating a repetitive victim. It has been a long journey, but I can't wait to see the beautiful things God does with my life.

Kris Jordan has two beautiful daughters and resides in Colorado. She is currently writing poetry and two books for her love of writing, and also writes newsletters, blogs and microblogs for her family-owned plumbing company. She adores volunteering with youth, particularly teens, art in many forms, and God. She has an exceedingly abundant and passion filled future. Kris Jordan is PlumbingGirl on Twitter and can also be found at GarvinsSewerService.com.

Escape to Hope

Ana-Christina Wadle

The pain was blinding as he head butted me repeatedly. He slammed me down and held my shoulders as he kept hitting and hurting me. I lived with being shoved and grabbed. I lived with being forced into the corner. Being pinned by my throat to the wall. I lived with being thrown around the room and smashed to the ground, unable to move. He threw things at me at close range; sometimes they hit and broke skin. I lived with having my arms wrenched around behind me a being controlled by that excruciating pain. I lived with my husband. And he was crushing me.

I lived with that, and worse. Regardless of the physical abuse, the psychological and mental strikes were even more damaging. More lasting. And no one could see what was happening inside my home. After the head butting incidents, my face was blacked and swollen from my forehead to my jawbones. I stayed home from work for a week, claiming the "flu." One of my little boys asked me what was wrong. "My eyes are sick, honey." I was depressed. I was desperate. I was desolate.

I lived on tiny island in Alaska at that time. If you watch "The Deadliest Catch," you might recognize it as one of the islands they mention: St. Paul Island, Alaska. It was very small, had a clinic but no hospital, and the counseling services were extremely limited. I felt like I had no place to go.

I had no idea what to do or how to get help. In the end, a special woman reached out to me and essentially changed the path of my life and the lives of my boys. She was a former professional counselor who'd ended up on the island for one year – the year I needed help so badly. She talked to me about boundaries and creating a life for me and my boys that didn't include abuse. She broke my heart by telling me that if I stayed, my boys would mostly likely role model after their dad. Turns out, she saved my heart by breaking it.

We planned my escape that night. I was frightened. If he caught us leaving, it would be brutal. We planned the escape Thursday night. The next plane was scheduled for Saturday. The planes only came in three times per week – and they didn't always land due to weather conditions. I didn't sleep again until Sunday night. I gathered all the cash I had (less than $400,) and asked for help from my mom and dad to be able to return to Colorado. I decided who I could trust, literally, with my life and the lives of my children, and enlisted the help of two friends. They were the only ones that knew that I was going to try to leave.

Saturday morning was horrifying. My body had gone into full fight or flight mode and I had to swallow my panic, hoping the plane would be able to land in the fog. I felt like I had to go to the bathroom every five minutes, but there was nothing there. My body was doing involuntary crunches. I literally couldn't stand up straight. A doctor told me later that it was my body trying to protect itself. It was tightening up my abdomen to protect my vital organs.

I took a few phone calls from the friend who was giving me updates on the plane and whether it would be able to land. Her end of the conversation was all business. My end was an act; I acted bright and cheery as I made fake arrangements for her to come pick up my five and seven year old boys for the afternoon so that they could hang out with her grandson. I couldn't believe what was happening and what I had to do to stay safe.

She came and picked up my two older boys in her little pickup truck and took off. I took my three year old (ostensibly to go visit a friend) and walked away from my house for the last time. My friend with the truck circled around the village and swung around to pick me up. As we headed to the tiny little airport with its gravel runway, I was sobbing. My heart and head were pounding. I hadn't slept or eaten since Wednesday night, and I was at the end of my physical and mental resources. My counselor friend met me at the runway as we were waiting for the plane to touch down. I was beside myself. She took over as a mom will do. I remember her firmly grasping my face, almost shaking me to get my attention. She looked at me, with her face an inch from mine, and said, "Ana-Christina! Ana-Christina! LISTEN TO ME. You are going to make it. You are going to get through this. You are going to make a difference for others because of this. ARE YOU LISTENING TO ME?" She had pretty well stunned me and helped me re-focus.

The plane came. My boys and I got on. One of my little boys asked me "Where is daddy? He needs to come with us." With tears rolling down my cheeks, I told him "Daddy's not coming, sweetheart." We landed in Anchorage where a good friend picked us up, took care of us for the evening and took us to the airport again for the red-eye flight to Denver. Sunday afternoon, I arrived with my boys at Denver International Airport with no luggage and a back pack. We started our new lives.

It was very tough at first. I look back at the first seven years and know that I was in a terrible place. When you survive a traumatic situation, you tend to simply go through the motions just to get through, day to day. I look back and know that I was terribly wounded, angry, and shut down – even with my boys.

I began a fundamental shift when I got **tired enough** of living in the anger, and the depression, and the denial. I was tired of pretending to be so strong. Single, working full time, and supporting a household by myself had gotten really old. I felt weak and drained and my life didn't have purpose. I asked God to come live in my heart. I decided to do things differently. And I did, step by step. I began the process of learning how to forgive. I started the road to forgiving myself. I set out to learn new skills and tools that I hadn't known or hadn't learned before in my life. I worked on setting boundaries. I worked on balancing my life.

I have struggled mightily. With the big things in life that happen like loved ones dying or loved ones caught in the cycle of addiction. And with the little things that pile up. Bills to pay, a house to clean, children to care for, cars that break down, health issues – the myriad of things that you simple need to take care of. I know what it's like to be way far down. And I know what it takes not only to get up, but to keep going. **I moved from victim to survivor to thriver.**

When you are faced with tough situations, when you are faced with your heart breaking, when you are faced with doubt and confusion – take a step. Even a little one. Then, another. And another. Just the act of taking baby steps will help pull you up and out of your despair.

I wanted to make a difference and share some of the tools that have helped me along my path. Tools that helped me when I was depressed. Tools that helped when I was doing ok, but just kind of floating along. So many people have helped me and my boys along our path. So many hearts have prayed for us. I wanted to give back. And pay it forward. In late 2008, I wrote and published *Tools of Hope – Simple Tools to Restore an Renew Your Hope* as a way to do that. I left my 20 year construction management career to begin pursuing my calling of sharing tools. I am a professional motivational speaker and trainer – I've trained over 1500 people this last year. In that same year, we spread over 1200 *Tools of Hope* books across the U.S. – all word of mouth.

Life is too short to keep floating, to just "get by." Life is too short to take for granted. Life is too short to allow bad situations to stay bad. I'm not talking about life being perfect. I'm not talking about it being all smiles and laughter. I know that life can be hard. I know that it can be heartbreaking and devastating. It is also amazing, and surprising, and beautiful. I know that keeping your hope – building your balance, resilience, and shifting your perspective – can make the bad times a little easier. A little less painful. A little more bearable. **Hope gets back up – Every Time.**

My name is Ana-Christina. I am building the life I REALLY want. I make a difference. I live with hope. I live moving forward. I live with encouragement. I live by taking steps. I live in faith. I live in prayer. I keep trying. I am growing and learning. I live knowing that if I died today, my life would be worth it. I am living and growing my legacy. No matter what you are going through, there is hope.

Take some steps. Reach UP. Reach forward. Build the life you REALLY want.

Ana-Christina Wadle ("Wad-lee") is an inspirational trainer and speaker, Legacy Coach, and author. She presents her Tools of Hope Workshops not only as a trainer and coach, but as a keynote speaker for a wide variety of companies and organizations. She was a single mom for ten years to her three boys, Colin, Nick, and Chris. She met and married her gift (and partner in constant-home-remodel!), Jerry Wadle in 2007. Her twin passions are helping survivors of any kind to learn to thrive, and helping the helpers. With her motivating and insightful trainings, she has worked with distinct groups such as victim's advocates, clinical staff, counselors, accountants, construction superintendents, police officers, SWAT officers, nurses, and sales professionals. Learn more at: www.TOOLSOFHOPE.COM or www.MyLegacyCoaching.com, Email: hope@toolsofhope.com, Call: 303.751.6813

I Married Young

Marie Gallagher

I was enlisted in the U.S Army, stationed in Ansbach, Germany in 1974. I was thousands of miles from home and feeling extremely lonely. I met a young man who worked as a driver for the officers in our headquarters company. He had a very negative attitude about Army life, civilian life, and life in general. I, on the other hand, was full of enthusiasm and joy for whatever adventures were out there in the world for me to experience. I loved what I was doing, and at the tender age of 18, I felt like I had everything going in my direction. I cautiously started dating this man with the negative attitude, thinking in my own Pollyanna world, if he could change his attitude and focus on the positive like I was, his life could be fantastic. I should have seen the warning signs coming. He was extremely possessive, verbally abusive, abused drugs, and had a general disdain for just about anything positive in life. I thought I just needed to try harder. We married a mere 4 months after meeting (I told you I was lonely).

The first physical beating took place one week before we married and continued off and on for 5 years. We had our daughter in 1977. She was just 15 months old when she witnessed her dad grab me around the throat to squeeze my life out. I decided right then and there that he had to go. We needed out of that toxic relationship. He left, and we divorced a year later. First strike out in the game of married love.

I was working two jobs trying to support myself and my young daughter when I met a new man. He seemed stable, friendly, happy, kind, and really liked me. He was about 8 years older than I, but that didn't seem to matter to me. I did have my dukes up, and after the last relationship, was entering into this one extremely cautiously. I surely didn't want to make another mistake. We decided to date, then to eventually live together and finally, can you believe this, I asked him if he ever wanted to marry. He seemed okay with the idea. Not overly happy, ecstatic; here's the love of my life happy, he was just okay with the idea. Again, I should have seen the warning signs. We married, but long story short, he was more interested in pursuing all of my female friends than he was ever interested in developing a long term relationship with me. He cheated on me throughout the marriage, and the last straw was when he cheated on me with one of my band-mates from a college band. I tried therapy with him and the therapist told me that I was the one with the problem! What? Oh no, I'm out of here was all I could think. Second strike out in the game of married love.

I moved to Denver in pursuit of a new life for myself and my child. I worked at a company selling survey equipment. I started corresponding with an old friend of mine from high school. We were always good friends. I could rely on him for just about anything. He invited me to visit him in a foreign country. I took the trip, ended up getting engaged. I thought, "What the heck, may as well give this guy a try." Well, we were better friends than we were married partners. Without going into a lot of detail, the relationship did not work out. We just were not meant to be married to each other. I felt so sad, so useless, so not worthy of a long, enduring relationship. I felt like a loser. Strike three in the game of married love.

I heard my mother say to me that I was just not the marrying kind. I felt stupid, hopeless, and sure that I would live my life alone as a single parent. That thinking lasted a short time. I met the man, and I was so scared that I ran. I wanted nothing to do with a long term relationship, and God forbid marriage. No way, no how; I thought I did not deserve another chance. This lovely man was so patient and kind. He told me he loved me, he loved my child and that he wanted to marry me. Oh gosh, I sort of freaked out and said not to mention marriage for at least 2 years. Don't you know that the two years passed as if it were just a few months. The love of my life then said to me, "What are you doing in October?" I said, "Nothing big, why?" He then mentioned that it was 2 years and that he still wanted to marry me. I swallowed hard, got choked up and said, "Even with my luck in the past?" He said, "Yes, absolutely, I love you, and I want to marry you." We married in 1987 and have been happily, joyously married for 23 years.

I could have given up, but I refused to lose faith. I knew in my heart that I deserved a marriage filled with love and respect. Besides, what kind of life lesson would that have been for my daughter if I had not kept the faith and trusted that there was a loving, kind partner out there for me despite the previous failed attempts? The point of my story is that if you open up your heart, and trust, love will find a way in.

Marie Gallagher is happy to report that she has been blissfully wed for 23 years now. She counts her spouse and daughter as the centerpieces of her life. She loves her work as a certified massage therapist specializing in pain relief for chronic stress, pain, injuries and trauma. She found that being present in life and showing up for what is - has made the profound difference. You can reach Marie at (303) 748-9130 to schedule bodywork. You can also reach her at: gsister2u@comcast.net -or- at the website: www.sisterjuice.mymangosteen.com

This Is Not Who I Am

Mary Owens

Usually my cozy dark purple robe made me feel warm and relaxed. This was anything but warming or relaxing. I was looking down over the five story balcony hanging by the belt of that cozy robe. I could feel the belt start to unravel from around my waist as my weight pulled against it. I thought to myself, if I land there I will be better off than if I land right on that spot. If I land there, I will be sure to die.

I turned to face my boyfriend who was holding the belt of my robe and ultimately my life in his hands. I could see the rage in his eyes and knew it was pointless to try and reason with him. I hung there watching the muscles in his arms bulge as it was everything he had in him to keep me in the air. I knew that the less I struggled with him the safer I would be, so there I was suspended five stories up with one person in control of my life.

The youngest of three girls, I was always happy and approachable from the time I was a baby. As I child I felt connected to my soul, but as I grew older I lost that connection and became lonely and scared. Being the third girl in my family I didn't feel very special. I did a lot of things to feel alive or to gain attention. Unfortunately I didn't feel very alive by doing the good things.

My parents were excellent parents and worked hard to give us a wonderful upbringing. Even with all of their love I felt unimportant. I was the youngest not only within my immediate family but in my extended family as well. I was just another child that my aunts and uncles had to try and remember. I didn't stand out to my grandparents either. At least that's what I felt inside. I could give you a thousand instances that would prove me wrong but I inside I felt I was just another body within my family.

This feeling of loneliness and feeling I wasn't special lead me down a dangerous path. I began thinking about suicide when I was in the sixth grade, about the same time I discovered alcohol. I didn't have any plans on how I was going to kill myself but at my core I hoped somebody would find me before I died. As I explored the different suicidal options, I realized that if I was going to attempt to get someone's attention there would most likely be pain involved and there was a risk I would actually pull the suicide off.

Realizing this cry for attention wasn't the best option, I turned to alcohol. Ah, the feeling of being light and carefree, I loved it! I found myself laughing with friends and being accepted into the cool crowd. There was still a feeling of emptiness in my heart, but when I was drinking I didn't care.

I used and abused alcohol on and off throughout high school. I had this inner knowledge that my life was something more but I couldn't reach it. I wanted people to see how special I was yet I felt lost in the overcrowded school. I did everything I could think of to get attention. I began to realize that this void in my heart wasn't about attention from a group of people. It was the attention of someone special I was seeking. I wanted to feel love. I wanted to feel that feeling you get when watching a movie where two lovers find their way to each other. They work to be together and at the end they melt into each other's arms. I wanted to feel love and to be special to someone.

That was about the time I found my first real boyfriend. He was charming and gorgeous, a George Michael look alike. It was the late 80's and George was at his peak and I felt like I was as well. The best part was that this guy was into me! I didn't know how to be a girlfriend or what was expected of me. I just knew that the feeling I was experiencing was even better than alcohol. How could that be? I felt more alive around him than I did while I was drinking. Having this knowledge, I turned my focus onto him and away from alcohol. Our relationship was amazing the first month, which in high school felt like forever! I loved everything about him.

We would sneak around to be alone together because when we were alone sparks flew! I was totally alive! While my relationship was growing, I was fading. I began to like what he liked. Music, sports, friends, anything about him was about me. A few months into the relationship I found out that he was going into the Navy and my life was shattered. I desperately wanted him to stay, yet he left and I was alone. The hole in my heart was stripped bare and bigger than before.

My image of this man was that he was the best thing ever. He was kind, gentle, gorgeous, and simply the best! That image was about to be destroyed. One summer afternoon I received a call. "Hello is Mary available?" It sounded very professional so I stepped up to the role and answered in my most mature voice that they were speaking to me. Then I felt the knife go into that wide open hole in my heart. "Mary, this is the Department of Disease Control. We are calling to inform you that you have been in contact with someone who had an STD, Chlamydia to be exact." My professional self was gone and tears poured down my face. I could taste the salt on my lips but felt as if it was being poured into my open wounded heart. The sting was intense and burning. I had not been with anyone else so I knew it was from him. Confused, hurt and naïve, I waited for his letter or phone call that would place the much needed band aide over my heart wound.

When we did finally talk he explained that he loved me so it must have come from someone I had been with. He was very convincing. I had to catch myself because for a brief moment I thought maybe that could be the case. I was even going over past drunken nights trying to figure out if something happened to me that I didn't remember. I even tested negative at Planned Parenthood yet they still put me on an antibiotic. At that point, something told me to be confident and I realized I had to put my foot down. Through my tears, a numbing headache, and a bleeding heart I insisted on the truth. He admitted he had cheated on me. Only months later did I learn the extent of how many times, but because I loved him and he filled this hole in my heart, I continued my relationship with him.

This relationship was intense and destructive to my self esteem yet I continued to see him. He found a loop hole in the system and was honorably discharged so he could come back home and repair our broken relationship. A couple of years went by, filled with allegations of cheating from all sorts of women. I finally had enough and let the relationship go. The wound in my heart had been stripped of the scab so many times; it now was a scar and was more difficult to penetrate.

The time in college proved to be challenging for me in the area of men. I attracted only the bad boys. If they were up to mischief, I was there to play with them. I wanted to feel free again and by no means was I going to let that wound in my heart be exposed to any more salt. It was all about protecting my scar, so I had a series of relationships but nothing serious. I wasn't open to it; at the time, I believed I just wasn't special. I spent years in relationships where I was treated the way I felt about myself, like a play toy. I sure wasn't girlfriend material because I could drink like the boys and play as hard as the boys! Who wants to take that kind of girl home to meet the parents?

In my hard playing days we would run around until all hours of the night. One night I was walking down one of the major streets in downtown Denver and saw this great looking guy. He was leaning against a brick wall, wearing a baseball cap, jeans, and a loose sweatshirt. He was sucking on a lollipop and his eyes were penetrating brown. I felt my heart leap for a moment and then I told it to settle down. I convinced myself that he was only eye candy and if I was feeling giddy it was probably the alcohol. I walked by him and our eyes met. I said hi and giggled but kept walking. I looked back and saw that a couple of other guys had joined him. They followed us into a bar. My guy was persistent! He wanted to connect with me and know things about me. Since I wasn't going to let him in my heart, I kept it surface level conversation. I gave him my phone number and went on my way.

A month later I was out dancing at a club. From the dance floor I saw someone familiar leaning against the wall staring at me. I was instantly pulled to look in his eyes and they penetrated my soul. I went to talk with him and he asked if I wanted to go and get some food. We ended up at a pizza place with a small group and that's when it happened. He made a comment about a message on my answering machine. I had saved a message from someone and he was quoting it. I was stunned. How did he know the message? How did he access my answering machine and why? This guy was so mysterious to me, I was hooked. What it was about me that had him looking in to my life? In a strange way, I felt special.

We became friends and even more, yet there was something about him. I knew he was so wrong so I never would admit that we were anything more than friends. I now know that was my soul screaming to me "don't let him near you; he is so wrong for you." This relationship was intense. When we saw each other it was like a beam of steel would reach out of our hearts and meld together to connect us. He was insanely jealous which caused many fights. This led to black and blue welts hidden under my layer of clothes. He was a smart guy because he never hit my face or neck and stayed clear of my arms. I was in this crazy spiral of mysterious suspense, and secrets. Strangely enough I felt 100% special to this guy. If I had the power to cause someone to be this enraged so many times I knew I had to be special. I was lying to everyone about the relationship.

I had cut off most of my friendships with people because when I went out I would run into him and that would lead to a night of him throwing me around my apartment. Mirrors and bed frames broken from my body crashing into them didn't matter to me. What mattered was the hearts I was silently breaking, my parents and sisters who would be devastated if they knew what I had gotten myself into. So I quietly accepted my punishment and lived in a world feeling deceptive and so profoundly important at the same time.

It was about 2:00 in the morning after the bars had closed. I had not gone out that night as I didn't go out very much at all. I heard a knock on my door so I threw on my cozy purple robe and answered the door. As I opened it, I was immediately pushed back into my apartment. I hit the glass table first and with much relief didn't break it. Then I was pushed over the back of the couch. As I tumbled to the floor I could hear him yelling, "Who was here with you tonight you slut!" I was disoriented yet this was nothing new. Using my skills of trying to talk him out of his insane thoughts, I began to beg and plead for him to listen to me. I had been alone, but this time was different. As I looked into his eyes, I could see the emptiness. He picked me up and took me out to the balcony. Without any time to realize what was going on, I was hanging from a five story building, praying if I had one more chance to show the world "this is not who I am" I would do everything I could to get my life in order. The rush of thoughts swimming in my brain were going so fast, yet time was standing still. How could I ever have let it get this bad? This was the last way I ever thought I would die!

Something from the Universe stepped in and I was back in my apartment. I sat quietly watching him as he sunk into the couch and went to sleep. I sat on my floor weeping. I could taste the salt from my tears again and this time as they reached my heart instead of stinging or bring on pain; I could feel them melting the iron away. I felt my heart screaming to come back and connect with me again. This time I allowed it to open and I began to listen to what it was telling me. I was strong and I would get my life in order.

I went for help and worked with a therapist on how to end this relationship in a safe way while putting my life back on track. I was still so ashamed that I had let my life get so out of hand. No one knew the extent of the danger I was in and in a strange way I think that kept the situation more controllable. The relationship was over in a matter of weeks by me standing up to him and telling him if he ever hit me again I would call the cops. I had the support of the Universe on my side, literally. Within 2 months of the incident, he was arrested for assault and placed on probation. He had anger management classes for 4 months as part of his sentence. As he went through these classes something changed. We agreed to end our friendship and go on our own ways.

I spent the next year looking into my heart. I recognized I was the only cause of my pain. Why was I reaching outside of myself to feel special? I realized that I would only feel special when I believed I was special. I created goals for myself and began to accomplish them. I discovered I was really good in business and able to create what I desired in a career. Most of all I designed rules about how men were allowed to treat me. I stopped looking to men to put the band-aid over my heart. My wound began to heal and without a thick scar over it. It was softer and smoother and so was I.

I know there are going to be bumps in the road and that's fine. I look at those challenges as gifts that provide valuable feedback, so I can get more in touch with my heart and soul. I'm sure I'll never be physically abused again and hopefully can inspire someone else to realize "this is not who you are." You are strong, beautiful, caring, and most of all special!

Ten years later from that night on the balcony, I work every day to empower people to live the lives they are born to live. Being on purpose in your life is your birthright! I am living proof. I speak to groups, writing, and coaching people through the times they are disconnected from what their heart is saying. Stop for a moment now. What is your heart calling you to do? My only request is remember to be who you are meant to be!

Mary received a Master's in Social Work from the University of Denver in 1997. She is a Certified Law of Attraction Empowerment Coach, a Landmark Education graduate and a Bob Proctor Coaching graduate. She empowers you to go from where you are in your life to where you want to be, using therapeutic techniques with the Laws of the Universe. Mary is the author of Mary's Moxie Talk newsletter and is an expert writer for Ezinearticles.com and SelfGrowth.com. She has been featured on the homepage of SelfGrowth.com as an expert writer on Success Skills. She has spent years studying the Laws of the Universe and how they play a part of our lives and relationships. For more information about her coaching services please visit http://www.LiveWithPurposeAndPassion.com

Trusting My Intuition, Choosing Me

Amy Schulstad

Growing up I was always encouraged to do things perfectly. Be the perfect student, get the perfect grades, be quiet, and don't speak out of turn. I had a life timeline in my head that I felt I was expected to follow: graduate from high school, go to college, get married at 22, get a good job, have kids, the perfect life. Boy, did I get my real life lesson! I found out that life doesn't always go according to plan and that's probably a good thing.

I met my soon-to-be husband at chiropractic school. Prior to that point, I really hadn't dated a lot or had a serious relationship. Jason seemed to be the perfect guy – smart, funny, athletic, dynamic, ambitious, charming, someone to whom everyone was drawn…including me. My parents loved him, because he talked and was open about me. Being open meant showing flaws, and flaws aren't perfection. We soon married and started our perfect life. We were going to open a practice together, be wildly successful and have a family. Looking back, I realize these dreams of ours were really his dreams. I jumped on the bandwagon because I didn't know what I wanted or what my dreams were. Kids? Sure, in 3-5 years after we were in our successful practice, had money, and because that's what you do when you're married, right? Although 3-5 years later I was feeling less and less like that's what I wanted.

That perfect practice together included a big office with a large overhead. I didn't feel we should have it, yet didn't speak up because I felt he knew best. He was extremely optimistic with the dreamer mentality that everything was going to be great, so I went along with it. Our practice did not take off like we were hoping and turned into a huge stress, financially and personally. We never had enough money, and since his philosophy was everything will work out, don't worry about it, I was the one who had to figure out how to get the bills paid. The sleepless nights were endless; the gut-wrenching pain of wondering where we would find the money to survive both in business and in life fell upon my shoulders. Some days I hid in our x-ray developing room, curled up on the floor, crying gut-wrenching tears, begging God to help us. Finally, practicality kicked in and we had no choice but for one of us to find a real job, one with a regular paycheck.

That person ended up being me. Since we needed cash immediately, I got a job as a server, with the intention of finding something more meaningful later after we were on our feet, and ideally getting back to chiropractic.

One serving job wasn't enough so it turned into two. I was working seven days a week asking, "Are you ready to order?" while my husband was healing people and being the doctor. Financially our stress became less but personally it was getting worse. I was just a server and he was the important doctor; he was the smart one while I was working a menial job. He felt like it was his responsibility to grow the practice and that I was playing everyday with no responsibility. There were nights, after both of us had too much to drink, when he would say, "You're just a server, you have no right to question how I'm running MY practice!" After awhile I started believing I was just a server as well. The fact that I had taken the same classes, graduated from the same school and had the same degree didn't matter at all. My confidence decreased daily, weekly, monthly, until two years later I woke up one day thinking, "How did I get here?" I was depressed and in despair. With no career and a non-existent relationship with my husband, we were living separate lives. On Saturday nights, he went to his brother's house to play video games while I stayed at home, drinking a bottle of wine and sometimes smoking cigarettes.

The low point occurred on a Monday morning. I had just come back from a weekend trip back home, my first trip without my husband in years, and I realized I was a different person without him. With him, I had gotten to the point of not speaking, saying my opinion, or sharing any part of myself, because he always overtook the conversation. I felt stupid around him. On this particular morning, I felt like a nobody, that I didn't matter. Yet I had a strong feeling I needed to do more with my life, and my purpose was bigger than what I was doing. I had experienced these feelings before, but this time I was ready to do something about it. The question was what.

Getting away from my current environment was the answer. I wanted to get back into practice but I didn't have the confidence to go back to our practice. It was his and there was no place for me. I wasn't sure I knew how to be a doctor anymore. I didn't want to live under Jason's shadow, I wanted to be me.

I ended up getting a job working for another chiropractor in Seattle, 1,360 miles away. I struggled with the thought of moving away from my husband, mostly of what others would think. It certainly wasn't the norm, and how dare I put my needs first? I always made decisions based on rational and logical thinking. This was not logical. Why would I travel half-way across the country to have a chiropractic practice when I already had one right there with my husband? In my desperation, I turned inward. For once, I listened to my gut, to my heart and made the decision to go. It didn't make sense, but I knew I had to do it in order to live. I told myself, my husband, and everyone else it was a training opportunity, a trial separation, and I would be back within a year. My husband was hoping I would develop as a person, get happy and come back to him a changed-for-the-better woman. Deep down I was hoping I would find happiness and I saw this as my opportunity to see if I could make it on my own and be successful, while having a fallback if I wasn't. I hadn't been happy in my marriage for quite some time, and this was a way to escape. The morning I left Denver, Jason and I shared a long embrace with many tears. I wondered if I was making the right decision. By the time I hit Fort Collins the tears were gone and my heart was filled with more hope and excitement than I had ever felt. I knew I was on the right path.

I knew no one in Seattle except for a great uncle with whom I was hardly acquainted. Within two months of living there, I had already made a handful of great friends. In the past, making friends, letting them in, and getting close, had always been a struggle for me. I knew I was in the right place because I was socializing, going out, having fun, laughing, living a life I had only dreamed about. Work gave me the opportunity to develop my skills as a chiropractor and instilled confidence I could be a good doctor. My biggest discovery was the feeling of happiness. Once I experienced how it felt, I knew the last five years had been void of it. What a turning point! I knew I couldn't go back to my old life. I couldn't live with the same person, live the same life and be happy. When Jason and I visited each other, I quickly reverted to the quiet, reserved, afraid-to-speak-up person I had been before. Although I knew things had to change and deep down I knew what I needed to do, I still resisted it. I didn't feel ready to be on my own. What if I regretted it? What if there really was only one person for everyone and I was throwing him away? What if I never found love again? All these questions plagued my consciousness and I found myself hanging on, telling him that I was planning on moving home sooner rather than later, even though in my heart I found myself never wanting to move back.

The time apart became easier for me and harder for him. I eventually moved out from my great uncle's place and into an apartment with a friend. At that critical point, living there felt more permanent than anything else before. I had my own place with a year's lease, friends that had become my family, and a sense that I belonged somewhere. Jason was increasing the pressure to move home. A couple weeks after moving in to my new place, I woke up with an intense, frantic feeling that I needed to make a decision. I needed to either give notice and move back to Denver or stay on a permanent basis and end my marriage. My heart told me what to do. Even so, I struggled with it for days. I couldn't talk with my parents about it. They had been married for 40+ years and felt divorce should only happen in severe cases. With help from my friends and parents, who ended up being extremely supportive, and some deep soul-searching, I found the strength to tell

Jason it was over. There were many painful conversations and it was not easy for either of us. This decision had weighed heavy in my heart. Now I felt like a ton of weight was lifted off my shoulders and I was free to live MY life, not someone else's.

I never regretted my decision. It hasn't been an easy journey and I am still paying (literally) for the divorce and its consequences. However, as a result of choosing me and my happiness, I experienced life in a way I never would have if still married. I eventually moved back to Denver and now have my own practice. With confidence in myself and my life, I know what happiness feels like on a daily basis. I make decisions that fit me, not someone else, based on my heart and gut as opposed to my head. It's those decisions that have fulfilled my life the most. Life is not easy-breezy, but it's my life and I look forward to the challenges because I know they help me grow and become a stronger person. Life, bring it on!

Dr. Amy Schulstad works with people to help them reach their highest health potential through chiropractic care at her practice, Awaken Possibility, LLC. Her mission is to not only help people awaken the health within, but also awaken what's possible within, help bring dreams to life, and encourage self-discovery. Check out her website www.chiropractorblair.com. She can also be reached at dramy@chiropractorblair.com.

I Will Remember You

Kelly L. Collins

It was 1973. My cousin, who was twelve at the time, was visiting from California. That far away land that I heard about in Beach Boy songs...she lived there! She had a beach, or at least so I thought. As I later discovered, Bakersfield isn't exactly near the coast. We had my kermit-the-frog green ball portable transistor radio and we were walking down the street to a corner store, entirely out of the boundaries my parents had given me. Sporting our extremely revealing Levi shorts adorned with patches of love and peace, rocking to the tunes she introduced me to... the sounds of Motown and the movements of the O'Jays singing "Get on board...join hands...join Love Train, Love Train." This was a far cry from my Salt Lake City upbringing and the innocent sounds of Donny Osmond.

She was by definition 'Out of Sight.' As if that weren't enough to have her little cousin, five years her junior, following her everywhere...she whipped out a picture of a *BOYFRIEND*. He definitely fit the description of a typical California surfer dude. After all, he was blonde *and* from California. He was an early version of Matthew McConaughey, with a West Coast accent. As I later discovered, the intensely hot farming community of Bakersfield was a good hour from any signs of water. Surfer no, party boy....yes! The impression was made. Someone to emulate, someone to admire and certainly a place I would move to when I was old enough. I wanted to be *just* like her! As I now know, regardless of whether the want is positive or negative, the Universe will often respond with a resounding yes to our desires.

Between the years of 1973 and 1980, I saw my cousin only sporadically, but always felt like the chick following my cool teen cousin's every move and behavior. If she listened to the hot sounds of Detroit, I listened to them. She wove wide brightly colored macramé belts, so I learned to macramé. I was naïve at the time, but discovered that during those later years, Teri was sexually abused by her step-father. The pain she felt would bring us together but in the end, it would separate us forever.

In 1981, I moved to California to live with my aunt and my adored cousin to try and get my own delinquent childhood behavior under control after an untimely pregnancy by an abusive and possessive high school boyfriend. My parents, exhausted and defeated, felt the only solution was sending me away to live with my aunt in California. To me this meant only one thing, I would get my lifelong desire for an older sister, my cousin. Although I knew my parents were very young, it was only after reaching my own thirties that I realized my parents were in their late twenties as I approached high school and my behavior was uncontrollable to two who were still immersed in their own growth and development. I was not parented. Not because I was not loved, but, because they themselves were too young and immature. This tumultuous time in my childhood was certainly not the worst time in my life, but I was a moth to the flame of substance abuse and paired behavior of covering emotions. The Don't Ask, Don't Tell family was fast on its way to claiming its two victims.

Not unlike the early seventies, I followed my cousin's every move. I had a job and lived in a house where I contributed by paying rent, I was an adult with adult rights. Not just the first place I drank alcohol, but it was the first place I learned to make blender drinks and party. Soon the substances were heavier and larger. We weren't unusual; we were just living in the post-disco era. Apparently we thought the pool parties and summertime in California should emulate Studio 54. Cocaine was the new alcohol. And in California, it was readily available. Teri's abuser was gone. My life, or so I thought, was in need of numbing and the ground was ripe. We were just going to say 'f___ it' and have a good time. And we managed, in the words of Gladys Night and The Pips, to 'make the best of, a bad situation.' We may have toned it down a bit, but, numbing the content was the goal.

All through the 80's we covered it up.

All through the 90's we covered it up.

Funny thing about your twenty and thirty-something body, it allows for lots of cover up! Not so much as we approached our forties.

Flash forward to New Year's 1999. We were ready to groove right into the next century. Not much had changed. My cousin worked tirelessly for an unmentionable international one-stop-shop retail presence. I was living 1200 miles away, but, we were in contact and we would always catch up whenever there were family events. It was a series of reunions; meetings at our grandma's cabin; weekend trips to Santa Barbara or a trip to Denver. Each time we drank and in the later years, we supported each other in our pain. Why was everyone so mad at us when we drank? Who cared if we drank two bottles of wine and passed out? Come to find out…nearly everybody.

As they say, 'Drink and Drive and You WILL Get caught.' And they were right. The spiral was slow and painful for us both. It meant lost relationships with family members who were no longer willing to tolerate the substance abuse. She married an intolerant individual who controlled and reminded her that she was 'less than.' I took my financial and personal relationship woes right into the cauldron. Eventually the wine covered the whine. The excuses were rampant. We would talk a couple of times a month. Usually our talks would last for hours. We would complain about our relationships; justify our drinking and discuss our alcohol related legal battles

Later, an auto accident involving drinking while driving coupled with a long history of addiction to pain medications forced my cousin to enter rehab in the Fall of 2008. She was there for 30 days and she was finally able to bring to the surface that which she tried to cover in mind and body altering substances. The abuse and the pain of her teen years were finally out in the open. And the abuse would have to be discussed openly with her mother for healing. She was ready. She was sober, at least for a few weeks. Rehab was a sanctuary in a way. It was a sacred space where she could tell her story, write her feelings and feel supported. There was no judgment, no condemnation, and quite honestly, no loneliness. But eventually, real life, relationships and experiences are reintroduced as part of the recovery. One must let go of that which no longer serves us.

During the same few months, I was arrested while numbing my own personal pain over the change of marital circumstances, home and financial stability. I thought my life was over. How wrong I was. This would be the pinnacle – that tipping point where one would discover an alternate path. Conversely, Teri would continue her downward spiral. What I did have, that my cousin did not, was a spiritual community to support me.

I did not go to my ministers. I did not go to the practitioners available to me. I did go to classes, read and immerse myself in the teachings of my church. Ultimately, what saved me is a very basic spiritual truth....You are Loved and accepted by God....You are *not* your Story and there is a triune nature in you. A credo taught throughout the ages, that you can live by. You are Body, Mind AND Spirit. Not one, not two of the above, but ALL of the ABOVE.

I tried working on my mind for healing. I read, intellectualized, discussed and analyzed myself to death. What's even more entertaining? Having someone else analyze you to death. They read about me in a book. It was my chemical imbalance; it was my missing childhood stage of development. Even better, it was that extra strand attached to my DNA. My room-by-room libraries were starting to resemble the self-help section of Barnes & Noble. Guess what? Analysis-Paralysis is what I had. By design, it was too much information and not enough practical living. A three-legged table cannot stand on two legs or less.

So, I went to work on my body. Going to the gym, controlling my serving sizes, more proteins, less carbohydrates , eliminating the faux foods, and whatever the dietary gurus of the day decided would cure my imbalance. This may make you look fit and possibly feel better, but it will only offer a temporary feel good. Just like drugs or alcohol. Alone, it is an insufficient coping mechanism.

I looked at all the religions for answers. Buddhism, Judaism, Christianity, Hinduism, Muslim. I attended services, prayed, meditated and try to emulate a life worthy of that which I had studied. I learned religion can be a replacement addiction. Just as with diet and exercise, trying to find wholeness and completeness in only one aspect of ourselves, is the danger when "God Becomes A Drug," (Booth, Rev. Leo 2003). And when it was all said and done, I realized that there really wasn't one answer. Buddha, Krishna, Mohammed and Jesus the Christ were *all* touting peace and love.

But the reality is that we are **all** of this. We are threefold in nature, The Holy Trinity; Mind, Body, and Spirit. Most religious teachings say that the Spirit is infinite, yet the mind and body are perishable. I would argue that ALL are full expressions of our Divine Nature. And while our post human incarnation body and mind may not resemble that which we know on this plane, they are Idea, Thought and Expression of that triune nature...all energy reassembled and therefore cannot be destroyed. In the words of Ernest Holmes, philosopher and founder of Science of Mind:

> Man is a threefold principle of life and action; he is spirit, soul, and body. From the Spirit he receives inspiration and guidance; in the soul he finds a perfect Law of life; and through the body he proves that he is a real individualization of the Invisible Principle. Man's mind should swing from inspiration to action, from contemplation to accomplishment, from prayer to performance. This would be a well-balanced existence. (Holmes, 1938)

One Friday morning this past winter, my mother arrived at my home with Starbucks in hand and a painful look of sympathy on her face. My cousin had ended her life in a California County jail, while incarcerated for violating her probation. On her path, the pain was insurmountable. Her three-fold nature on this plane of existence would no longer be expressed. Or in reality, her lack of a fully expressed three-fold nature was in transition.

There was shock; there was numbness on my mother's face expressing the realistic fear that this very well could have been her own daughter not so long ago. She had been there to comfort and support me in my own pain and now the spotlight was on me. What would Kelly do without her cousin? Would she fall apart? There have been many moments since that I have been tempted to numb myself beyond comprehension. But, it is all too evident here that following temptation to cover pain is not a suitable option. Like tobacco, which they say 'May Be Hazardous to Your Health.'....what it should say is....THIS WILL KILL YOU!

Teri was living unconsciously. In the words of Eckhart Tolle (A New Earth,

2005), she had a very strong pain-body that she identified with. I, on the other hand, decided to release my own pain-body and therefore the patterns of physically contaminating my body beyond recognition. I decided that despite my IQ, I don't necessarily know that I know. In fact, I know very little. This, I believe is what they call surrender. And finally, I have released all of what I know and intend to move me forward to Prayer and Divine Guidance coupled with a healthy balance of ingestion and expression.

I miss my cousin and I am sure I will for a very long time to come. I can not purport to having figured it *all* out. I do know, however, that the seeds were already planted and that I was ripe for change. I am living my life now as though I am standing on the fulcrum of a see saw. Once I was seated on the edge of one end, just waiting to see if someone would sit on the other side, lift me up, cause me to stay grounded or balance me out. It works much better, I have discovered, to stand in the middle myself. Balancing it out using each aspect of my being; mind, body and spirit. I have racked up quite an arsenal of tools in my toolbox from a pint of Cherry Garcia with a side of Ghirardelli filled with caramel (not always a bad thing) to spiritual development classes with intensive self-exploration. Now I know that the list of comforts can never be too long; that surrender and an approach of seeing what is next to be discovered works better than numbing and closing me off from a life well lived. My life has been changed for good and changed for the better. In a way, her loss of life has gained me my own.

It is with a heavy, heavy heart that my cousin will not be along for this ride and have the opportunity to follow me for a change. Her decision was much too close for my own comfort level. It very well could have been me. In the words of Sarah McLachlan, 'I will remember you.' The question is…Will You Remember You?

Kelly Collins has been a Licensed Mortgage Broker for the past 27 years. She holds a Bachelors degree in Psychology with a minor in Women's Studies and an emphasis on Religious Studies from the University of Denver. Kelly is a certified Zumba® fitness instructor and is also in pursuit of becoming a practitioner with Mile Hi Church of Religious Science. She lives with her family in Lakewood, CO and can be reached via e-mail at KellyCollinsEMC@gmail.com.

I Choose to Love Me

Elana Perry

I am truly blessed! For years I have lived a charmed life — one filled with love, success and some failures. Dare I say a life that for all intents and purposes was somewhat uneventful. For that I am eternally grateful and I give God all the praise and honor. However, there have been several extremely impactful events in my life that have made me the woman I am today.

I still remember it like it was yesterday. I was only 7 when my parents announced they were going to get a divorce. I felt my hands begin to shake and I felt the blood rushing up to my head, my heart began to beat faster and faster and I thought I was going to faint. It was as if someone had just thrown a brick through the window of my life. My whole world shattered in that moment. Our lives were about to drastically change forever. A million thoughts began to encircle my mind. Things like: Was I to blame? Did I ask for too many toys, clothes and food? Had I been a bad girl? Why was this happening? Will we ever see him again? Now, of course, I realize that none of these things were true or my fault but you couldn't convince me or my sisters that we weren't to blame. I adored my dad!

My daddy was strong, outgoing and extremely talkative. He would talk to anyone, anytime and on just about any subject. The joke around our family was to not ask daddy a question unless you had an hour to spare and wanted to get the encyclopedia version of the answer. He was a fun-loving man, always whistling a tune or singing a song, so much so his sibling nicknamed him "Byrd."

The news of this pending divorce devastated me. I remember sobbing and saying, Daddy, don't go! Please, don't go, Daddy! Don't go! As my tear-filled eyes surveyed the room I noticed that there wasn't a dry eye in the house. The pain my parents both felt seemed to permeate the room. He left the house for a few weeks and stayed at my uncle's house until the divorce was final. Don't go, was all I could say to his back in a whisper as he walked out the door.

My mother has been and will always be my rock. She is my hero and one of the strongest women I know. She, too, had been broken by her decision to divorce, and the divorce had rocked her to her core. For weeks, I would sometimes sit outside my mother's bedroom door, and I could hear her crying. She probably thought no one knew of her pain. But I did! I could see it in her eyes. I felt it when she entered the room. She did her best to mask the pain but I was always watching, always listening. During this time we saw very little of my dad. Perhaps his pride wouldn't let him admit that his marriage was ending but my sisters and I missed him dearly.

The doorbell rang, DING DONG! It sounded as if we had the bells from the Sistine Chapel inside our house. It was so loud, the sound was deafening, drowning out my thought of who it could be waiting outside. I could tell something was wrong because my mother stayed in her room and didn't rush to answer the door. It was my dad and my uncle Bernard. The time had come and the divorce was final. My dad had come to pick up the rest of his things. He was really going to leave us. The divorce was final.

I remember following him from room to room with tears streaming down my face pleading with him to not leave. It was as if someone had turned on a faucet of tears. I felt helpless; I felt hopeless; and I felt afraid. I would have, in that moment, promised to give up anything: my favorite toy, my favorite dress, even Christmas (which remains my favorite holiday) for him to stay. I could tell he was sad but he was a man and as the saying goes, "real men don't cry." A whirlpool of thoughts began to resurface, like who will take care of us? How will we make it? Who will protect us? Who will love me? Deep down I knew the answer — "Mama would." She always has. That gave me the solace I needed to keep going even though I was still very sad.

When he and my uncle had finally finished packing his things into my uncle's rusty old blue truck, he hugged my sisters and me and told us, "Daddy will always love you!" He kissed us on our foreheads and drove off into the dark of the night. As I stood in the front door in my Winnie the Pooh PJs and watched, the headlights from the truck grew dimmer and dimmer, and I thought, he was really gone! I cried for months.

It had been six months since that dreadful day of watching my dad walk out the door, but today, I was happy because it was MY birthday! I was turning eight! I called my dad and proudly proclaimed that it was my birthday and that I was 8 years old, as if he wasn't aware. He promised to take me and my sisters out to celebrate. We were so happy! It had been months since we had seen him even though he had only moved across town.

I got dressed in my favorite pair of purple pants and purple, pink and white striped shirt for the occasion. I was beaming with pride because my mother had allowed me to pick out my outfit all by myself. My sister and I waited on our red velvet plastic covered couch. We waited and waited and waited until we began to sweat from the plastic. HE NEVER CAME! But it was my birthday, I thought. He never came! I was hurt and furious. Missed visits, birthdays and holidays soon became the norm. You see my dad had remarried and didn't tell us. We weren't even invited to the wedding. I believe he only remarried to hurt my mother, but we were the casualties of that decision. He later converted his faith to Jehovah's Witnesses, a faith whose members don't believe in celebrating birthdays or holidays. At least that was what we were told. How convenient! I have **never** received any birthday present or Christmas gift from my father. To think of it, I don't have anything tangible that my father has ever given me. NOTHING! Not a necklace, a rusty old Volkswagen beetle car (my favorite car back then), a dress or even a pair of shoes. Now that is sad! Over the years we saw less and less of my dad and stepmother.

Now, fast-forward fifteen years into my future: I am now in my early twenties. I'm cute, well built, smart and successful. I thought, hey, I was a really good catch and any man would be lucky to have such an accomplished young woman on his arm. But that wasn't how I really felt deep down inside where the real me lacked self-confidence. I was wounded and scared of being alone. I believe all little girls need know that they are OK, pretty enough just the way they are and valued. Often their daddy is the first male figure to provide that type of validation. Oh, how I longed for some guy, any guy, to validate and love me.

The phrase, "You're just like my dad," was a badge of honor my girlfriends would bestow upon their boyfriends. Perhaps it was because their dads were there for them, loved them and validated them. Not me... As a result, I ended up dating more than my share of losers! I did eventually use that phrase — just not in the same context my girlfriends had.

As a little girl I loved birthdays, Christmas and Valentine's Day. I would always go above and beyond with the gifting during those celebrations. Therefore, I always tried to make sure whomever I was dating at the time would feel extra special on those days. I recalled dating guy(s) named David, Clay, Mark, Paul, Steve, Richard, Reggie, Robert, etc. etc., and the list goes on and on. Did I mention that I kissed a LOT of FROGS on my quest to find Mr. Right? In my twenties and into my thirties, I needed so desperately to feel loved that I accepted things in a boyfriend that went against all of my morals and values, just to have someone in my life. If he was funny, fun-loving but smoked or drank, or just wasn't a nice guy. I dated him. I seemed to fall for the notorious bad boy. I often felt like I comprised many of my core values in my quest for love.

I remember my grandmother telling me once that the "way to a man's heart is through his stomach" so I learned to cook! I might not be a Paula Deen or Rachael Ray but I could hold my own. On several occasions I prepared a romantic five-course dinner for my boyfriend. A feast fit for a king, complete with candlelight, wine, dessert, "the works." You know the type of meal that takes damn near all day to prepare. I waited and waited and waited and he never came. None of them ever came. They would always stand me up! The drippings of candle wax and an empty bottle of wine were my lot in life back then. Unfortunately, a pattern had developed. I was feeling more and more desperate and needy. I needed the love, attention and the acceptance.

To win them back, I would give birthday gifts, or Christmas presents or even Valentine's gifts and the outcome was always the same. Nothing! It was never reciprocated. Just like my childhood, I began to ponder and question my self worth as to why all of the men in my life treated me so poorly, as if I were nothing. I questioned whether I was pretty enough. Was it because I wasn't thin enough? Why me? Questions seemed to plague me. Just like when I was a child, I would change my hair, the way I dressed, lose weight, gain weight, did this or that chasing guys' approval or acceptance of me.

Now I can laugh and often think, it's too bad the book *He's Just Not That Into You* by Greg Behrendt hadn't been written yet. I could have saved myself some heartache and kept a few more dollars in my pocket. I had an epiphany, "Wow, you're (they were all) just like my dad." After years of that type of hurt, emotional abuse and abandonment, I became disillusioned with men and the ideal of finding someone to love me. I took a long sabbatical from relationships.

During this alone time, I began to do some self-reflection; I read all type of books from the Bible to self-help books and relationship manuals. It was during this time that I began to find my own self-worth. My mother, with God's help, taught us to be strong, to be kind, to be women of our word, to have honor, humility and pride and to treat others as you would treat yourself. To quote from the acclaimed poet Maya Angelou whose poem "Phenomenal Woman" vividly reminds us of our inner strength and beauty. "I'm a woman Phenomenally. Phenomenal woman, That's me."

Looking back on those years of lack, low self-worth, I am grateful for every day we struggled, every tear I cried. It wasn't until I began to love me for me and see my own beauty that I could appreciate me. Each experience enhanced me, helped me to grow and transformed me into the woman I am today. It gave me the strength to choose to love me! Once I began to love my curves, my short hair, my mocha skin and my full lips, once I began to "Love Elana" I opened myself up for the world to love me.

In 1997, I was determined to step outside of my comfort zone and do the things I truly enjoyed, even if that meant going out or doing those things alone. Now that was really a stretch; I hated to be alone. I hated to be with me! I decided I would attend a Friday night open mic poetry set. It was free, so what did I have to lose? It was there that I began to hear the call of one poet in particular, Bryce Perry. He quickly became a featured poet with his readings on love, romance, intimacy and eroticism. Most of the women in attendance would sit on the edge of their seats when he got up to speak. He was a soft-spoken man by nature and extremely cool, but not bad boy cool. He seemed to be a gentle, yet strong kind of cool, almost beatnik in nature type cool. His deep, baritone voice would caress your ears and carry you away with him to whatever fantasy place he was painting with his words. As I listened, a conversation would always erupt in my head, "Why was this brother always talking about me? We hadn't met. Why was he describing so vividly the life I wanted with my soul mate? The children, the passion, and the house, the love I wanted. Who was this man? Snap out of it, girl, remember our…NO Men pledge," I would catch myself saying aloud.

Soon I found myself eagerly awaiting Friday poetry sets. It didn't matter if I went alone or not. Wow, I had made progress. I was feeling more confident and my self-esteem was getting stronger. After weeks of attending he finally got up the nerve to ask me out for, as he said, "dessert." He later told me he had noticed me right away the first night. From our first date we both knew we were meant to be together. True soul mates! He told me he had noticed my inner beauty and thought it strange that the person he had fantasized about and wrote about in his poetry was real and he had found her. It was me! He saw me and loved me before even meeting me. We dated for only seven months before he proposed. We have been happily married for 11 years now. All because I chose to love me!

It is my hope that through my successes and failures, triumphs and defeats, that you, my friend, will gain wisdom, hope and love — so you too can choose to love yourself! And gain the courage to speak your own truth no matter how painful. You just might find that not only will it prove to be therapeutic for you, but it will, in most cases, help someone else along the way. Through this story I hope you see that I chose to love me! Be Blessed.

Elana Perry is a writer, social entrepreneur, humanitarian and Personal Financial Coach / Independent Consultant for Primerica Financial Services (PFS). She is dedicated to educating and helping middle-income individuals, families, companies and organizations achieve financial independence and debt freedom. She lives in Denver, Colorado, with her husband, Bryce, and their sons, Mylz and Mekhi. For a free financial needs analysis visit her Web site at: www.primerica.com/ElanaPerry Email: elanacperry@primerica.com Phone: 303-472-3783

How Clarity Brought My Freedom

Linda Anderson

I have many memories from my childhood. I remember big happy Christmases where the wrapping paper was flying with lots of laughter, fun, and toys. I remember wonderful food my mother would make and how I loved bedtime stories with her. I also remember my father fighting with my sister, fights that were terrible and ended with the police being called and taking my sister away. I remember teasing my older brother just to get him in trouble because it seemed to win points with my father. I remember thinking my dad could fix anything and knew everything, that he was the smartest person ever! There was love in my childhood and there was abuse, I just didn't learn to recognize the abuse until much later.

This is what I have decided makes gaining clarity the hardest. Life is not always bad. Something bad happens, but then it is minimized and forgotten. So when another bad thing happens they never accumulate.

As I got older, I sometimes reflected on things that happened in my early childhood. I compared with my friends, and I knew that my family was a little different. I heard my family stories. I learned my father molested my sister at a young age and that was why they fought so much. She ran away and got involved with drugs during her teenage years when I was too young to understand. I knew how hard my brother had it too. My father constantly picked at him for no reason. It was as if he couldn't do anything good enough. They were both twelve years older than me, so it was just normal that they were both out of the house by the time I was six years old.

My family settled into a routine then. My father would go to work to support us, and my mother would take care of the household and me. She would also wait on my father constantly. He would come home and drink until he went to bed each night, and if my mom gave him everything correctly, and I was nice and quiet, we had a good evening. I learned very early that if you didn't cross my dad, he didn't get mad. It wasn't that hard for me (or so I thought) because I was his favorite.

I always knew I didn't like the way he talked to my mother, but I knew better than to get involved for my own safety. I really never saw them fight, because they never did. There was no screaming or hitting or throwing furniture anymore. My mother and I were skilled at this point in not making him angry, and it was a full time job. I wasn't aware at the time that it was a job. It was my life.

As I became a teenager, the need for understanding all these unfelt emotions became unbearable. I was very interested in sex and alcohol, and I started both at age thirteen, as soon as I could find them. I found that drinking numbed all the emotional pain I felt, and boys would give me the attention I wanted as long as I gave them sex. It seemed as though life got even harder. I drank whenever possible but kept my grades up and never got caught doing anything wrong because to get in trouble at home was not even an option. The last thing I wanted was to be compared to my sister in my father's eyes. She had gone to prison when I was thirteen, and it devastated me.

In the eleventh grade, I met a boy who didn't just want sex from me but actually wanted to date me as well. His family had issues too, so we could relate. We also drank together. A lot. He would sometimes not treat me very nice, but I would dismiss it as him having a bad day or someone else had pissed him off. Plus, that was the relationship dynamic that I was taught. The woman would handle the man and his mood. It was my job, right? Right before our senior year I met up with one of my old friends and cheated on my boyfriend. I felt horribly guilty and couldn't believe what I had done. I was never going to do such a thing again, and I was never going to tell him. But he found out anyway. He broke up with me and gave me a silent treatment that sent me into a frenzy of self-hate. I begged for forgiveness. I stalked him. I wanted any chance I could have to prove to him I was sorry. He finally gave in, and we not only got back together, but we also got engaged. We were married right after high school graduation. He never let me forget how awful I was for doing such a terrible thing to him and that I was lucky to have him. And I believed I deserved it all.

Being out on our own was more difficult than I had anticipated. There were bills, and our little high school jobs were not enough. So I got a second job, and since that seemed to keep us afloat, he decided he didn't have to work anymore. While I continued working thirteen hours a day, he was discovering crack cocaine. During these first four years of our marriage, I got pregnant with our first son. Working so many hours throughout my pregnancy and his infancy I could barely keep track of myself much less notice what was going on with my husband. Most of this time was a blur for me. Whenever I was around my husband, I couldn't do anything right. I wasn't bringing in enough money, so I worked harder. I could be a good wife, I just had to try harder and prove it to him. Maybe then he would treat me nice. If only he saw how hard I was trying, but he didn't. Finally his parents saw that something had to change for us. They got him a job with his brother in Denver, Colorado. If we moved, things could be better for sure, right?

Wrong. Things only got different. My working situation improved, and we were both making more money than we ever had, but he was still angry. I still wasn't good enough. I didn't clean the house properly or cook well enough. I still did not know my place when it came to my mouth. But he didn't hit me, so I wasn't being abused, right? It was my job to take what my husband gave me, so that his life could be better.

During this time I started to notice how he treated our son. It reminded me a lot of my father and my brother. I didn't like it. He was constantly getting into trouble for no reason, and I took to trying to control my son's behavior so that his father wouldn't have to punish him. This made me hyper-vigilant, and I had to be aware of everything that was occurring to try and prevent violent outcomes. This made me tired.

At this same time, I was experiencing something else, something new. I was working as an assistant in an oral surgery office, and the more I got to know my boss, the more I liked him. This was a strong, intelligent man, who was also kind. He was happily married to a woman he spoke highly of. He never raised his voice or told anyone how horrible they were. We were like a little family, and I loved going to work. I never knew work could be enjoyed. My boss back home was just as abusive as my father and my husband, so I thought it was normal. How could I know anything different? It was all I knew. Fairy tales were fiction. Life was difficult and hard work, right?

This went on for the next ten years. Life was tolerable because I was so happy at work. When things were bad at home, I drank. That lessened the pain. At age twenty-eight, I had our second son. This was purely a surprise because I had no intention what-so-ever of bringing another soul into this household. But, as with all things that came my way, I decided this was my responsibility.

Things were certainly getting harder at this point. We bought a house, and with another mouth to feed, finances were getting tight. My husband was once again telling me that I didn't make enough money. It was my fault we couldn't pay the bills, and once again I got a second job and he quit his to work for himself, which brought in very little money.

I always thought if I could only show my husband more love, more understanding, then he would see that things weren't so bad. If I showed him I was a good wife, I could make him happy. I decided maybe my problem was depression. I went on medication, but that didn't do it. As I was contemplating psychiatric help for my inability to do things right, I discovered a book called "*Why Does He Do That?*" by Lundy Bancroft. I thought to myself "Why *does* he do that?" and I bought the book. This book changed my life. As I was reading it secretly, my husband was getting madder than ever. After one day of him yelling at me for not having the house clean before he woke up at noon, I was desperate. I looked in the back of the book, and there was a national hotline for women in crisis. I thought I wasn't really an abused woman because he never hit me. But I didn't care about that on this day; I had to talk to someone. If they told me I was crazy, maybe they could tell me how to fix it too.

They absolutely did not tell me that I was crazy, and they got me in touch with my local women's shelter where I was going to secretly start counseling. Then something amazing happened. Right before I started counseling, he hit me. For some reason, I waited through 17 years of being in this situation before he hit me. I knew right then that the only thing wrong with me was I was letting this man hurt me and my children, and something needed to be done about it and fast. I just didn't know where to start. My woman's advocate helped me create a safety plan to be free of abuse.

One day it happened. We were in an argument. Unlike my childhood, there was always a lot of screaming and name-calling when we argued. He was so mad at me this time that he stormed out of the house. He had left. He never left. This was my chance, and I knew it! I called to my oldest son and told him we were leaving fast and that we were going to New Mexico where my parents lived. I threw random clothing into laundry baskets, grabbed them and my youngest son, who was three years old at the time and quickly got them in the car.

Leaving only a note for my husband saying I couldn't handle the abuse any longer and I was leaving him. I had no idea of when he would return and if he caught me leaving or what he would do, and I did not want to find out. I remember stopping at a grocery store about two hours away from home and just knowing that he would be there. That in the next aisle he would be standing there, around every corner. But he wasn't there. I stayed at my parent's home for almost a week. When I returned, I rented an apartment before I saw him again so he couldn't talk me into coming back.

I compared the experience to that of jumping off a cliff. And that is exactly what it was like. I landed hard. I was in unknown territory. I had never had to take care of just myself before, and I certainly did not know who I was. I remained in counseling for almost three years at my local abused women's shelter. She taught me that I wasn't crazy and what had happened to me all of my life was not my fault. I had choices and I could take care of myself, living the life I wanted and deserved. During that time, I got my divorce, with partial custody of my boys, and made a new life.

When I left my abusive situation, I started to notice other areas of my life that did not serve me. My boss, who I had liked so much, retired shortly before I left my husband and sold the practice to a young surgeon. He was the first of a series of employers who were abusive. After changing jobs several times, I decided I couldn't work in the medical field anymore.

All the personal work I had done during this time after my divorce led me to one of the most caring men I have ever met. I was open and honest about what my past was like, and he accepted me for who I am. I accepted him as well. He is patient and understanding. We moved in together and take one day at a time. Almost two years later, I love him more than ever and have finally found my best friend. He has also supported me in establishing my business so that I can be my own boss.

I continue to learn more about myself and help my boys grow to be the best they can be. We are taking these lessons that have been given to us and using them to have a better understanding of ourselves and the world we live in.

I am sharing my story because I want to reach other women who may be in an abusive situation. If it feels wrong, then it probably is. Trusting your intuition is key to understanding what is happening. I would encourage anyone who may be in this situation to talk to a professional. We can never know too much about ourselves and why our lives are the way they are. With clarity comes understanding and the ability to change your situation.

Linda Anderson lives by the foothills of the beautiful Rocky Mountains in Lakewood, Colorado with her loving boyfriend, his daughter and her two sons. She has a personal assisting business, which is growing steadily, and she is enjoying running her own business. She loves to travel and is always looking for more ways to grow together and individually. She reads and plays the violin in her spare time. She looks forward to the rest of her life with hope and optimism. She desires to help society understand what domestic violence is and put an end to it. She can be reached at lindahssco@ yahoo.com.

Disillusionment to Enlightenment

Susanne Kind

I grew up in Queens, NY with five other siblings and two loving parents. My mom was a stay-at-home mom until I was 10. Dad was frequently out of the house with one of three jobs, as well as refereeing and going to school at night. In spite of what seemed to be a normal upbringing, a sense of not belonging festered. I somehow believed that everyone knew how to do life, how to socialize, how to play sports, how to do basically everything, and I'd missed the boat.

In an effort to belong, get attention, approval, and love, I got involved in all kinds of things at a young age. Sex, drugs, and rock-n-roll were what it was about, and I was certainly living in the fast lane. I believed I was wiser than most and didn't need to waste my time with studying or sports.

When I was 17, I met the first man who stopped me in my tracks. I had dated previously, but I maintained a sense of independence. I didn't allow others to tell me what to do. But when Chuck walked into my life, for some reason I was ready to surrender. I became completely immersed in life around him, and couldn't seem to let go. Even when the first beating occurred, three months into the relationship, I hung on thinking tomorrow would be different. My grades suffered terribly, and I barely made it out of high school as a result of my obsession. When I was 18, I became pregnant with our daughter. Through my pregnancy the beatings continued, and I believed I had to stay because I couldn't imagine being a single mother. The worst beating was still to come. When our daughter was two days old, we were at his mother's home and after something I said, he unleashed such fury that my face was disfigured. The police were called and they asked me "What do you want us to do?" I turned away, unable to summon up the courage to say, "Take him away." That night, as I lay down beside him, I couldn't believe I was there. I looked like a one-eyed Cyclops. I'd like to say I left the next day, but I didn't. It took until my daughter was almost two, when she yelled out as he was hitting me, "Daddy stop hitting mommy." That was my wake up call. I realized if I couldn't leave for me, I had to leave for her.

While I did leave the relationship, I was soon to find he was not my problem. For awhile I went on as a devoted mother, fully immersed in raising her and loving every minute of it. But soon a feeling of unrest started settling in, and I began to date again. Very quickly into the dating scene, I began using my tales of woe as an excuse to drink and drown my sorrows. Before long, drugs came back into the picture. For the next two years I drank and drugged and sought out people who drank and drugged like me. I went from dating an artist to dating a man whose best friend was a Hell's Angel.

Working full-time, spending a little time with my daughter, putting her to bed and racing out so I could party to 3, 4, or 5 a.m. I was clearly addicted and invested more and more energy feeding my addiction. In 1987 my family had enough. My mom said "Do something or else." I tried several avenues but could not stay stopped. I was good for a few days and then off again. In July, I went out drinking, this time for almost two days. Family, friends, co-workers, and employers were very concerned.

I went back to my mom's home confused, lost, and tired. I knew I couldn't live this way any longer. I went to a 12-step program the next day but knew I needed to take stronger action. There was an amazing organization who offered free counseling to people like me. At a counseling session, it was decided a rehab program would be best. A few days later, I checked into a facility located around four hours from my home. My family agreed to care for my daughter while I was away. I stayed there for 35 days with a lot of excuses as to why I was different or too young or not that bad. I finally got serious in the last week of rehab and realized this was life and death. With the support of a 12-step program, I have been sober since.

My daughter did not escape my antics unscathed. She had a very challenging adolescence. I tried many approaches to help her find her way on the road of life, through the many sharp curves she encountered along the way. Her father passed away when she was just 13 years old, and she ended up in and out of hospitals for depression and suicidal thoughts. Sometimes I didn't know if I had enough courage for both of us; life just seemed way too difficult at times. And if she chose to take her life, what would I do? It was at that point I realized that while I might have gotten sober for my daughter, whether she chose to live or die would be her choice. I had to choose to live, and trust that no matter what, it was possible to enjoy life.

In 2005, after having worked as an Assistant for almost 20 years, I felt it was time for something new. I went back to school and got a 4.0 in Human Resource Management, but concurrent to this, I found myself at an orientation for a school that I had never even once considered. This was the School of Integrative Nutrition. Every day after that orientation, thoughts of the school would tug at me, until finally one day, I took action and enrolled. That school opened up my mind in ways I had never considered, or even thought possible. While I wasn't suffering with any major illness, I had been prone to migraines and mild depression. But at this school, I began to learn the power of food, the power of thought, and the power of choice. I started experimenting with different dietary theories to see what made sense for me. One of them was a macrobiotic diet. And within a few short months, I noticed I was feeling and looking considerably different. The migraines and depression that I had grown accustomed to were gone. My PMS was gone. The breast tenderness around my cycle was gone. I noticed I had more joy and more energy than people half my age. In fact, I could run circles around my daughter! It absolutely rocked my world that I could dramatically impact my mood, just by changing my food!

Dramatic changes were to continue. I began taking huge risks left and right. I took up scuba diving, resigned from my corporate position and opened my own practice. I very quickly had clients who loved what they were experiencing as a result of working with me. I started giving workshops on health and wellness. One woman told me that when she listened to me speak, I reminded her of Wayne Dyer!

I followed another whim and that was to try a Tony Robbins seminar. I had never heard of him or read any of his books, but someone suggested it and off I went, walking on fire after having only gotten off the airplane just a few hours before. On the way home from that seminar, I had so much energy and resolve, I knew there was so much in me I needed to share. I began working on a book. Ideas were popping out of my head, left and right. It was so much fun! And I didn't stop there! To continue to face my fears, I jumped out of an airplane, and a few months later, as part of another seminar, climbed a 50 foot telephone pole, danced at the top and then leaped onto a waiting trapeze bar. Mind you, I'm afraid of heights and get vertigo when watching a movie about heights!

More events and seminars brought about more change. In September of 2007, I flew to Colorado for the first of three consecutive events, in three different states. While there, I met a man with whom I had a few brief conversations and didn't really give much thought to after the weekend ended. However, fate had other plans. After the 2nd time I bumped into this man, while surprised to see him again, I downplayed the coincidence. However, a casual friend was insistent that I email him. The most I would commit to was a brief "how do you do," which prompted a very enthusiastic response. We continued to correspond, and over the next few weeks, we found that we would both be at the same seminar the following month. Now that got my attention. In December of 2007, I began to get to know this man I had previously thought I wasn't interested in. What I quickly discovered was that this man had attributes I had once only dreamed about and hoped for. In fact, the year before I had played a game with a close friend where you discuss in detail every characteristic your ideal partner has, as if it already was happening. During that game, I said, "My guy is so amazing, he loves decorating the Christmas tree." Guess what - this man, my partner, might as well be called Father Christmas! And what was beyond my imagination was that without having known my previous story of abuse he told me it was his desire to devote time to helping women heal from abuse! I truly cried. I was intrigued and terrified.

So, I continued to remain slightly aloof. But he called me from Colorado two days before New Years and asked if he could come to NY to visit me. I was speechless. I mean, we hadn't even kissed yet! I said yes. Our first date was to a restaurant appropriately called Caravan of Dreams. In hindsight, I clearly stepped into a Caravan of Dreams beginning that night. Our next stop was to see the movie, Kite Runner. As I glanced to my right, I couldn't believe my eyes. This man, practically a stranger, weeping over the abuse we witnessed in that movie. I was quite moved and wanted to know more.

We began to date, long distance, over the next nine months. At the end of September of 2008, terrified, I drove from NY to Colorado to join him. Here we are over two years later, and it has been nothing short of magical. He is the man I always cried, prayed and wished for. We have the utmost respect, excitement, and devotion for each other. We encourage each other to reach our highest heights. Life is fun, work is fun, and learning is fun. We continue to seek higher learning together professionally, physically, spiritually, and emotionally.

Since coming to Colorado, I decided to take an old wound and do something positive with it. I signed up to become a volunteer at the Safehouse Shelter in Longmont. I briefly worked with a legal advocate, who provides support to women seeking orders of protection. I remember how terrifying that process had been for me many years ago. If I could provide that warm smile a woman needs as she takes this courageous step, then I know I've helped. Currently I am a mentor for a program within Safehouse called TERA, Teens Against Relationship Abuse. God bless these kids who are stepping up to help educate their peers on what's healthy and what's not. I wish I had that support when I was 17.

Throughout my sobriety there have been many ups and downs. One of the best gifts I have received throughout this journey is a knowing; knowing that I am an amazing being with so much to give others. Today I get to live in the solution instead of creating problems.

Today, I am developing a local presence with my health and wellness practice as well as building my national clientele through the Internet and other mediums. Most of my clients are long distance and have given me great feedback on how well that is working for them. I love what I do and trust that the Universe will guide me to where I am needed most. I continue to make self care a priority. If I am to teach others how to have balance in their lives, it's important to me that I walk the walk. Juicing, meditating, mentoring students from the nutrition school as well as from the teen program is a way that I can give back. I host monthly teleclasses on a variety of topics to help others learn how to best care for their bodies.

I also work with clients individually, exploring how to connect with themselves on every level!

My partner and I recently became non- denominational ministers and facilitate classes on how to reconnect with yourself on a very deep level, leaving with an understanding that there is no separation. We envision reaching out to all communities, facilitating healing whenever and wherever we can. We conduct a weekly blessing right from our home where, through intention, we give blessings to people from around the world who are in need. In addition to our work with Oneness, we travel around the country as volunteers for Tony Robbins' programs helping people transform their lives as they take the first step and make a choice to walk on fire! I also must share that my daughter is doing extremely well today. She has created a very exciting life for herself, and she too has learned to celebrate herself.

Many years ago I heard the phrase 'beyond your wildest dreams'. I am now experiencing this in my life. If it weren't for the love and support of my family, friends, counselors and coaches along the way, who knows where I would have ended up? I count my blessings daily and pray that I continue to be open and aware of how I can best be of service to others, as has been done so freely for me.

Susanne Kind is the CEO of Your Kind of Nutrition, an International Health and Wellness practice. She is a Certified Holistic Health Coach, an International Health and Wellness Speaker, an Ordained Minister, and Oneness Facilitator. She is a graduate of the Institute for Integrative Nutrition, Tony Robbins' Leadership Academy, and Oneness University. Susanne is available for corporate workshops, speaking engagements, individual and group coaching, and Oneness Blessings. For more information, you can email her at yourkindofnutrition@gmail.com, our website: www.yourkindofnutrition.com or call (631) 882-8398. (631) 882-8398.

Health & Healing

Finding My Voice

Donna Mazzitelli

January 2007 started out like any other new year – filled with the hope and promise of new growth and success in the year ahead. Since moving to Colorado at the end of 2005, it was also time for my first annual checkup in our new home state. I expected that appointment to be like every other I'd had, uneventful. My appointment turned out to be anything BUT uneventful.

When I got to the office I checked all the boxes as usual—no for every condition, disease or medication. The only item that had changed was that I no longer experienced a monthly flow. It appeared I was now in the next phase of menopause and I could now officially call myself Crone, having entered the third stage of life. I was coming to terms with leaving behind my first two stages of the female life cycle – that of the maiden and mother – and beginning to embrace this third aspect of the goddess.

My appointment continued pleasantly enough—a female doctor who seemed to have time to really learn about who I was, what brought me and my family to Colorado, and how everything was going since moving here after a lifetime in California. Next came the exam portion—listening with the stethoscope, feeling around glands and lymph nodes of the neck, palpating my breasts and conducting a pelvic exam. All was going well until she continued to palpate my right breast and started asking questions. She'd found a suspicious lump that I'd thought was just another fibrous area.

What transpired from that day – January 20th – until my diagnosis on Valentine's Day 2007 was a whirlwind of tests and emotional ups and downs, the height of which were middle-of-the-night calls to my closest friend in California. Once the diagnosis came in as Grade 1 cancer—the least aggressive grade—and the size was estimated at about 1 cm., what was left to determine was the stage, which involves analysis of whether or not the lymph nodes are involved.

Everyone—family, friends, and doctors—expected me to consent as quickly as possible to the next biopsy (if I was considering a lumpectomy) or schedule my surgery (if I intended to have a mastectomy). Initially, I seemed ready to follow their advice: choose one of these two options and take immediate action. However, as I sat with these choices—especially in the early morning hours – a little voice started to whisper so quietly that I almost missed it completely. This quiet stirring, which started out almost like a gentle breeze, carried questions on its current. Are these your only choices? Is this what you want for yourself? Are you sure? Are you really sure?

Over a period of days, that gentle breeze within me crescendoed into a howling wind. And as a result, what I did next shocked and terrified those closest to me. I said STOP! I need to WAIT! I said NO to everyone and their advice, whether they were medical professionals or laypeople. I needed to give myself the gift of time: to gather more information, consult with more practitioners (especially those outside the traditional medical community), and time to consider ALL my options. What I've come to understand is that my need to pause was the beginning of finding my own voice again. When and how did I lose it? Where had it gone? And would I ever reclaim it?

As a small child, I remember having a beautiful voice. It was happy and playful. It was strong and clear, lyrical and melodic. Sometimes it was sad and tearful. It was the voice of a child who knew that anything and everything was possible. It was the voice of a child who was in touch with her inner being – a young girl who knew that the world was her oyster – who was clear about what she did and didn't want. Somehow that voice began to fade as I grew older.

One incident which I remember very clearly stands out as the beginning of my fading voice. I was four or five years old. It was dinnertime and my family and I were sitting around the table. My father, who was sitting to my right, asked me to pass something to him. I was so busy eating that I really didn't want to be bothered with having to stop to get the butter or salt for him, so I simply and honestly told him no. I was *in the moment* enjoying my food.

What happened next shocked me (and apparently my Dad as well). My father reached with his left arm and back-handed me across the side of my face. It was so swift and had such energy behind it that I was knocked off my chair and onto the floor. I began to cry. Apparently, my father left the table and went into the bathroom where he cried as well. My father never took such a drastic approach to discipline again. That action left a lasting imprint on both him and me.

I learned a valuable lesson that day—a lesson in how I needed to live from that moment on. It was the beginning of my understanding that in order to be accepted and loved, I needed to do what others wanted rather than what I desired for myself. I needed to think before I spoke in an attempt to not make waves. And I needed to NEVER SAY NO to the adults in my life!

I was raised during an era when phrases like, 'children should be seen and not heard,' 'speak when you're spoken to,' and 'don't argue or talk back to grown-ups' were the mottos of the day. Respecting adults meant never questioning. Honoring thy father and thy mother was an important rule to follow and when you did it right, you were applauded for being a pleasant, agreeable child. As a result, adults enjoyed having you around.

I wanted to be loved more than anything else, so I began to conform and do exactly what seemed to please my parents. I wanted to be acknowledged for how well I did things. When my mother called me a cry baby or when one of my relatives called me the local waterworks, I felt very hurt and ashamed but I never protested. I would just try to stuff my feelings and get quiet as quickly as possible. Eventually, I learned to not show those emotions that express vulnerability or sensitivity. I learned to suck it up.

As a teenager, I did attempt to find my voice again, but it was tempered with the voice of reason. I can remember challenging my father about double standards for men and women. The actions he condoned in my male cousin's life were absolutely forbidden in mine. My father went to great lengths to protect my virtue and believed that women needed to remain chaste while praising my cousin for his many conquests. I tried protesting and arguing to persuade my dad that men and women should be treated equally, but my protestations fell on deaf ears. Eventually, I realized it was better to keep my opinions to myself.

As I grew from childhood into adulthood, my desire to please and be accepted transferred from my parents to teachers, professors, superiors, colleagues, and experts—which of course included doctors. So here I was in February 2007 faced with the challenge of once again doing what others wanted me to do in order to please them and make them feel safe and comfortable—in order to not make waves. Complete the tests, pick my course of treatment, follow it unquestioningly, and trust that the experts knew what was best for me, my psyche, and my body.

Somehow though, when faced with such life-altering news, that voice that I'd long ago buried began to resurface – first, as a knot in the pit of my stomach and an ache in my throat, and eventually as a racing heart, sweaty palms and gasping breaths. My voice was becoming more difficult to ignore with each passing day. Having cancer finally gave me the impetus for speaking my truth. As I began to awaken to what was happening, I was both saddened and angry that it took such a big message from the Universe to shake me into the realization that it was time to begin speaking up and speaking out. Along with these feelings was the deep knowing that if I didn't begin to stand up for myself at this point in time, then I might just never do it. I was afraid of the potential consequences of remaining silent.

So speak up and speak out is exactly what I did! And I paused so that I could decide the course of action which was right for me. This included connecting with my intuition as I chose books that seemed to call to me or to jump off the shelf into my arms. It continued as I chose people to work within the holistic wellness arena—acupuncturist, homeopath, intuitive, alternative physician, and more.

Ultimately, after much reading, searching, working with others, and some deep interpersonal work, I decided to take an integrative approach to my treatment. By the end of May, I came to understand that FOR ME it was important to take pieces from both camps rather than to choose one or the other. Both conventional medicine and alternative medicine had something to offer me at the time. So, on June 11th, 2007, I underwent surgery and combined that with other alternative practices I'd already begun.

Using my rediscovered voice, I actively participated in the planning of my surgery and post-operative course of action. My surgeon understood there were conditions to my surgery. For instance, I was operated on during the 4th quarter of the moon because that is the optimum time for healing. I conveyed to my surgeon my desire to work with physicians who would understand our relationship as a partnership and collaboration towards the achievement of my perfect health. With her assistance, I looked for an oncologist who would support my post-operative path. Today, cancer-free, I am moving beyond my oncologist and beginning work with a naturopath whose focus is holistic wellness.

And today, I actively strive to reconnect with my voice on a daily basis. I realize it is very easy to slip back into the patterns learned during childhood, especially on matters which don't appear to be life-threatening. Yet, I've come to understand that it is just as important for me to express my desire to have a cup of tea rather than coffee as it is to choose a course of medical treatment. It is equally important for me to take time for myself each day—away from all the demands of work and family—nurturing myself and connecting with my inner core.

Today, I choose to continue the journey of reconnecting with the time in my childhood when my thoughts and feelings were pure expressions of my true self—when joy and bliss was simply the way it was. I am learning today that I am no ordinary being, much in the same way I understood this as a very small child. I am coming to understand that I am here at this particular time in history to play a very special role – here on this planet to realize my true purpose. In order to bring that essence into the light, I understand that I must embrace my true self by letting my light shine forth, no matter the consequences.

Reclaiming my voice and my true essence – apart from my past roles and traits – is an ongoing process. It takes time and much courage. It takes constant vigilance. Having denied my authenticity for so many years, it is sometimes difficult to separate my true identity from the identities I've taken on to cope with the world around me. As I continue to open up to my authentic self and allow my true voice to ring out loud and clear, I am often amazed, awed, and astonished at the depth and breadth of what resides within. As I recognize my own power, my luminosity and my divinity, and continue to give voice to my authentic self, I feel a deep sense of appreciation and gratitude. And...as a my spiritual self and my physical self, along with my inner- and outer-world personas, integrate more and more, I marvel as I come closer to who I was always intended to be: a whole person, a radiant being of light with a marvelous destiny yet to be fulfilled!

With this deep knowledge, I step out a little further into the light each day. I open a little more to reveal the brilliance of the colors that have always been a part of me. As e.e. cummings once said, "It takes courage to grow up and become who you really are."

Donna Mazzitelli is a writer and author of the Bellisima Goddess blog. She enjoys writing articles for magazines and online publications and is currently working on her first book. As an advocate for Mother Earth and her inhabitants, she enjoys teaching workshops and leading green wisdom circles in an exploration of green, healthy living. She shares her passion for creating a green lifestyle with individuals, families and businesses through her company, Bellisima Living, LLC. She loves working with individuals one-on-one to bring a deeper shade of green to their lives. She currently resides in Castle Rock, Colorado with her husband, twin teenage daughters, and loving pets. To learn more, visit her blog at www.bellisimagoddess.com and her website at www.bellisimaliving.com.

Live Like You Were Dying

Rhonda Barry

It was August 27, 2002. Swallows chirped happily outside my office window as the sun streamed across my desk. But at this moment, simple pleasures almost seemed like an annoying distraction to the constant flood of chatter filling my mind. *What have I done with my life? What kind of mother have I been to my children? What legacy will I leave behind?*

What haven't I done yet that I really wanted to? The questions whirred on and on in my mind.

First one tear, then another, trailed down my cheek, landing silently on the surface of my desk. It had been a long and tiring six weeks of sleepless nights tossing and turning, and large wine glasses filled to the brim, hoping for a moment of relief or distraction, as the throbbing pain in my side grew stronger with each worried thought. My mind drifted back to the last appointment with my gynecologist six weeks earlier and the concern in her voice as she shared the results of the ultrasound. The ovarian cysts weren't shrinking as she'd hoped. In fact, they'd almost doubled in size. It looked like surgery was going to be the only option.

But surgery was not something that scared me. I'd always healed well and since I was self-employed, time off wasn't an issue. I actually breathed a sigh of relief that at last this issue was going to be resolved. It was her next few words that gripped me. "There's a blood test I'd like to do to see if there are cancerous cells present." Cancer? Cancer!

First, the word screamed in my ears and reverberated there. Then it seemed to fragment and dissolve as my body went cold and my mind numb. I moved robotically as she instructed me to lie back so she could examine me, pressing here and there. "Does this hurt? What about this?" as she manipulated first the left, then the right side of the pelvic area.

Is it possible that the pain could be both intense and dull all at the same time? So confusing. My mind filled with everything; then nothing. Nothing making sense. A pause, the look, the unspoken question. The doctor pressing this time on my breasts, first on the left, then on the right, then the left again, her brow furrowed.

Her lips began to move and I heard the words 'mass', then 'large solid mass', 'surgeon', and 'biopsy'. Only fragments of the sentences registered in my mind. I felt like I was observing myself on that examining table, like the proverbial fly on the wall, disconnected from the feelings of the woman being examined on the table below.

As she quietly closed the office door behind her, I mechanically rose and dressed myself, retrieved my keys from the belly of my purse, putting one foot in front of the other, wanting to escape to the safety of my car. I don't really remember driving those first few blocks away from the clinic. Idling at a red light, a sudden strong urge gripped me. "I need to talk to Mom!"

As the light shifted from red to green, I clutched the steering wheel with one hand, while I fumbled with my cell phone in the other. "Please be there. Please, please, please, please."

"Hello?" Her gentle, familiar voice. Thank God she was there! I felt calm and safe for a brief instant until I remembered the reason for my call, and the dreaded words caught in my throat, escaping in jagged breaths. I pulled over to the side of the road, unable to see the curb as tears flooded my eyes. Mom then did what she does best. She reassured me that everything would be fine, and she would be there for anything I needed.

So, here it was, six weeks later, as I sat at my desk in my office, and stared at the next day's appointments in my calendar. Tomorrow I would hear the results of both tests — the blood test and the biopsy. I'd been trying so hard to be brave (my mother labeling me as stoic) pretending everything was just fine, painting on a grin whenever anyone was around. But behind that smile the constant chatter continued in my head and the uneasy feeling in my stomach persisted. Thankfully, only one more night. I silently dreaded spending the evening at home, with the clock slowly ticking away each second.

The ringing of the phone startled me. I checked the caller ID, knowing that I would not be able to have a productive, focused call with a client. Oh good. It was Dave, my husband. I put on my happy voice, not wanting to reveal the hole of depression I'd dug for myself. He was calling to suggest that I have an evening out with the girls — perhaps a nice dinner and relaxing glass of wine. He would take care of the dogs and his own dinner. Oh, what a wonderful idea! Blessed distraction was just what the doctor would have ordered!

A few hours later, appetite satisfied, a warm glow from the wine and great company, I unlocked the back door of the house and stood, dumfounded, in the back porch. Five steps above me was our closed kitchen door, papered from top to bottom with bright white poster paper. My eyes darted to the drawings first. There was my company logo that meant so much to me; then one of my favorite things in the world, a decorated Christmas tree; and another favorite, shooting stars, scattered all over the paper. My focus moved on to the writing. A message from mom, one from dad, one from each of my children, one from Dave himself, my siblings, my friends. Encouraging, loving, heartfelt messages. A sob caught in my throat as I realized Dave had spent the entire evening calling family and friends for messages of support for me. And there they all were, in bright colors, an 8-foot message of love. I couldn't take my eyes off of that door.

My heart began to swell, and deep inside me, something began to bubble up — the truth. I was *not* alone. I was dearly loved. In fact, I was surrounded by love. And I knew that whatever the results tomorrow, it would all be okay. I had all the love and support I needed to handle whatever was before me. I slept like a baby that night, wrapped in the warmth of those messages of love.

I attended the appointments with renewed energy the next day. At both appointments I received miraculous results. No abnormal cells. No cancer. I would be fine. I was going to live.

I also knew from this moment on, my life would be different. I would begin, that very day, to create the life I wanted. To leave a powerful legacy. To BE the mother, daughter, sibling, friend I wanted to be. To live *purposefully*. To make my life a masterpiece.

These experiences — the ovarian cysts, the solid mass in my breast, the dreaded threat of cancer, and the reminder of the incredible love and support that surrounds me — gave me three life-altering ah-ha moments. First, I was reminded: *Life is short! Why was it my tendency to wait for the Universe to remind me of this? It was so very easy to get caught up in the day-today patterns, living my life unconsciously.*

While I am very fortunate to have a career I'm passionate about, no amount of business or financial success can replace the joy that spending time with family can bring. Nothing is more treasured than a child greeting me with a leaping hug, or cradling a tender newborn as they drift off into a peaceful sleep, or watching with pride as my grown children lovingly parent their offspring.

During those long, worrisome months of 2002, the Universe helped me to internalize and accept the reality that yes, indeed, life IS short for us all, myself included! Any day could bring news of an illness. Any day I could face accidents or injuries. Any day I could confront a drunken driver. Any day could provide a life-altering experience for ANYONE, ourselves, those we love and adore or those we simply pass on the street.

I've come to realize that there's incredible beauty in the message that "Life is short." For any day can also bring precious, memorable moments, like the one that Dave created for me on August 27, 2002. It can bring joy and laughter. Heartfelt conversations and connections with others. Precious memories; when I take the time to really pay attention. So today, I listen more. I connect more. I hug more. I smile, laugh, dance and play more. And I challenge myself to *be* more.

I love listening to the song, "Live Like You Were Dying," released by country singer Tim McGraw in August of 2004. What would *you* do differently if you knew you were dying? Would you go sky diving? Rocky Mountain climbing? Would you love deeper? Speak sweeter? Give forgiveness you've been denying?

There is great benefit in living like we are dying. Life becomes sweeter. More dynamic. More precious. More filled to the brim with glorious moments we can savour through to our last days here on earth. Harriet Beecher Stow said, *"The bitterest tears shed over graves are for words left unsaid and deeds left undone."*

Next, I learned that *a terrible experience can be turned around when someone cares enough to create a special moment*. It was amazing how quickly my focus shifted from illness to love and support as I stood in the back entryway on that August evening, looking up at the poster paper covering the door. What an incredible gift of a magical moment. I have learned to acknowledge that I create my life on a moment-to-moment basis and, in every moment, I have a choice in what I create for myself, and for others.

Medical research shows us that oxytocin (the feel good chemical) is created in our body when we think good thoughts or have pleasant experiences. When we are the recipient of an act of kindness, our oxytocin levels go up, and we feel good. When we see, or hear about an act of kindness, our oxytocin levels go up. Here's the really cool thing. When we DO an act of kindness, our oxytocin levels go up! I learned I can make myself feel good simply by pausing to remember some of the special moments others have created for me, or by creating a special moment for someone else! How exciting is that?

Finally, I learned I *have so much more love and support than I realize*. Often, when my life was not working the way I wanted it to, I felt all alone in my discomfort or misery. I've found over the years that focusing on what's NOT working in my life only creates a downward spiral.

Sometimes I put on a mask of everything's just fine, while I suffered alone and in silence. I hesitated to ask for support. I didn't want to appear weak or to bother others with my troubles. But here's what I've discovered. Often the people in my life *wanted* to help but didn't know how they could. Or they weren't even aware there was a problem. It's amazing when I take stock of how many people I have in my life to love, and who love and support me. I am literally surrounded by love and support, but with my focus elsewhere, I failed to recognize it. So, now I take stock. Who are my cheerleaders? Who always listens and supports me? Who disregards my bad habits and idiosyncrasies? Who can I always count on?

It's been said that the more we send out, the more we get back. I have found that to be true in my life tenfold. With kindness, I can be the veritable pebble in the pool, creating a ripple of love, a river of oxytocin to heal myself and the world, one moment, one kindness at a time.

With my heightened awareness of our precious, limited time here on this earth,

I have been on a quest to discover ways that would allow me to squeeze every ounce of joy from each and every moment. I found myself surrounded by wonderful ideas. Books, movies, conversations, and the lives and stories of others have all been the catalysts and inspiration to take life-enhancing actions.

Now years later, I think often of those days of 2002 and the lessons I learned, both in the doctor's office and on my back porch. To this day, tears surface, my heart swells and the words get stuck in my throat when I remember or share these extraordinary experiences. And on a regular basis I think fondly of Dave, his big heart, and how he cared enough to create a moment for me that I'll remember until the day I die. While Dave and I still have engaging conversations and occasionally dinner or drinks together, we are no longer a married couple.

But that, my dear friends, is another story.

Known by her clients as the 'Wizard of AHs', Rhonda Barry has been leading transformational seminars and corporate programs for over 25 years. She is a published author, whose time is spent writing, designing and facilitating corporate and personal development programs, running her hypnotherapy practice, volunteering (in the community and beyond) and spending time with her family. Her soon-to-be released book, Pretend Birthdays and Other Memorable Moments reinforces her learnings of August 2002, as she shares a multitude of stories to help others create memorable lives on a moment-to-moment basis. She currently resides in Saskatchewan, Canada and can be reached at soulgardener@sasktel.net or through www.EnlightenedLeadershipforWomen.com.

Healed To Become A Healer

B. Grace Jones

Moving to Alaska began as a spectacular adventure. My life reached a peak I had never imagined possible. After my 40-hour workweek, I explored Alaska on weekends and holidays. I built a tight network of wonderful friends and was literally on top of the world. Six years later my world came crashing down, dragging me into three years of total disability in the isolated, great white north. Ultimately, that led me to something even more spectacular.

For two decades I had pushed through pain, fatigue and various symptoms to work full time in Oklahoma. The diagnosis was Mitral Valve Prolapse, a heart condition. Medications and physical therapy treatments were prescribed. I raised a family, divorced, and fell in love with Alaska during a vacation. Increasing job stress and burnout in my graphic design career signaled new physical symptoms layered on top of old. I packed and headed north, seeking a less stressful job in Anchorage.

Updated medical tests showed I had NO heart condition. My confidence in Western medicine diminished, and I phased out medications. I managed the pain via physical therapy, heat, exercise, diet, and essential oils. I studied personal growth, spirituality, and healing. I was on the path to gain better health and independence.

Menopause signaled depression and insomnia, which affected my work performance. Personnel changes created incomparable stress. I had done my best to adapt, but I had compromised my personal values. I wanted to change my career to the Healing Arts. I visited two career counselors, who advised against it. I was stuck trying to survive at work and make the best of a deteriorating situation.

A decade from retirement, I felt financially unprepared. A subliminal driving fear began to rule my life. I kept my job and started a business to create more income. I rented the spare room, was a vendor at two fairs and took two trips outside Alaska, all within four months. It was a great recipe for stress overload.

During the second fair, I came down with a terrible sore throat and within a week was too ill to work. Completely baffled by waves of debilitating fatigue, I pleaded with God, "*What is happening to me? What did I do wrong?*" The answer came to me, "*This is not all about you.*" I knew then, whatever this experience was, somehow it would help me to help others.

Diagnosed with mononucleosis, I did not recover for months. Numerous tests and medical consultations determined the diagnosis of Chronic Mono and Fibromyalgia/Chronic Fatigue. Western medicine had little to offer, but I was locked into that system by medical insurance. Payment for alternative therapies had to come from my disability benefits. Even with that brutal scenario, I was determined to find a way to recover.

It felt like the worst flu I ever had, plus a 300-pound weight on my chest and a plethora of other symptoms swirling about. I could not read one paragraph without needing to rest 20 minutes. Even listening to music would exhaust me. Bathing was an infrequent, elongated chore punctuated by rest periods. The hardest thing I ever had to learn was how to do *nothing*. It was mandatory that I find solace in stillness and silence as my muscle tone wasted away. The second hardest thing I had to learn was how to ask for help. I had to call on family and friends to grocery shop, clean house or give me rides. I was often too fatigued to answer the phone, but just hearing the message would lift my spirit, "*Somebody cares.*"

Repetitive relapse cycles proved any forward progression had to be in micro-units. After six months I tried the treadmill at home for two minutes which produced shin splints. When finally able to walk outside briefly, it was a tentative blend of toddler and elder. My brother reported our 90-year-old mother could walk faster than me.

It felt as if I was moving through wet concrete, but I did my best to research alternative therapies. I could barely sit at the computer and sometimes pushed beyond safety to seek salvation from a living death. I learned Feldenkrais, bought an expensive massage bed, heat packs and cushions. I experimented with essential oils, supplements, diet changes and received Johrei. All offered minimal symptom management, but I was grateful for any negligible relief. My total disability created an intense desire to find something to heal me, not just manage symptoms.

One theory is that Fibromyalgia is triggered by a trauma. I reviewed my life to determine the onset of symptoms and when they increased. I identified the possible traumas, but didn't know what to do about it. My previous experience with traditional psychotherapy had not provided any effective solution. I had done much personal inventory in 12-step work, which enabled me to deal with it on a conscious level. I owned my part, as I cleared away the wreckage of my past.

The first two years disabled, there was no way I could travel. I longed to see my mother, and wanted to meet my new grandson. I finally gained enough recovery to attempt it, but I required wheel chair assistance, pillows, heat packs, blankets, essential oils, and much meditation to endure it. A four-hour delay and heavy fatigue required I lie on the floor at the airline gate. The trip was entirely too much for me, and I lost two months worth of gain.

I returned home to discover a shock: the loss of disability insurance benefits without prior notice. I had to make a desperate, heart-breaking decision to leave. Alaskan winters were too hard for me. Keeping my condo would be a financial drain. I had to move before winter's impending arrival in less than two months. I was powerless to do much of anything myself.

Thank God for family and countless friends. Again, I had to ask a lot of them to do really huge things. I could barely make decisions of what to keep and what to give away. I was totally overwhelmed. I made a plane reservation and lists with instructions. My perfect home disintegrated into chaos beyond my control. That was my perception anyway. Upon entry to the central packing area, previously known as the living room, a friend exclaimed, "Oh! Everything is in Divine Order." All I could do was walk away from the mess with no sense of emotional closure. My tears were abundant as my plane took off, and I watched my Anchorage home disappear far below.

My dear mother opened her heart and home in Kansas where I grew up, but made it clear she wanted us to live independently. It was the first time I had spent any length of time there since Dad died. My grief was doubly magnified. I missed my Alaskan home, and my Dad in this home. Mom and I were just beginning to adjust when my oldest sister was discharged from the hospital and needed to join us. We sat on Mom's couch like two invalid bookends. It was difficult for everyone, but we struggled through it with love and tolerance.

I unpacked with indescribable difficulty, since any storage space for my things first had to be cleared of my parent's decades of accumulation. The plan was to remodel the basement into an apartment for me, but I stayed with Mom until that could be managed. My oldest daughter spent a week clearing and redecorating the basement living room. Finally, I had a space that felt like mine even though I was sleeping upstairs in the guest room. (Gratefully the stairs are equipped with a chair lift.) It was months before I was able to resume my micro-units of attempt at recovery.

My friend in Oklahoma, Linda Esser, had told me about a powerful tapping technique she was practicing. She said it had healed people from Fibromyalgia. I thought, *"It might work for those who are still able to function, but she doesn't know how sick I really am."* I was not able to travel by car to Oklahoma. The four-hour trip would require three days of rest plus a driver. It sounded strange, but I did my best to search online for the demo videos to try it. I watched testimonials, but the fatigue would overcome me before I could find the "how to" videos.

I had hoped to keep ties to Alaska and arranged with a friend to inhabit his duplex in Anchorage the next summer while he worked in Denali Park. With minimal energy recoup, I headed north. As usual, I made the trip in two segments with a one or two night layover in Denver allowing me to rest with family. My ability to be a passenger in a car required my seat to be reclined, my eyes closed, plus the radio and driver had to be silent. Even that was exhausting.

Back in Anchorage I unpacked and sorted things left behind. Then I resumed micro-unit attempts of recovery. I reported my return to Linda. She suggested I start making a list of my entire life's hurts and traumas in order for her to teach me the healing technique. I slowly began to work on the list.

Faithfully seeking a way to completely heal, I continued to study spiritual and healing masters. I listened to audio books as I continued my massage bed treatments and essential oils. I practiced many types of meditation but still struggled with the practical application of concepts. Desperately, I inquired of God, *"What would I do if there were an earthquake, if I had no electricity for the massage bed and my supplements fell into a crevasse? How would I manage to survive?"* I knew there must be a way to be healthy without the aid of equipment or consumable products, and I was determined to find it.

After two years and ten months I had slowly regained limited energy when I realized I was spiraling down into relapse again. My pain and fatigue increased and my digestive system would not tolerate much food. I cried out in desperation to God, *"Where is my teacher? This student is ready."* I knew if the student is truly ready the teacher has already appeared, so I began to inventory my life to discern who it might be.

I called Linda, who had recently completed certification as a practitioner of the healing protocol she had suggested. It's called Faster EFT, Emotionally Focused Transformations, developed by Robert G. Smith. My list wasn't complete, so I called to ask what she knew about fasting, since my body would not assimilate food. She immediately began to teach me Faster EFT over the phone. I was still skeptical but desperate enough to try. During the first phone session half my pain vanished, and the release of fatigue was dramatic.

When Faster EFT worked immediately, I was gratefully amazed and had an instantaneous, synchronous revelation. *"This will work on anything, if I use it. This will be the healing wave that carries me out of the sea of disability. I will do this as my new career in healing arts."* Enthusiastically I practiced the techniques daily. I visited Robert's YouTube channel to study and practice more. Linda continued phone sessions for several weeks to address and release the emotional charge of past traumas. I purchased Faster EFT training DVDs to learn and heal more.

Within ten days of daily practice I was able to grocery shop without the motor cart, stand in line without extreme fatigue or pain, and sleep without a pill. I noted in my journal, *"As I walked outside, I could feel the big difference in my muscles . . . so much more relaxed and fluid, kind of like pudding. My jaws were not in spasm, but relaxed and springy . . . I have not had any flicker of depression, nor felt lonely . . . I even did some bending and reaching . . . some of my leg aches are now the good kind, from rebuilding muscle. I am really getting my life back and way better than before. This is stellar spectacular!"*

My healing progressed daily as I practiced Faster EFT. In six weeks, at the suggestion of both Linda and Robert, I began to share the skills with others and help them improve their lives. I was impressed that everyone I worked with experienced a positive effect on some level. It didn't take their belief, only willingness. It's a simple system that works if you use it.

Physical strength and stamina increased with regularity as I continued daily tapping. In four months I left Alaska and returned to Kansas for winter. I supervised the completion of the basement apartment remodel and created a place to call home. Two months later I began driving weekly to Oklahoma City to take the Faster EFT practitioner course. Classes met every Monday and Tuesday evening for six months. At first I paced myself slowly, making it a three-to-four day trip. By the end of the course I was able to make it an overnight trip.

Today I am highly energetic and building my worldwide business as a Faster EFT practitioner. When symptoms arise, I use the techniques to heal every area of my life. Faster EFT enables my conscious and unconscious mind to communicate with each other and my body. It releases stress, clears the negative emotional charge of past traumas, changes unconscious automatic behaviors and replaces them with a deep inner peace and joy. These skills enable me to change my perception of my past and the world around me. I experience the freedom to change how I feel. I am free from pain and fatigue, free to live longer, be happier, feel more love, and make more money. Faster EFT gives me the power to control my thoughts and emotions. Any time, any place, I can effectively use these simple skills to practice the spiritual concepts that were previously beyond my reach. I continue to heal my life and teach others how to heal their lives. Thank God it's not all about me.

When I returned to Alaska the second summer, one year after I began daily practice of Faster EFT, my M.D. was very impressed with my recovery progress. After examining me, he stated, "Well, you can't argue with success!"

Grace owns and operates Denali Dragonfly Options, a worldwide healing arts practice, where she is primarily a Faster EFT Practitioner and Life Skills Coach. She presents public seminars and does private client sessions over the phone, Skype, and in person. She is writing two books, one is her story and one about how Robert Smith developed Faster EFT, including the techniques. Grace is her own best testimony to the power of practicing daily Faster EFT. For more information, contact Grace at (405) 443-4086, www.DenaliDragonfly.com or email DenaliDragonfly@gmail.com.

My Wellness Journey

Erin Reas

One hot June morning at forty years of age, I started feeling faint. I thought it was from the heat since my house did not have air conditioning. I went downstairs where it was cooler and starting having chest pain and shortness of breath. I went to the hospital and had a number of tests done. I was told that I had experienced a heart attack. I was in shock. I was only 40 years old. I considered myself to be a healthy person. I overlooked the fact that I was overweight and did not exercise. I had a habit of stopping at McDonald's some days on the way to work to get a Quarter Pounder with cheese.

When I was in the emergency room, I vowed I would start exercising. A day or so after coming home from the hospital I decided to take a walk around the block. I couldn't believe how hard it was to walk such a short distance. Less than a week after the heart attack, I was back in the hospital with a blood clot in my leg. After a few days, I was able to come back home, but had to be on medical leave from work for a while so that I could get better.

Later in the summer, I went back to work. My life was almost back to normal. However, even after experiencing such major events, I didn't make many changes in my life. I no longer stopped at McDonald's on the way to work but I was no longer taking walks because my heel hurt.

I decided I wanted to change what I did for a living. My hospital pharmacist job had a lot of stress and required me to work weekends and holidays when I preferred to be with my family. I wanted to make big changes but kept getting side tracked by things going on in my life. I was busy with my job and family. I did not make time for myself.

Months went by and the next thing I knew, a year had passed since my heart attack. I now weighed even more than when I went into the hospital due to snacking and not exercising. I had joined Weight Watchers online several months before as part of a New Year's resolution to lose weight. However, I had regained all the weight I had lost when I was going through a particularly stressful time.

The turning point was when none of my clothes fit. I ended up going to a plus size store for the first time in my life to buy new ones. I realized I needed to do something if I wanted to prevent having a second heart attack. My son was about to start sixth grade and I wanted to be sure I was around to see him graduate from college some day. I decided that when school began in September, I would join Weight Watchers and go to the meetings every week.

I followed through on my decision. I requested to be off work every Friday so I could attend my Weight Watchers meeting. That was an important step in taking care of myself. What a huge difference it made.

I started eating better and exercising. I walked during my son's soccer practices. After the soccer season was finished, I worked out at a gym. In January I signed up for a kickboxing class and loved it. I looked forward to going to class every week.

I was steadily losing weight. My goal was to reach a healthy weight and maintain it. I did not care how long that took. I figured that if the weight came off slowly it was more likely to stay off.

By spring I had reached a healthy weight and felt great. I enjoyed picking new recipes to try. I was in better shape than I had been in years. Now I was ready to make other changes in my life.

For some time I had thought about becoming a wellness coach. It seemed like a natural fit with my pharmacy training and experience as a diabetes educator. In September 2007, I went to a Circle of Life training program. A year later I became a Certified Circle of Life Health and Wellness Coach. I discovered that I love coaching people and helping them make changes in their life.

Now I have my own coaching business. I have maintained my healthy weight for 2 years. Last summer I completed an 11 mile hike in Glacier National Park. I have changed and grown so much from the overweight, out of shape, unhappy person I was four years ago.

I learned several important lessons during my journey to wellness. The first is when your body talks to you, *Listen*. I was not feeling well the day before my heart attack but I went to work anyway. Second, make self-care a priority. Self-care is not only important for maintaining health and wellbeing but also helps in making positive life changes. When I was always putting others before myself, I found it difficult to move forward with the changes I wanted to make in my life. Third, the secret to making big changes is to keep taking one small step at a time. Don't let life get in the way of starting or continuing on the path towards a goal. Last, it helps to have support in achieving goals. I have been surrounded by supportive people while making significant changes in my life. Their encouragement made a world of difference to me.

As a registered pharmacist, wife, and mother, Erin Reas has learned the secrets to reducing stress while managing multiple demands on her time. Erin is a Certified Life and Wellness Coach who helps busy professional women reduce their stress and reclaim their excitement for life. Erin assists people in designing their own personal action plan to create a healthy and satisfying life. She teaches Tai Chi Easy classes in addition to leading workshops and providing individual and group coaching. To receive a free copy of "Simple Ways to Reduce Stress" or schedule a complimentary consultation, call 313-429-3214 or email erin@erinreas.com. www.erinreas.com.

Adapting to Change:
What I Learned After the Diagnosis

Michelle Wilson

Not long ago I didn't have to think much about food allergies, sending special snacks to school, checking labels obsessively, or bringing one cupcake to a birthday party. These were things other families had to do, not ours. We have friends whose children have severe, life-threatening allergies, so we understood their cause for caution and concern. My kids missed their peanut butter and jelly sandwiches when they couldn't bring them to school, but we adapted easily. It wasn't until I had my own increasing symptoms and diagnosis, that food ingredients took on a whole new, more personal meaning.

My symptoms were not particularly dramatic at first and I attributed most of them to being a busy mom. Fatigue and brain fog, primarily... most moms can relate to that! I had some bloating, but hey, that's normal too, right? When my son was in the toddler phase, I was sleeping, eating and exercising pretty well, but the sleepiness was getting intolerable and the lack of focus and poor memory was frustrating. I saw a holistic nutritionist, chiropractor and my doctor. I learned a lot, but no one put all the pieces together. Probably, because I didn't recognize and describe enough of my symptoms.

Women out there, did you know that you should see your doctor if you are bloated for more than two weeks? I learned it can be a symptom of ovarian cancer - scary! Nurse relatives confirmed my belly did not look normal. "See what my stomach looks like at night? I think it might be related to wheat..." "Don't stick your stomach out." "I'm not!" They urged me to see my PCP right away, who ordered ultrasounds, blood tests, and then an endoscopy.

I now have celiac disease. This is actually an autoimmune disorder, not an allergy, however, like an allergy, my body can't tolerate a common ingredient in many foods. It was most likely triggered by the stress of my second pregnancy and the adjustment to two children! I now go to great lengths to avoid gluten, a protein found in wheat, barley and rye. The disease can take many years to diagnose due to the variety of symptoms. In fact 1-3 percent of the population has celiac disease, but 97% of those people do not know they have it! After seeing several traditional and non-traditional practitioners over the course of a year, I finally had an answer. I could never eat foods with gluten if I wanted to avoid serious symptoms, malnutrition (caused by damage to the intestines resulting in mal-absorption of nutrients), and the increased possibility of cancer.

My husband and I knew we needed to test our kids since it is a genetic disorder that can be present even without symptoms. However, the testing for celiac disease can be complicated and we were unsure of how to proceed with their nutrition for awhile. As it turns out, they don't have celiac disease now. I feel so fortunate that we only had a few months with our kids on a gluten-free diet. It was not easy! It takes effort and a more expensive grocery bill to accommodate special foods! I definitely have a new appreciation for families whose children have allergies, especially with multiple ingredients to avoid. As for now, my children can go back to having graham crackers and goldfish at school or pizza and cake at a party, although we do limit gluten and will test them regularly. My husband thought it might be easier for our kids to go gluten-free than for me, because it's all they will know. I disagree. It's hard to be different
from your peers and not be able to participate in childhood social events in the same way, but it's hard for me too!

When it is just me, I feel a bit selfish. It is not a life-or death allergy, my kids are healthy and I don't have a terminal illness. I shouldn't have anything to complain about, right? Well, I do value recognizing and owning our feelings, rather than denying them. In any situation, we can always find those less fortunate with whom to compare ourselves, but in order to be truly authentic, I needed to process, own and then keep moving through my feelings.

As I went through the process of adjusting to a life-long change and a new way of shopping, cooking, and eating, the five stages of grief developed by Elizabeth Kubler-Ross kept popping into my head. You know the ones. They've even been used in sitcoms and SNL like skits and are well known and applied to all kinds of situations. Well, they seemed to fit for me, even if it wasn't the original intent of the stages. Perhaps you'll see yourself in these if you are adjusting to a life change.

Denial: I knew acquaintances who had celiac, but didn't think I would have an actual diagnosis. Even months later, I thought the tests must have been wrong. It just couldn't be that I could *never* have many of my favorite foods again! However, the longer I was away from gluten, the more obvious the symptoms became. It was confirmed for me when I had about 1/2 cup of regular pasta by accident. I thought all the spaghetti in the fridge was gluten-free and added it to my chicken parmesan with GF bread crumbs. By the end of the meal, my husband asked, "What have you been eating, because you've said about five of the wrong words?" (we determined that was another symptom - my brain really doesn't work properly when I have gluten). "Well, I haven't eaten gluten in months, so it must just be mommy brain." That night, I was so sleepy, I went to bed about an hour after dinner, the next morning I looked like I was 5 months pregnant, and 24 hours later the joint pain in my shoulders and hands kicked in. Yep, that's my reaction to gluten. We figured out there was regular pasta in the fridge from a night I worked late and they had gluten-full spaghetti. I had grabbed it unknowingly and suffered the consequences! Now it is sinking in...it is not even psychosomatic.

Anger: "OK, this is just beyond ironic and not fair!" As a teenager I had struggled with an eating disorder and so much of my recovery involved having no forbidden foods. I felt that I had made peace with food and the ideas of moderation. Letting go of the all or nothing thinking continues to be helpful for so many women I see in my therapy practice who struggle with eating issues. This is just ridiculous. I don't even want to cheat or I'll suffer for days after. The worst is when I am trying so hard and a crumb in the silverware drawer or a new vitamin I forgot to check brings on symptoms. Sometimes I never figure out the culprit. In rebellion (during the early days after a frustrating tour of the grocery store), I bought Twizzlers. Yes, red dye, corn syrup and everything I knew wasn't the healthiest, and I didn't even check the label. True story: I didn't realize until days later that they contain wheat. Flour is the second ingredient, who knew?

Bargaining: Fine, I'll do this gluten-free thing for awhile, and maybe it will cure itself. I'm still not sure it can actually be an auto-immune disorder. The tests weren't completely thorough and maybe they were wrong. Maybe if I get more medical opinions there are treatments out there that can cure allergies, right?

To be honest, I couldn't seriously stay in this phase long. If bargaining worked and I did have ovarian cancer, I would have traded that for celiac disease in a heartbeat. If given the chance, I would take upon myself any illness that my children could possibly have. So there you have it, I would have chosen my current fate over many other options.

Depression: I've definitely had my share of pity-parties. This especially happens while grocery shopping when I calculate about 75% of the foods probably contain gluten, even in trace amounts. If you have never checked labels for the common allergens, you would be surprised! If you have, you know nuts, dairy and soy are everywhere too. Today I wanted dried cherries. Too bad they were processed in a factory with wheat! In the past I've almost had a crying meltdown before a dinner party. What could I possibly eat in someone else's home without feeling high-maintenance or bringing my own food? I never fell into a deep depression, but there were moments of sadness as things kept sinking in. Little things like not being able to have the pretzel my son offers from his plate, never being able to have a girl scout cookie from my daughter's brownie troop, or needing to make special birthday cakes for the family if I want to participate.

Acceptance. In my life and in my work with clients, this concept has become so powerful to me. Sometimes it feels like radical acceptance: why would we want to accept something negative? It seems we are taught to fight or avoid what we don't like in our lives. I'm realizing it is often our resistance that brings us suffering, and it is only through acceptance that we can find peace. When we start accepting what is, we can move on instead of staying stuck in the other stages. This process of grieving an old life and adjusting to a new way of being is an ongoing one. There are still times it hits me. "Oh...this is another food I can never have." As I learned in a seminar years ago, sometimes we recycle through those stages in waves.

Most days I try to recognize all the wonderful foods I *can* eat. This is a perspective shift I can choose daily. When I look at foods found in nature, I have tons of delicious choices to enjoy. Fortunately for anyone with gluten intolerance or food allergies, we live in a time with many alternatives and better food labels. I am starting to experiment more with "G-free" baking, I bring my own cones to our favorite ice cream stand again this summer, and my supportive husband just moved the silverware drawer away from the gluten toaster oven (yes, we have two!).

Michelle Wilson, MA, LMHC is a psychotherapist and life coach in private practice in Andover, MA. She's grateful her husband enjoys cooking and she treasures hugs and kisses from her kids even with gluten-covered fingers or faces. Michelle has over 15 years experience helping women reach their goals and create a life they love and is the founder of Inner Oasis Counseling and Coaching. She enjoys working individually with women to help them manage stress and find more calm and joy in their lives and she offers workshops, retreats and teleclasses on her MOM OASIS principles for women around the world.

Please visit www.InnerOasisCounseling.com or www.TheMomOasis.com for more information and FREE RESOURCES for creating more peace and joy in YOUR life!

Royal Warrior Goddess

Ginny Martin Fleming

Every day, I pass a place in my home where an elegant lady inspires me. There is a female face who reminds me of the utter despair from which I have come. Along with an assortment of crystals, quotes and other meaningful trinkets, this is my spiritual altar.

At the end of a women's retreat years ago, we were given a blank white plastic mask of a female face mounted on a dowel rod. We used the many assorted craft supplies provided to adorn the masks to represent ourselves – our newly conceived highest expression of the women we were becoming. That evening we went around the circle explaining ours to the rest of the group. We admired the impressive creativity and thoughtful choices of decorations teeming with meaning. Each of the empowered women had courageously met, dis-covered, and created a new vision of themselves that weekend.

My mask has beautiful smoothly painted, peach colored skin and rosy cheeks with pale pink glitter. My princess warrior goddess wears a strand of dangling golden yellow beads for a headband, with a sapphire blue jewel above it at the center and sky blue glitter spreading out from the jewel on either side. A real peacock feather, all golden, chocolate, teal and green, shoots up from the left side, signifying my connection to God's glorious world of nature. Six strands of ribbon – wide purple satin, medium textured gold, and narrow shiny silver – stream down from the right side with regal flair. I am a worthy, royal child of God, learning to love myself and boost my self-esteem.

Translucent sequins line the eyes to represent seeing with clarity and truth. Shiny azure sequins wrap around the top of the dowel rod, under her chin – the throat chakra supported and strong. And my favorite part – a short green stem with a white silk rose bud and three green leaves emerges from the left side of her dainty mouth, her elegantly curved lips parted slightly, painted a dusty rose. This gentle warrior goddess speaks her truth with compassion.

On the altar beside her is a small clay figurine I made at a healing conference several years prior to the women's retreat. Our instructions at that workshop were to get in touch with our emotions and to shape something out of the wet gray clay expressing them. My little Ginny is sitting on her knees with her legs tucked under her, torso bent forward, face buried in her hands, her long hair falling down around the sides of her head. She is making herself small, inconspicuous, hiding her tears, her shame. I remember fresh tears rolling down my cheeks, dropping onto the cool lump of clay as I formed her. I felt deeply the anguish of my life at that time as I defined her features and smoothed her shirt, her jeans. When she dried, I took the ivory colored piece of art home with me and I entitled her "Despair."

The day after my thirty-first birthday, I woke up terribly sick with what would be diagnosed a year later as chronic fatigue syndrome (CFS). My daughters were one and four. Housebound and often bedridden for the first two or three years and during numerous relapses throughout the past twenty years, I have had many dark days and even more sleepless nights. Besides extremely debilitating fatigue, daily pain, constant headaches and a host of other symptoms, insomnia has been perhaps the most frustrating part of this bizarre disease. To feel so exhausted and not be able to sleep for more than an hour at a time, for a total of maybe four hours of broken sleep night after night after night, even with prescription drugs, is exhausting!

The grief of all the losses – the inability to exercise, to travel, to participate in my kids' school activities or social activities; the loss of many friends, my marriage; the loss of my former life, my former self – has left me with as much emotional pain to heal as physical pain to endure.

We all have our crosses to bear – chronic fatigue and fibromyalgia just happen to be mine. But as my mother taught me early in life, "It's whatcha do with whatcha got" that counts. From the outset, I was determined to heal, and have explored many fascinating modalities and therapies I would most likely never have tried otherwise. I discovered helpful tools for keeping my sanity that can be useful to all people, and I share them with others when I can. One of the quotes I tore out from a page-a-day calendar says, "We cannot do great things, only small things in a great way." I still have it posted by my kitchen sink where I see it daily. And when I can't get out of the house and participate fully in life, I still try to do even little things with great awareness and love.

In many ways, CFS was a perfect illness for my Type A personality. I became a more conscious parent, emotionally and physically present for my daughters in ways I might not have been if well. I developed empathy for others' pain, grief and challenges, letting me effectively minister to others, one on one. I've come to be known as a safe, compassionate listener who makes herself available to others. It is one rewarding way I maintain social contact and a sense of value.

I have experienced and learned many alternative healing practices – from homeopathy and nutrition to kinesiology and chiropractic; from flower essences and aromatherapy to energy balancing and crystals; from astrology and numerology to rebirthing and tarot; from Reiki and EFT to Theta Healing and Bowen; from bio-feedback and meditation to acupuncture and massage; from psychics and medical intuitives to … well, you get the picture – it's been quite a journey!

Perhaps the most helpful tools that have carried me through even the darkest hours and to which I have consistently returned again and again, have been journaling; feeding my mind with positive quotes and books (and audio books and music when I was too sick to even read or write); and kundalini yoga and meditation. The first two practices I had started as a teen. I just happened upon (there are no accidents!) a kundalini yoga instructor early on in the illness who taught me things that pretty much saved my life in the years to come.

About three months after I got sick, I walked into my first health food store and picked up a local wellness directory. Too sick to travel far, I found the closest alternative healer in the area and made an appointment for intuitive counseling and flower essence therapy. I was a fish out of water as I entered HarDarshan's home, was asked to remove my shoes at the door, and then was gently and lovingly guided through her "green" home, fifteen years before that concept ever had a name. We went into her sunroom, which was filled with dozens of live green plants, a bird perched in a hanging cage, and we sat down on a long, comfortable sofa. There I was introduced to kinesiology (muscle testing), which is how Har-Darshan selected the flower essence remedies to treat my symptoms. A reference guide listed information about each remedy and what it was good for, which provided insight into the emotional/mental aspects behind physical symptoms. For example, broccoli was good for courage, in addition to treating my chronic sore throat. I was *fascinated!* Food for thought for my journaling as I pondered each of the dozen or more remedies my body said I needed.

When I learned that HarDarshan also taught yoga, I was immediately interested. I knew I wanted to spend more time around this peaceful, loving, light-filled healer. She invited me to attend a class and offered to drive me, as I was too ill to be able to predict my ability to drive from day to day, sometimes hour to hour. I decided to give it a try. I didn't realize this type of yoga was different from others, but I immediately felt "at home" with it, and have been practicing kundalini yoga and meditation ever since.

A man named Yogi Bhajan brought kundalini yoga to the west in 1969. Thought to be reserved for the higher castes in India, this ancient form of yoga is really a technology for our times – a practical discipline to help us counteract the stress and negativity in the world around us, to ground us, center us, and enable us to function more effectively in the world. It utilizes a combination of physical exercises, breathing techniques, meditations, and mudras (hand positions), and by using sound current (chanting mantras). It truly addresses the physical, emotional, mental and spiritual aspects of the individual. I can personally vouch for that.

"Sat nam" is the "seed" mantra which instantly attunes us to our highest self and is used throughout many of the exercises, even if only "vibrated" mentally – "sat" with the inhale, "nam" with the exhale. It rhymes with "but mom" and means, "Truth is my Name" or "Truth is my Identity." I liked that.

About the time I made the little clay figurine, HarDarshan gave me an assignment: a 31-minute meditation to do daily for 1,000 days. If I missed a day, I would need to start all over. I was just desperate enough at the time to give it a try, and too stubborn and determined to give up. Mostly, it was something I *could* control in my rather uncontrollable life situation.

So for two years and nine months I meditated, chanting the prayer for protection every single day or night. Sitting cross-legged in easy pose, I chanted "Aad Guray Nameh, Jugad Guray Nameh, Sat Guray Nameh, Siri Guru Devay Nameh". With the palms of my hands together I lifted my arms from the prayer pose position at my chest upward and out, then back down to my chest again and so forth, with the rhythm of the mantra. Often I did my meditation after lunch when Caroline was in school and during Hallie's naptime. As she got older, Hallie sometimes stayed in her room, but gradually came more and more often to my bedroom, bringing paper and crayons or a puzzle to work quietly by my side until she got sleepy. Then she put her sweet little toddler head in my lap while I continued to chant softly. In those tender moments I performed the arm movement with one hand, while stroking my precious child with the other. My little yoga baby.

I must confess that there were many days when I did not feel light and blissful and peaceful. Sometimes I was downright pissed off about having to do the exercise and it was a chore, a burden, and I cried to get through it. Sometimes I was so sick I had to just lie down in my bed, forget the arm movements and just mentally vibrate the chant when my throat was too swollen and sore to even speak. But I did it! And the experience of completing such a commitment of discipline changed my life. At the end of the thousand days, I was a royal warrior goddess!

Since those early days of CFS, I've had other life issues to deal with, as we all do. I've survived a divorce, breast cancer, and several other difficult health challenges. I have also raised two beautiful, successful, independent daughters, have learned to trust and love again in my rewarding, healing second marriage, and have attracted the most amazing women friends into my life. Sometimes I still forget to trust my intuition, my body's wisdom, and I rush from doctor to doctor seeking the latest and greatest advice and treatment options. But when I'm in my home and I go past my spiritual altar, my royal warrior goddess reminds me to go within in one of the myriad of ways I've been privileged to learn. I return to a more disciplined practice of kundalini yoga and meditation in my peaceful room over the detached garage, burning my Nag Champa incense that has long served to center me. I breathe in deeply the prana, the life force the universe provides to us all, and breathe out any negativity or things which I need to let go. I breathe in love, and breathe out fear, I breathe in "sat" and exhale "nam," and I am "home."

Prior to having children, Ginny was an Account Executive for a high tech advertising agency. Before getting sick in 1990, she had her own free lance marketing and public relations business. Today, Ginny's passion is empowering other women through private healing sessions, rich friendships, and teaching kundalini yoga and meditation. She is also a writer and lover of books. When not escaping to their little beach house, Ginny lives in Wake Forest, NC with her husband, Michael, and her sweet 15-year old golden/border collie, Bailey. Contact Ginny at gmfleming1124@gmail.com.

The Bedpan

Jan Haas

A long stay in a hospital doesn't do much for one's self confidence. I had just spent sixty days in a hospital Intensive Care Unit, forty nine of those on a ventilator, and was used to having a nurse at my beck and call. Because I had been in a drug induced coma for so long, I didn't always know my physical condition. When any number of doctors would ask me how I was doing, I looked to my husband Tony for the answer. I experienced helplessness and hopelessness because I couldn't take care of myself. I had become a specimen for doctors to observe, poke and prod, and I felt like I was losing myself in a very sterile environment. Emotionally and physically, I had a long road to recovery. Not even the luxury of 8 pillows in an adjustable bed could make up for my loss of all things familiar. The beeps of machines, the clank of IV poles, and intercom pages for doctors reminded me that I was not at home. As I became stronger physically and moved to the general surgical floor, the test of my emotional strength was just beginning. Although there were many significant moments during my initial 100 days in the hospital, a turning point for me came in the form of a bed pan.

One of the biggest adjustments I had to make on the new floor was less medical attention from the nurses. At no other time was this more crucial than when I had to go to the bathroom. One night, I turned on the light for my nurse to come help me relieve myself and still ten minutes later I was waiting. Now mind you, in the hospital, they don't look too kindly on you if you try to get out of bed yourself and use the toilet, especially if you are just out of ICU and still attached to a feeding tube and IV's. When you add a bum knee and a pair of crutches and an open wound to the mix, it is a potential disaster waiting to happen. A bedpan seemed like the right thing at the time. Finally, the haggard nurse arrived and helped me get situated as comfortably as I could be on the cold bed pan. I then asked the question that changed my life in that moment.

I asked the nurse, "So how many people on this floor do you have to adjust bedpans for?" She looked me in the eye and said, "You are the only one." I was startled. Even today, as I run this conversation through my head, I can't guess whether or not she was telling the truth. Maybe I was the only one. It didn't seem possible since I was on a surgical floor and there were many people recovering from all kinds of surgery. Maybe they all had catheters. But I felt truth in that statement for me, and something inside shifted. I knew that now was the time for me to step up and become more responsible in my own healing. It was time for me to help myself. No longer would I do what was the most convenient, if you can call a bedpan convenient. I vowed to push myself to the next level whatever it was so I could get out of the hospital and be at home with my family. The very next night, with the nurse's help, I walked on crutches to and from the bathroom, and gained some self respect.

Never in a million years would I have thought I would spend 150 days in the hospital with a near fatal strep infection I contracted after the birth of my third daughter. I didn't know I would have seven surgeries by the end of the year. I didn't know that I would turn blue the first time nurses sat me up on the side of a bed, or that I would celebrate making a single pivot from bed to chair. I didn't know how amazing even an ounce of ice water could taste after having a tube in my throat for so long. I really didn't know just how wonderful it would be to sit in a mesh wheelchair under a stream of water for 20 minutes, my first shower in months. And I didn't know that I would live on IV nutrition for 6 months and that the open wound on my abdomen the size of a football would finally be closed surgically after almost a year of frustration and pain.

What I did know however, was my husband was at home with a newborn and two other daughters under the age of 6. I knew my mother was living at our house so she could help with the girls and visit me during the day. I knew the nights were the loneliest, yet some of the best healing conversations occurred in the midnight hours with the nurses who became my friends. I knew a hospital is as far away from normal as you can be, and it was not a place I wanted to spend much more of my time. And I knew I would do everything in my power to get well enough to go home. I chose to keep moving in a forward direction.

After the bedpan shift in awareness, I realized I had been moved out of ICU for a reason: I was well enough to start taking steps to heal myself. Every day, I would focus on doing something just a little better than the day before. Maybe it was just one more step in the hallway, or 30 more seconds to improve my balance, or an extra set of exercises for eye-hand coordination. Slowly but surely I did get better. I gradually moved from two crutches to one, pushing my own IV pole to the bathroom. I learned how to stand in the kitchen, first by holding on to the counter and eventually standing without support. Then I moved to holding a spatula, helping to make a cake. Eventually I could make a meal by myself. One of the most important things I had to do was regain strength in my fingers so I could put a ponytail in one of my daughters' hair. I know that sounds simple, but being a part of the girls' day to day activities was what I missed the most, and fixing their hair brought me joy. Focusing on doing something new or better than the day before is how I finally regained my health.

I wish I could say that all the steps I took were in a forward direction. When one is recovering from any illness or injury, it really seems that you take two steps forward and one back. Sure there were setbacks, and at times I was so overwhelmed I wanted to give up. There were days when I changed the dressing on my wound 12 times. I carried my food around in a backpack pump attached to a central line in my chest, and at times, the 'baggage' was an emotional burden. I cried my frustrations into a mini tape recorder, just to have someone hear me. I called my aunt in my times of desperation. She would allow me time to grieve, and then set me back on task, asking me what I was going to accomplish that day. She became my *PMA coach,* helping me keep a *Positive Mental Attitude* in the midst of challenge. More than anything else, I wanted to be a mom to my little girls, and I would find the strength inside of me to push through the pain or obstacle of the day. I had faith that something good would eventually come from this illness.

Although getting home was my first focus and healing completely was my second, I still had to live the challenges of the moment. I couldn't wish them away, not do the work, and be someplace I wasn't. This was my life in the present moment, whether I liked it or not; I had to learn to breathe, face forward, and take on the challenge. Amazingly, at the end of the day, I could usually look back and see grace in action: where I was touched by a nurse's kindness, a card in the mail would bring a smile to my face, or a visitor would tell me what an inspiration I was. I began to find myself in a position of gratefulness, that I touched people through my willingness to walk this journey, even in the midst of pain. And in the times when the world was so dark and I felt so drained, I would lie in the motherly arms of God and rest in the quiet peace. It was in hope-filled moments I found the courage to continue to walk the path toward healing. Even in the darkest moments of my illness, I found the light of God shining through. Even though it is not an experience I would want to repeat, I have been changed for the good and I am glad that I can look back and see how far I have come.

One might think that after returning to health after something so long and traumatic, all other journeys would be easy. So why is it I struggle with the same issues over and over again in my life? Just when I think my life is flowing smoothly, I hit an obstacle and lose my balance. Like many women I know, I focus mainly on work and chores, and I struggle with adding fun and play into my life. This past January, I slipped on the ice and broke my wrist, leading to surgery and the insertion of a three-inch plate thirteen days later. The first two weeks were difficult because my hand was so swollen I couldn't use it at all. I am not good at DOING nothing. Luckily, I had friends and family who helped with chores and meals so I could rest and heal.

During this time I reflected back on all the challenges I faced when I was so sick fifteen years ago. Just like before, there were good days of healing, and days when I didn't feel like progress was being made. The biggest battle I had was with me, letting myself know that it was okay to let others help me, to rest, and to not be DOING something every minute. I worked at self kindness and love. I adjusted my goals and refocused my attention on healing.

With the help of tools such as journaling, meditation, and prayer, I continue to learn to love myself, trust in the pace of the journey, and balance my time between work and play. I wish I could say that I have learned how to stay in balance, and that it will be smooth sailing from here on out. Yet I know there are many obstacles to come that might temporarily halt my forward motion. This is the life I have been given, with all its ups and downs. I can be a victim and sit on that bed pan, and look to others to change my situation. Or I can step up, become a part of the game of life, and create something good out of whatever life brings.

George Leonard, author of Mastery, says that the traveler is fortunate if the path is profound and complex enough to make the destination two miles farther away for every mile she travels. I am a fortunate traveler, becoming aware of how Divine Love works in my life through all things. There is no good and bad, only opportunities to be my best. Even though I don't know what's around the next corner, I know it is all part of the process of becoming the best I can BE.

Jan Haas is the founder of The Present Path. As a balance coach, author, and speaker, she is passionate about empowering others to accept and embrace their divine power. On her blog, Jan inspires others to embrace their own worth and divinity, and shares ways to balance mind, body and spirit so that The Present Path becomes an easy journey. Jan lives in Denver, Colorado and has been married to her best friend Tony for almost 25 years. Their three teenage daughters are a reflection of Divine Love in action. To learn more about Jan and receive a free healing meditation MP3, visit www.thepresentpath.com.

Finding Your Path

I Find Myself Painting

Marcella Nordbeck

I am happiest when I paint. The world falls away and it's just me, the blank canvas, and the wet, sticky paint on my brush marrying us to one another in the creative process. Gone are the day's worries and, in their place, a calm surrender to trust that the painting, like life, will unfold and reveal itself to me in its own time. I often have an idea of what I want to paint, but when it's finished and I step back to take it in, the final results are usually something different and better than I could ever imagine.

Painting gives me a voice to express thoughts and emotions that can't be articulated, that have no words. Be it feelings of happiness or joy, sadness or fear, painting is like a release valve on my heart. I learned the hard way that without it I am prone to stuff emotions until the pressure builds up so much that I feel like I'm going to burst, expressing myself in less constructive ways.

My earliest memory is painting by my mother's side – I was three years old. I watched her draw an outline of a bear on brown construction paper. She handed me a paint brush dipped in black paint. As I colored in the form with my ebony tipped wand, mom returned to her art project. I don't recall what she was working on, but I do remember the feeling of connection I felt to her as we each created something that had not existed before.

I often think of these early years as the lean years – the years that my single mother, who was an art student when I was conceived, struggled to honor her creative yearnings while trying to support us financially. She simultaneously held three part-time jobs as a waitress, putting herself through nursing school. Eventually mom graduated and received her nursing license, the lean years finally behind us, but along the way she stopped drawing and painting. To survive and support us, she pushed aside her self expression and desire to be an artist.

Although the necessity to provide took my mom down a non-artistic career path, she still managed to incorporate art into our lives. We visited art museums during summer vacations to Chicago and New York City. Occasionally the two of us would spend Saturday afternoons exploring the Detroit Institute of Art where we were drawn to the black and white photography exhibit first.

The most extreme measure mom took to expose me to art was when I was a sophomore in high school. She obtained fake identification for me so I could attend the Robert Mapplethorpe photography exhibit in Cincinnati. At just fifteen, we didn't know if I would pass for eighteen – the minimum age to view his explicit and controversial images. But at five feet, seven inches tall I got into my first art gallery exhibit. They didn't even ask to see my ID.

Until this experience I passed the time in Ms. Cronenwitz's art room drawing a still-life – a bowl of fruit, an old pair of shoes, a skull from the science lab (if we were lucky), always placed over draped fabric so we could shade in the shadows of the folds and creases. But after seeing Mapplethorpe's work, I had a new appreciation for the human form and I began looking at my mother's book of Tina Modotti's photographs. Others may have seen nude bodies, but I saw the shadows and contours around the slope of a breast or the curve of a hip. I spent hours in my bedroom listening to music and dragging acrylic paint across my canvases duplicating the female silhouettes depicted in Modotti's photographs and wondering, not only what my gangly teenage body might look like as I grew older, but who would I be? What would I do with my life? What would become of me?

The hours of solitude in my bedroom drawing, painting, and listening to music were the happiest moments during those tumultuous teenage years, but when I looked around my art classes at the work my fellow classmates created, I felt inferior. My confidence further deteriorated during my junior year of high school, when I was encouraged to consider where I wanted to go for college and what I wanted to study. A friend's mom took us to an event at a local university where student portfolios were displayed. As I flipped through pages of drawings and paintings, photographs and pastels, the self-sabotaging voice in my head got louder saying, "I can't draw. I'm not creative. I'll never be able to paint like that." I squashed the creative spirit within me before I really had a chance to express it.

My self-doubt, coupled with the belief that art was a nice hobby, but not a means for making a living, influenced me to major in English instead of art. I loved to read and write as much as I loved to paint, and received the highest grades in my literature and composition classes, so it made sense. It also helped that Dr. Sax, who was head of the English department and my professor for most of my English classes, encouraged me to pursue my literary passion.

Not being brave enough to take a job in publishing in New York City or Chicago, following graduation I stayed close to home and worked in advertising in Detroit for eight years. I spent the first few years on the account side of the business as an Account Executive, but, eventually, I worked as a Print Producer where I was able to collaborate in the creative process with Art Directors and Printers. Finally, my creative spirit was finding a small outlet. However, the sixty-hour a week ad agency schedule left little time for a balanced life, allowing for my personal creative expression.

In my late twenties I was living the life my mom desired for me – similar to the one she created: college degree, secure job, marriage and home ownership. Though it provided financial stability, I spiraled into a dark depression and was hospitalized when it became life threatening. Having followed a path motivated by seeking approval and validation from others, I no longer had the desire to live.

My breakdown, or what I prefer to call my breakthrough, gave me a reintroduction to art in the form of art therapy. During the week I was an inpatient in the hospital, spending my days in a double-locked psychiatric unit on suicide watch, I passed time between therapy sessions coloring my way through a box of Crayola crayons. As I wore down the colorful wax, I awoke my inner child, my creative spirit.

Once I was stable and no longer a threat to myself, I was released from inpatient care to a month long outpatient program where daily talk therapy sessions were accompanied by an hour of art therapy, five days a week. Each day after lunch, I would run from the hospital cafeteria to the art room where I would be the first patient to dive back into stenciling spirals on a cloth book bag (an image prelude to a series of future paintings) or gluing small tiles onto a wooden trivet. It didn't matter the medium; I was a desert soaking in the rain after a long drought of creative denial and emotional suppression. While the other patients talked about the adjustments to their medication cocktails, I was lost in the wonderment of reconnecting with the creative side of my self.

The years that followed my hospitalization were a series of trial and error, figuring out how to take responsibility for my happiness, while balancing financial needs with creative space. When I was initially released from the outpatient program, it was clear I could not go back to my job in advertising. The sixty-hour workweek was not conducive to a balanced, healthy lifestyle. I tried everything from retail sales and management, freelancing as a visual merchandiser, to answering phones in a call center. I even took a marketing position for two years, but when it proved to be as stressful as my ad agency days I walked away, finding a job as an administrative assistant. With the work experience I had gained over the years, I was overqualified to work as an admin, but the forty-hour workweek provided the structure and financial stability that I needed, while allowing time to be creative.

Changing my career path to support a healthy frame of mind was not the only major lifestyle change. The most difficult decision I made to support my emotional well-being was ending my marriage. My husband supported me the best way he knew how during the darkest days of my life. But as I began my journey of self-exploration, I realized that we had different ways of defining happiness and wanted different things for our lives.

One of the benefits of living on my own again and renting an apartment was how simplified my life became. This freed up time for me. I was no longer spending weekends working on home improvement projects, like peeling old wall paper or weeding gardens. Instead of painting dry wall, I finally had the time to paint on canvas, my preferred surface. I enrolled in painting classes with Detroit artist Shadia Zayed, my first art classes since the few electives I had taken twelve years earlier in college.

Within a few years I found myself in a healthier relationship and renting a house. But before I lost my sense of self, and my commitment to honor my creativity, I read Elizabeth Gilbert's book *Eat, Pray, Love* and challenged myself asking, "What do I really, really, really want?" Sitting each morning in meditation I kept hearing the word paint as if someone were whispering in my ear. With our rental home improvement projects only half-way completed, I abandoned them, purchased new art supplies, and made it my mantra to make more time to paint.

When an opportunity for us to relocate from Detroit to Denver presented itself, I leapt at the chance to move somewhere where we didn't know anyone, somewhere I would have little distraction in following my heart's desires. Six months into living in our new home state of Colorado I summoned the courage to submit my painting, "Infinite Love," to a juried art show. Much to my amazement, and delight, it was accepted into the exhibit.

A couple of weeks later, while attending First Friday Art Walk in the Santa Fe art district, I met Denver artist Laurie Maves who asked me if I was a painter. I had never thought of myself as one, but before I could think, the words, "Yes, I *am* a painter!" flew from of my mouth. Then Laurie asked if I was showing anywhere and because of the juried exhibit I could honestly say I was! Although I was only showing one painting in my first group art show, I was showing.

From there doors of opportunity began to open within the Denver art scene. I began to show more work, in larger shows, and with greater exposure. Just ten months after arriving in Denver I was invited to be the Featured Artist of the Month at Michelangelo's Coffee and Wine Bar. My first solo art show included nineteen paintings made up of eleven acrylics and eight acrylic washes – similar to watercolors. The show was a huge success for this budding artist. And because I sold five paintings the night of my opening reception, I was asked to extend the show another month.

A couple of months later I was invited to serve on the event planning board for the Denver Art Society. It's a non-profit whose mission is providing free art classes to children in Denver. Board members have the opportunity to plan and curate art shows while organizing fundraisers to raise awareness and money to end artlessness in Denver. I was honored to be invited to serve on the Denver Art Society board, as I know all too well the perils of not incorporating art into one's life. It is my hope that each child who is exposed to art early on will discover a healthy and constructive avenue for self-expression. Maybe they won't have to hit bottom like I did to discover their calling and follow their joy.

Throughout my journey I kept a journal of my experiences. Shortly after I started showing my work, these private entries evolved into a public art blog titled, "Observations of an Artist." It is an avenue for me to share both my trials and successes as I navigate the Denver art scene, searching for the truth of who I am, both as an artist and as a woman. Tarcher/Penguin, the publisher of Julia Cameron's book, *The Artist's Way*, endorsed my blog. When they learned I was writing about my experiences following the 12-week course outlined in Cameron's book and blogging about it, they asked for permission to post my blog on their website.

The most rewarding aspect of honoring my creative spirit is the effect it has had on my relationship with my mother. When I went back home to Michigan for a visit, we spent an afternoon at our old haunt, the Detroit Institute of Art. As we walked through the museum's exhibits and shared which photographs and paintings spoke to us, I realized art is a language my mom and I use to connect with each other. By the end of the afternoon, I felt she finally understood that everything I've been through – life threatening depression, hospitalization, divorce, multiple career changes, relocating, and finally honoring my creativity – has made me the woman I am today. She's talking about taking art classes again. By honoring my creative spirit, I gave her the permission and inspiration to rekindle her creativity.

As I broke the rules I was raised to live by, and followed my dreams to be a painter, mom was concerned for my emotional and financial wellbeing. It was scary to be hospitalized, to leave a successful career, and to end a marriage to find myself, but it was worth it – every scary, uncertain moment. Today, feelings of depression are a memory far away. Instead, I find myself painting and I am happy.

Marcella Nordbeck lives in Denver, Colorado where she paints abstracts with acrylic, acrylic mediums, and mixed media. She also shoots candid photographs documenting the Denver art scene. Inspired by her studies of the world's religions, New Thought philosophy, and her experiences in meditation, her mission is to, "send out love into the world one painting at a time." She only participates in art shows in which at least ten percent of the proceeds from the sale of her artwork support a charity or cause. When Marcella is not painting or taking photos, she writes a blog about the Denver art scene titled "Observations of an Artist." To contact Marcella, email her at: marcella. nordbeck@gmail.com. To read her blog, visit: http://marcellanordbeck.blogspot.com/.

Living at Choice

Candace French

On January 1, 2000, I awoke next to my husband of eleven years and felt relieved that we had survived Y2K and the huge celebration the night before. That day, I enjoyed a phone chat with a lifelong friend of mine. Our conversation felt like a tapestry weaving together all areas of our lives. Towards the end of the conversation, we talked about relationships and my friend Gerri commented "If Dr. Phil was on Oprah 20 years ago, I would still be married today."

With curiosity in my voice, I asked "Who is Dr. Phil?"

Gerri chuckled and replied "You obviously have not been watching Oprah lately."

No, as a full time working woman at U S WEST and mother, I hadn't. So, on the first Monday in January, I started taping the Oprah show and watching it in the evening. I quickly discovered Cheryl Richardson among other Oprah guests committed to helping people living their best life. What clicked for me was Cheryl's idea of taking time in your life for self-care.

That summer Cheryl led her "Finding your Passion" workshop at Mile Hi Church in Denver. At the workshop, one of the exercises unearthed a deep seeded passion of mine: to help others live a more heart centered life so they can make a bigger contribution to the world. During the exercise, she asked a series of questions and I realized something incredibly profound. I had buried my passion years ago.

After graduating from Ohio State University with a Bachelor's in Psychology, I landed a job in my profession of counseling. The challenge for me was that most of my clients at the state funded hospital were verbally abusive and even physically threatening. As a result of this unpleasant work experience, I buried my passion and convinced myself that I could put my psychology degree to good use in a sales career. I didn't realize at the time that I was selling myself short and putting a knife in my heart's desire of helping people transform their lives.

Fortunately, during Cheryl's workshop I realized two things. The first was that having the right support in place increases your probability of success by over 90%. The second was that I immediately fell in love with the coaching profession. Soon after, I enrolled in a coaching certification program and started a Life Makeover Group. That led to future turning points in my life.

The first turning point was during the summer of 2002. I was sitting in the midst of a sea of people in Las Vegas attending an event that was a departure from my day job. The event? It was the launch of CoachVille, a global coaching community and school. I found myself feverishly writing everything he shared. Who was the he I was enthralled to learn from? He was Thomas Leonard, founder of the coaching profession, CoachVille, Coach U and author to many books. I noticed him glance at me and my efforts to capture his every word. He paused, then he turned his head up towards the entire audience and said "I invite you to simply sit back, relax and allow every cell in your body to soak in this experience." I panicked. "What! Let go of my pen, my security blanket?" I froze, clutched harder at my pen and wrote faster. After over 20 years of successfully leading diverse groups to drive customer satisfaction and annual revenue over $100 million for a large corporation, I found myself feverishly writing every thought, word, belief and idea he shared. What I was learning was like water to a thirsty person. Little did I know I was sitting in the essence and true energy of my encore career, professional coaching, a profession that has changed my life and the lives of my clients.

Then something very significant and powerful happened. At one point in the conference, Thomas invited an individual to be laser coached by him. A woman volunteered and stood up from the audience. She shared a couple of minutes about the struggles of her life and her desire to change it. Thomas responded "So, you want to transform your life without blowing up your marriage." The laser coaching session was complete. I was fascinated with how quickly Thomas was able to get to the truth. I was not only curious about the laser coaching process, but, I noticed a feeling about how I could transform my life without blowing up my marriage. At the time, I felt I was on a treadmill. Despite my awareness of taking time for my own life and practicing self-care, I felt chained to taking care of others especially the men in my life. I was ignorant to the fact that the harder and longer I worked, the more struggle and unhappiness I felt. My ignorance was not bliss. It was unconscious suffering.

Over a year passed as I continued to fuel my desire to refine my coaching expertise through participating in CoachVille conferences and graduate coach training. I loved seeing the lives of my clients unfold in magical ways, like flowers blooming in the spring. I yearned to experience the same quantum leaps in my own life. Then, in February 2003, Thomas Leonard died suddenly and tragically. I felt deeply saddened.

About six months prior, though, Thomas Leonard had connected with Tom Stone. It was through their collaboration that I connected with Tom Stone. Once again, I was at a turning point as I found myself being drawn to his work called

Human Software Engineering. It was and remains to be the most powerful road-map to higher consciousness through identifying and deleting the "bugs" and "viruses" in our "Inner Human Software" that keep us stuck in self defeating thoughts, feelings and behaviors. I became certified to coach and train the 12 Core Dynamics and eventually mentored others in the training program. I loved integrating this new approach to coaching as I could see my clients release years, even a lifetime, of pain that was holding them back from experiencing a more fulfilling life. My client's lives transformed before my eyes. It felt magical and still does to this day as I continue to feel such great satisfaction in helping others clear their past and step into their new lives.

Then, late one cold snowy January night, my life dramatically changed. I found myself waking to a family crisis. In less than five minutes my entire life crumbled, my dreams shattered and I felt destroyed. After an unpredictable act of violence by my husband, I knew with great certainty that my marriage of over 18 years was over. I took our daughter, our dog and guns and left. Indeed, my own life was at the crux of being transformed. Over the next two years I unraveled what I learned to be an oppressive and emotionally abusive relationship. Despite all the work I had done as a coach, I discovered I had been living in a web of denial and fear over the shame of being divorced. The intricacies of the enmeshment were astounding. The more I learned about relationships and worked with a therapist, I more I realized that all my life I had given up my dreams to the men in my life. The men included my dad, brothers and husband. I did what they wanted me to do so they could be happy. I never felt at choice. Even worse, I felt I never had a life I could call my own.

Through my own personal journey, and perhaps because of it, I learned that I have an inner strength and a willingness to receive support from others that can guide me through any situation great or small. Things are usually never what they appear to be and I am committed to truth and consciousness in every relation-ship, especially the one I have with myself. With every choice I make, my life feels like an adventure unfolding in surprising ways every day. I am a single parent going after my dreams and not settling for good enough. My daughter, Lauren, and I are learning from each other. I continue to work a corporate job to support myself and my daughter while being more passionate about building my coaching business. I feel more empowered, fulfilled, and at peace knowing that I am grace-fully preparing to transition into doing the work of my dreams fulltime.

To this day, I remain committed to empowering women in living a more con-scious heart centered life through coaching, speaking and workshops. As a Hu-man Software Engineer, I teach my clients the Power of How Techniques, support them in releasing trauma and using a host of conscious living techniques and processes including these four simple, yet powerful, practices called:

"The How to Live a Conscious Life" Process™

- Stillness – Be still and connect with your heart's desire
- Intention - Clarify your intentions. It is through clarity that you achieve focus and through focus you become more empowered.
- Attention - Pay attention to your self and to your surroundings. By your self, I mean your body's sensations and what they may be telling you. For example, a knot in your throat could be a sign that you are having difficulty expressing yourself. Or, feeling the hair stand up on the back of your neck could mean that you are judging someone else and overlooking the oportunity to love that part of you. Also, pay attention to what shows up that is an unexpected, yet welcomed, surprise. These synchronicities are the guideposts that affirm you are living a con-scious life in alignment with your truth.
- Breathe - Give yourself a deep breath to create space for you to respond instead of react. It is in this space that you move into possibility and choice. Feeling that you are at choice is the cornerstone of feeling empowered. Creating consciousness in every breath.

I invite you to start with just a few minutes a day and expand that time and space for yourself everyday. Throughout your day, pay attention to your breath so you can create a bigger space for yourself to be at choice and step into living a more conscious heart centered life.

Candace French is the founder and president of the Center for Intentional Living, an organization dedicated to empowering women to live an extraordinary life. As a Certified Coach and Human Software Engineer, she can show you how to transform your life through transforming your relationships. She loves teaching life skills in the art of conscious relating through individual and group coaching, speaking events and workshops. She also enjoys being with her daughter and is passionate about how they learn from each other. For fun, Candace enjoys the outdoors, especially camping, bicycling and exploring new places around the world. Connect with Candace at Candace@CenterForIntentionalLiving.com and visit her web site, www.CenterForIntentionalLiving.com.

A Student of Experience

Molly Hall

The customary question I forever dreaded and allowed to destroy my existence anytime I walked into a social situation was, "where did you go to college?" I would always answer truthfully, "a community college in Western New York" but I always had an inauthentic, daunting feeling of fraud deep in the pit of my belly. Although it was true, I did *attend* ECC in NY, I do not have a college degree. Not only am I a college dropout, I a *community* college dropout.

I never had a burning desire to attend college but I did what was right and enrolled in community college to tryout some courses until I figured out what I wanted to do. It was August 1990, when entering my 2nd year, that my father opened up a tavern and I began to work there in the evenings to make some extra cash. Very quickly I was attracted to the real world and how one night of bartending could pay my month's rent. I quickly got to know the regulars and enjoyed the sense of community in this tightly knit Irish Catholic neighborhood. I also had a full time job in city government that provided benefits and all the perks. I quickly realized I was making more money than my college educated peers, without the suffocating debt. There was no going back to college. With wisdom, I now realize it was not all about the money and undoubtedly not about a chosen career path. It was truthfully about a deeply rooted sense of community during this time in my life and the impact it would serve towards creating a bigger future for myself.

Yes, I was making a fine amount of money in my young 20's and having an absolute ball. I lived this life for eight years until the day my dad decided he was finally ready to retire and hand the successful business over to my older sister and me. My sister was ready to start a family and I felt this nagging sensation to not only listen but, follow my heart. I would like to pronounce this was the pivotal point with a frisson of energy that electrified my very being with the skies opening up to an awakening of possibility and transformation. But it wasn't. My head was telling me this would be a great business to have for the rest of my life but my heart was telling me another thing.

I am that person that has that intangible quality of getting it done with compassion and ease. I have always been the person people call on when they have a problem, the one whose opinion is asked, the one whom people always look to when they need someone to trust to get the job done or breathe life (and sense) into a murky, cloudy and confusing situation. While that might be a great compliment, that intangible quality is hard to express in a resume. It doesn't show up as a *skill* or a certification. There is no major in 'trust me to get it done', especially when you are missing the degree part. Often the inability to articulate and measure this feature results in being liked, known, and trusted without being able to really solidify the value. If truth be told, I felt so very stuck and not sure what my life offering was.

A friend of mine was living in Denver, Colorado and we got to talking. I took a HUGE leap of faith and for the first time in my life, I trusted my heart. I sold everything, and travelled across country for five weeks to give the Mile High City a try as my new home. Just three hours outside of Buffalo and I had an absolute panic attack. "Judy, I can't do this. Drop me off at the Cleveland airport, I'm going back. What did I just do?" Judy turned to me without skipping a beat, "The way I see it you have *nothing* to lose. Treat this like a five week vacation and when we get to Denver you can hop on a plane and slip right back in to the life as you know it." OK, that was a plan I could and would embrace. And that was my precise plan, I'm headed eastbound once we exit I-70.

Three weeks after arriving in Denver I landed a job and began serving in the Estate and Trust attorney entrepreneurial world. I started this job at The National Network of Estate Planning Attorneys as an Administrative Assistant. Nowhere near understanding the path, I just began to unleash my passion that would lead me to my primary aim in life and creating a lifetime profession. I loved my job and met a lot of great people that are still in my life. In March 2000 the company decided to hire a life and business coach to come in and support the attorneys with growing their businesses and finding a work/life balance. And naturally I was assigned to support this coach because remember, I have that intangible quality of getting it done with compassion and ease. I remember that day so very clearly. It was March 2000 and the first event was in Orlando, Florida. We were at the Crowne Plaza outside Disneyworld and my job was to assist our new leader in any way possible. I wasn't sure what that meant or if I was doing it "right" or not. We had never met, not even as so much as talked on the phone. I was assigned and was supposed to do my job even though I wasn't quite sure what that looked like. But I was eagerly ready to assist.

We started the day at 8 a.m. sharp and I met my new boss for the first time along with the rest of the class he was instructing, or really coaching. The day started with a discussion of living your life by design vs. default, stop hiding out, long term and short term suffering. I had never heard or seen anything like this. The closest I had ever come to any type of self improvement at my tender age of 29 was Chicken Soup for the Soul. After the first break I checked in with the speaker/leader (a.k.a. my new boss) and he greeted me by saying "I don't know who told you that you are stupid and why you think it is ok for you to show up in my program with zero confidence, but you are not stupid. You need to let go of that and start being or you will never grow into the person the world needs to see." No lie. This was my first introduction to not only my new boss but my calling to living a bigger life.

The truth of the matter is this was my first calling to face the scary truth that I kept buried so deep inside, or at least I thought I did. The truth was that I believed "I am a fraud. I am not worthy. I am uneducated and unequipped. I am working within an industry of the world's top intellects and I am stupid." For the first time in my life there was someone that saw through me and my story within hours of being in the same room with me. More importantly, he called me on it and gave me permission to let that which was not serving me anymore, go. I had the choice to live in that truth that I had created that fit me so well for so many years or step up to a calling of purpose, to accept my new boss' invitation to be present as a student of experience. This was not just a call to accept this position as not just a new job role, but a mentorship, a spiritualist experience.

My path of self discovery was a long process that took me over eight years to truly feel, embrace and believe in my core that I was not only worthy but I had a tremendous amount of knowledge, insight and authenticity to share. Over the past twelve years I have grown and worked closely with presidents and founders of national organizations, master level marketers, entrepreneurs and coaches. I can't help but practice the coach way of doing things on a daily basis in my work and my life. Without the privileged schooling I have been blessed to receive I would not be the woman, professional, mother, friend or wife that I am today.

We hear time and time again, "you're so lucky" or "as luck would have it." Well truth be told, luck is when opportunity meets preparation. Twelve years after leaving my home town with zero confidence in myself or my future, intentionality or purpose, I can say I am lucky. But, I believe I am manifesting my luck. The irony, last Tuesday I was driving up to Vail with my two remarkable kids to escape for a few days and soak in our breathtaking Rocky Mountains. Symbolically, just reaching my favorite part of the hike up the hill, where you reach the peak and get your 1st glimmer of Summit County, I received a call on my cell phone from one of my favorite highly respected CPA and CFP clients with a personal favor. "My son," he said, "is at a pivotal point in his college education where he needs to declare a major. He has no idea what he wants to do. I can't get through to him and he is lost. Can you talk with him?" Say what? ME? But I agreed and I loved every minute of my calls with Anthony. Not only did I aid him in finding direction, but I have a new found hope for today's youth. I was utterly inspired after talking him through the very process that has gotten me and so many other lost souls to where they are. After our second call, Anthony excitedly exclaimed he was going to double major in International business with a French minor and we are currently looking into how he can study abroad next year. But Anthony didn't choose a major because it was the right thing to do, or to please his parents or feel smart. He, with some guidance, looked inside himself to find the future that would fulfill him in a way where he could make a difference for others and he uncovered it. I am not serving as an advocate for not participating in higher education. In fact, it is my greatest wish that both my eight and four year old children experience the marvelous world of university and all it has to offer.

My sole purpose and intent is to inspire people who feel like they are on the long, painful track of life in a day to day job that does not provide passion, excitement and purpose and encourage them not to look around but look inside. Look inside your organizations, the people in your life, and what resources you have direct access to. Stop looking at them as bosses, teachers or supervisors but rather look at them as mentors and keys to unlock experience for you. Your path may include higher education, or it may not, but whichever path you take – make it a path you *choose*, a path that abundantly fulfills you and moves you in the direction of a life with purpose, a path of experience.

Don't confuse a good job (stable, easy, and convenient with a decent paycheck and benefits) for living a life you love. The necessary element is locating your passion keys and living within your passion zone. What allowed me to unleash my unique ability and stop taking it as that's just what I do was finding my passion keys. Identifying and living by them has allowed me to create a career and a life I love because it is in line with my primary aim - to empower every life I touch in a way that makes a difference for them.

I firmly believe it is essential to identify the elements of your passion keys and *your* personal definition of success. It is hard to be successful if you do not know what that means for you and to you. The definition *is* different for everyone. Whether you are feeling out of control or uninspired by your current job or excited about a new one, there is hope. And when there is hope, anything is possible. Living a life of passion allows a new career, a path – a no (new) degree required, no night classes needed way to take control of your professional life and *learn to run your life, and stop letting it run you*. Just like it's possible to achieve success at work, while still keeping boundaries between your work time and your personal time.

If someone would have told me twelve years ago that I would be sitting where I am today, I would never have believed it. But it all started with others believing in me and my willingness to simply be present in a way to be able to see (and receive) their belief.

My greatest hope in this world is to help others unleash their personal passion and then guide them in creating it in their professional life.

What I know to be true is that my sole gift and passion are SCREAMING at me loud and clear and show up in everything I do. I vividly remember completing an exercise about two years ago to tap into what I am committed to in life and what motivates me – my story is taking me right back there. Not only do I aspire to work in a community environment but I *CREATE* community; that feeling of love, acceptance, compassion and experience through stability and validity of relationships. I am not inconsistent in my love and support of people, I show up ALWAYS not when I feel like it or it suits my needs. And luckily, I have built a career around that and community will always be a principle for me, as a student of experience. In fact, I am so passionate about making a difference my book will be published in 2010 about helping the employee create outrageous passion in their work.

Molly Hall is the co-owner of The Ultimate Smart Solution™ a National Training company designed to help business owners and the team that supports them to power-fully connect and grow their business in a way that produces results where everyone wins. The Ultimate Smart Solution™ is the only training company in the country for employees and business owners alike to create an understanding of how to run a successful business in a way where everyone wins. www.theultimatesmartsolution.com

Business Should Be An adVENTURE

Sabrina Risley

Mistrust, doubt, worry, fear, misgiving, anxiety, suspicion, uncertainty. Perception or reality? We all experience these emotions. We all live with them at some point. For many, doubt, mistrust and worry can seem invigorating, stimulating, exciting; without which some view their lives as boring and ordinary. But what happens when these emotions become restrictive, limiting and restraining? Have you ever felt a level of anxiety such that your stomach aches, your throat compresses and your chest tightens? It's a feeling we want to escape and the cause of which we often want to avoid.

That's exactly how I felt when I thought about sharing the secrets of my business with others and partnering or affiliating with businesses. I was fearful of feeling stuck in a professional relationship that, if it didn't work out, would result in getting burned and cut off from what was previously a friendly, professional relationship.

You see, people can turn on you. I learned that in 7th grade. I recall having a wonderful childhood, playing on a variety of sports teams with friends. I attended a Junior High school into which children from multiple elementary schools fed. Many of the friends I had grown up with attended the school as well. We had the opportunity to make new friends but I preferred to remain in the comforts of the friends I had from elementary school. We had fun joking around and being silly. We even had inside jokes… wow, that was always fun! One inside joke I never quite understood was my girlfriends saying "TA" at recess. TA. TA. Select girls in our group would say TA. What did that mean? I never said it because I didn't understand what it meant.

One day, my friend Kris pulled me aside to let me in on the joke. She cautiously explained how I was the brunt of the inside joke. TA meant "tag along." They thought I was a tag along, I wasn't a leader. I just went along with what the group wanted to do. I lingered and never contributed. Kris was very worried about my reaction and, of course I was hurt, very hurt. In fact, I was devastated. I had never encountered anything like this in elementary school. In fact, when I was in 6th grade, I was popular and was elected Vice President of our school, winning the election by singing a personalized campaign jingle at the school assembly to the tune of "Oh, I wish I were an Oscar Meyer Wiener!" Yet, just one year later, I had no idea this cruel Junior High joke was on me all along!! The friends I knew and trusted had turned on me and were making fun of me.

As a result of the joke, Kris and I distanced ourselves from the group and became best friends. And, as you can imagine, I learned that you can't trust people, not even your so-called friends. They can turn on you in an instant, without warning or cause and you have no power over their actions against you.

Fast forward now to September 22, 2003 when I incorporated my business. I was gainfully employed at a corporate job I had had for 9 years, climbing up the ladder of success. I was a Corporate Director of a national organization with more than 26,000 employees. The company's culture was quite negative, to put it kindly. Corporate employees were over-worked and under-paid, not an uncommon experience of many at the time. I knew within my heart that I was ready to leave and had intended on resigning by the end of the year, just 3 short months away. However, sometimes the Universe has other plans in store for us.

Just two short weeks after incorporating my business, my boss called me into his office and told me the news. I was being laid off. I have to admit, I felt very lucky. I was a chosen one, after all, it's what my colleagues and I were waiting for all these years. The idea of resigning and leaving a healthy severance package on the table was a rough thought to see through. I actually felt this layoff was coming and already had my office packed into boxes when I was given the news. My severance included eight and half months of pay! With butterflies in my stomach, I knew this was the start of a whole new world for me. I was officially an entrepreneur, and with a little financial cushion, I had some time to really get my business off the ground.

Since this was my first business venture, I didn't know where to start. I had a vision to connect businesses through networking events. I was detail-oriented, organized, efficient, and began successfully coordinating and managing numerous professional networking events. I moved with caution and worked situations out as they presented themselves. I put myself on a budget and spent my pennies wisely. I did all the normal things a business owner does to get started, fulfilling every role in my business from web designer to salesperson. Meanwhile, I had two young, active boys and a spouse who spent 75% of the time traveling for his profession. I found myself working much of the day and well into the night, around the kids' sports schedules, homework, and play-dates. I was exhilarated by my work, despite my demanding schedule.

Three years into my business, I was doing it all. I soon found myself unable to quiet my mind enough to fall asleep at a decent hour. When I finally slipped into a slumber, I soon found myself awake, fighting bouts of energy in the middle of the night, sometimes keeping me up for 4 hours at a time. I couldn't shut my mind off. I had so much on my mind; my bedside table was cluttered with lists and sticky notes of ideas and things to do. I found myself physically exhausted and emotionally drained. I was growing my business, albeit at a snail's pace, all on my own and without support or assistance of any kind.

While I noticed small businesses partnering and affiliating all around me, I refused to move in that direction. You see, in one instance, a fairly prominent partnership between two local businesses had dissolved abruptly after enjoying a few years of bliss. The dissolution of the partnership came complete with a second helping of misunderstandings, miscommunication and back-stabbing. Both companies suddenly found themselves with half the number of supporters they had enjoyed the previous year during their partnership.

This is when the fear solidified for me. Nothing lasts forever, right? I resisted the idea of researching potential partners for compatibility and working out a plan to ensure the relationship would be mutually beneficial, transparent and trusting. A partnership, also known as a joint venture, meant teamwork with another business to further common goals and interests, resulting in optimization of resources and expansion. There were countless benefits to partnering with companies that had solid reputations, with similar business plans and goals, however, I was opposed. I had unfortunately witnessed colleagues get burned after their seemingly perfect partnerships soured, reminiscent of the friends who turned on me as a child.

Because I had been the brunt of an inside grade school joke and suddenly found myself privy to the detrimental affects of a business partnership gone bad, I avoided exposure to such vulnerable circumstances. When I thought about partnerships and joint ventures and the need to be transparent in the process, I was paralyzed by fear. I questioned my value and worth and was terrified to reveal my weaknesses, afraid others would realize I am not as strong as they thought. One detail I quickly learned during my corporate years was that I was rewarded whenever I just figured it out on my own. That belief transferred over to my business. I recall thinking "everyone thinks I've got it all together but what if they figure out I don't? Will they still support and approve of me? Will they turn on me realizing they no longer have use for me?" The exposure of admitting I might need help and advice was horrifying to me.

After three years of working on my business, I started to notice the bottom line. My severance package had long run out, and while my family was financially stable, I was not contributing financially. When I looked at my life, business and relationships, I was attempting to be the perfect person who was all things to all people. I was overwhelmed, frustrated, and started questioning why things weren't working for me. I had no outside employees and was actually proud to claim that

I was doing it all on my own. I was working so hard, yet not reaping the benefits.

One day, I was asked to coffee by a new colleague. She wanted to bounce some ideas around. She was a competitor of sorts and well-respected in the community. During our meeting, she asked about my business. Cautiously, I shared *some* of my aspirations, goals and plans. I shared more with her than I had with anyone outside of family. She offered advice, and very good advice, I might add. But I couldn't understand her motives. "There had to be ulterior motives," I thought. Why was she offering *me* advice when *she* should have viewed me as a competitor? The ideas she gave me should have been used in her own business. After our meeting, I thought long and hard and replayed our conversation in my head, desperate to understand her motives and fearful I had opened up and revealed too much.

I waited for something bad to happen. I waited. And waited. But nothing bad became of it. She didn't get out a megaphone and scream my dreams to the world. She didn't bad-mouth me. In fact, after our meeting, she began connecting and referring me to her circle of influence. As a result of sharing myself, she understood where I was headed and that I was serious about my business. Soon, I realized that we were forming an informal, spontaneous partnership *and* nothing bad was happening as a result! This was a great first experience that warmed me up to the idea of partnering with others. Looking back, I realize I lacked the ability to identify when a potentially good partnership opportunity was right before me. Luckily I didn't let this opportunity slip past me.

On a separate occasion, I was approached by a competitor who wished to discuss a potential affiliation between our businesses. We knew of one another and had established mutual respect, but had never met or talked at length. So I was eager for our meeting and the potential to join forces. We shared two and a half hours worth of information without signing confidentiality agreements! It turned out our needs were not as compatible as we had hoped and therefore an immediate partnership was not pursued. Oh no! Upon this realization, my stomach churned to think of all the information I willingly disclosed. A competitor now had all this juicy information about me... my general business plan and aspirations, my weaknesses and limitations, even how much revenue I was bringing in! Now what? What must they think of me? We are not a good fit for one another. What did I do or say that they didn't like? Why am I not good enough for them?

I grounded myself and identified the negative self-talk that was running through my head. I *was* good enough, just not compatible at that moment for a partnership with *that* company. In fact, it's not just that my business was not compatible for them but they were not compatible for my business either! Not only is partnering with other businesses crucial for growth and expansion, but partnering with the *right* business is just as, if not more, important. I reminded myself not to internalize and take the situation personally.

Still today I continue to meet with businesses for consideration of potential joint ventures. At the very least, I expose myself to the opportunity to get to know someone on a deeper level and discover commonalities. I have come to realize that collaboration, joint ventures and operating as a community is, without question, a wonderful and fulfilling way to grow a business exponentially. I have no doubt my business would have turned a profit much sooner had I risked ventures with others in the early stages of my business. It wasn't until I got over my fears and put my ego aside that I was able to make that shift.

It took me 4 years into the start of my business to overcome my fear of trusting others. I am still very careful when I consider partnerships with others, however I now welcome partnership opportunities and see them as an incredible way to share in the abundance and make new friends. Still today, I am reminded of those first few years where my business struggled as I tried to do everything on my own, lacking trust in others and myself. I cannot imagine going back to my old way of thinking as I am now supported by a gracious community that lifts me up when I struggle, props me up to take the next step and nurtures me to carry on when I think I am incapable. I am supported by a generous community that has taught me the importance of giving and being open to receive.

In 2007, Behind the Moon celebrated its 3rd anniversary. I was excited to have made it past the point at which most new businesses fail. I recall that eight fans attended our anniversary celebration and realized I had a lot for which to be thankful. At our 4th anniversary, 21 celebrated with us. I couldn't believe we had nearly tripled our attendance. In 2009, more than 150 fans celebrated our 5th anniversary and more than 200 attended our holiday party. Even today, when I think about it, I get goose bumps and a lump in my throat, not from fear but from excitement and hope. I know I could never have done it alone. Collaborating with over fifteen other businesses with similar target markets, my business had seen its greatest success yet.

As of this writing, my business has welcomed over 1,200 new participants (customers) in the previous twelve-months as a direct result of partnerships and joint ventures. Participation at our networking events has doubled and even tripled in some locations, and due to the high demand of our groups, we've expanded to new cities. Behind the Moon has amazing possibilities that have yet to be discovered. I know the success I'm experiencing would never have been realized had I not learned that transparent partnerships can be mutually gratifying. Since making the shift to collaboration, the future is wide open.

What's your story? What is holding you back from trusting others? Do you have something to lose? Have you considered what you have to lose by trying to do it all on your own? If you're always turning around to watch your back, who's navigating your course? Give trust a chance and open yourself up to a partnership.

At the very least, you may gain a new best friend who will want you to tag along and who will be there to watch your back.

Sabrina Risley founded Behind The Moon, Inc.® in 2003, a Colorado-based networking and referral group organization that sets itself apart with its motto "grow your business by helping others grow theirs." Behind The Moon offers more than a dozen networking events across Colorado's Front Range as well as referral groups that attract professionals who network to give rather than get. You will find Sabrina speaking to audiences about the Power of Partnerships, Effective Networking Techniques, and Principles of Service and Giving as a means to grow a business. Living in Parker, Colorado, Sabrina enjoys health and fitness-related activities, and spending time with family, friends and colleagues. Sabrina can be reached at Info@BehindTheMoonInc.com or via www.behindthemooninc.com.

Creative Awakening

Melissa Kline

Through writing, I have found my life's true purpose. Whether jotting in a notebook or clicking away on a computer, there is always hidden meaning to be revealed. Behind every word a magical lesson awaits. I am an eager student, mystified and curious. Writing has taught me many things, but my eyes have only just begun to open. It has taken many years for me to fully recognize and appreciate this beautiful gift that has been given to me.

My writing evolution started with my upbringing. As an only child with an alcoholic father and a struggling diabetic mother, I was often left to my own devices and created imaginary worlds to escape. These circumstances are what formed the foundation for my gift. I was so good at creating and imagining that it became my life. It was how I survived, how I coped, how I broke free.

Through school I learned that I could put these visions and worlds of mine on paper. I wrote my first book at the age of six. It was called *The Easter Bunny* and I remember feeling so proud and excited about this new concept. I thoroughly enjoyed constructing the story and paid special attention to detail. My teacher was very impressed and my parents gave me praise, saying I did such a great job. It was an extraordinary achievement, and so my writing career began.

I first attempted to create books outside of school when I was twelve years old, right after my parents' divorce. I needed an escape. I created two books; one a mysterious love story called *The Story of Manchester* and the other was a horror tale, *The Doorknob*. I even took the time to create book jackets with colored construction paper and I drew detailed illustrations. I'll never forget the experience of writing *The Story of Manchester*. For the first time I could feel, smell, and taste the things my words described. I saw scenes in my mind like a film and tried as best I could to convey it on paper.

A year later, I went to Boise, Idaho to visit my grandmother. Like any typical thirteen-year-old girl, I was bored stiff. I needed something, though I wasn't quite sure what it was. I clued my grandmother in and she suggested I go to the loft and shuffle through her collection of books, which turned out to be numerous boxes of romance novel paperbacks. I flipped through them one by one and remember thinking they were corny. I was disappointed. In that moment, a surge of determination shot through my being and I thought to myself, *I can write something way better than this! In fact, I think I will.*

I got out my trusty notebook and pencil and started creating. I scribbled day and night, filling up page after page. I was so inspired I didn't want to do anything else. I remember thinking how cool it was that I could create my very own world and make the characters do whatever I wanted them to. These characters became more than made up personalities. To me, they were real people and I belonged to their world. Not only did I write about them, but when I wasn't writing, I was thinking about them. Forget reality, I had my own, and it was better than anything I'd ever experienced before. Maybe that's why I chose the title, *My Reality* for that book.

After creating that first novel, filled with teenage angst and drama, I continued to write and escape until I ran out of steam. I had written multiple versions and decided to end the book with one of many dramatic options. From there I edited and revised for years, still staying in touch with my characters and slipping away into their world whenever I needed to. I did this off and on until I was twenty years old. I was so attached to my characters, who had become my life, that I didn't want to do anything but be with them in my spare time. I modified, reworked and redrafted myself silly and after endless rewriting, I began to get exhausted.

Something changed when I went to Grants Pass, Oregon to take care of my terminally ill maternal grandmother in the spring of 2002. I created another story! This saga, titled *Tyann*, was about two of the main characters from my original novel. I poured my heart and soul into the book, so excited to finally have some fresh material and a new adventure. This was my escape from my grandmother's imminent death and the experiences I was having as a caregiver on a daily basis.

During a weekend visit from my boyfriend I got engaged, and we were married shortly thereafter. My life changed in big ways; although my writing continued to be an escape from the difficulties I was experiencing as a young woman. I played with other characters from *My Reality*, but none of them really resonated enough to write a complete book. My passion wasn't fulfilling me the way it had in the past. I guess you could say I felt stagnant. Luckily, that didn't last long.

My first big transformation as a writer came with having a baby. I didn't realize it at the time, because it all just happened naturally, but right after my first son was born in 2004, my inner novelist went through a drastic metamorphosis and I was forever changed. Not only did I birth a baby, I birthed a new me as well. As I watched my son grow and develop, creativity stirred from within.

I got a great idea to explore a different character on a different journey. This time, thanks to technology and my husband's thoughtfulness, I *typed* away like a madwoman on my new laptop computer. I was on a roll, my heart bursting with enthusiasm, though I really had to work at it. My time was limited between dishes, laundry and a drooling toddler. Despite this, I made it work and adapted to a new way of writing. One hundred thousand words later, I had written a complete book about a teenage girl and all of her dramatic quests. I was so excited that I started to wonder what I could do with this masterpiece, which I eventually titled, _Colette_. I wanted to share it. How would I do that? I wasn't sure, but I was going to find out. With a spirit full of optimism and nothing to lose, I submitted it to publishing houses.

Twenty rejection letters later, my spirits started to fade. I wasn't sure exactly what I had done wrong, but I wasn't very enthusiastic anymore. I was confused. Why was it so hard to publish this glorious book I had put so much time and energy into?

I didn't let this stop me. I was a bit disheartened, but I decided that I would just move on and continue to write. Deep down inside I knew I was good enough. I wanted to share my gift with the world and I wasn't going to give up.

Thank God for my intuition, because I wrote two more books. After my poor attempt to publish _Accepting Hannah_, I began _Storm._ It was unlike anything I had ever created with underlying spiritual messages and a mysterious twist. I knew from the very beginning it was unique. My craft was getting better and I was evolving.

I sent _Storm_ out into the publishing world with a little more optimism. I thought I was over the rejection from _Colette_ and tried again because I knew this was _the one_. I even branched out for the first time with sharing, letting friends and family read my work.

Over the course of a year I sent _Storm_ to every publishing house that would take it. I got great responses – some of the best and most valuable feedback from editors. The overall message was it was a beautiful book, but its format wasn't strong enough for the market. I was glad to receive some useful information, but disappointed my book still wasn't good enough – in their opinion.

I guess you could say that in a way I gave up. I didn't give up on my writing, but I did give up trying to publish for a while. I questioned what was wrong with me. Why wasn't I good enough? Were they out to get me or was my writing truly not impressive?

On top of all of my questioning, I came to a painful realization - my imagination was different. I no longer used my books as a complete and total immersion. They were still an escape, but I didn't lose myself the way that I had as a child. I worried that if I didn't become the characters and entirely absorb myself that I would not be able to write anymore. I had to adapt to be a mother _and_ a writer, I just wasn't sure it was going to serve my creativity.

Even though I struggled with uncertainty, I continued to write and started _A_

Soul's Journey. This book about a teenage boy on a spiritual path came out of no-where. In a way it mirrored what I was going through. As this novel flooded out of my mind and onto my computer, I had a sense my writing was getting better. It took me a while to realize, but as I revisited my old stories I noticed vast improve-ment. As a result of my willingness to open up and share my work, I had changed and grown. I realized as a self-taught writer, I needed the guidance, wisdom and viewpoints of other people. Advice, suggestion and constructive criticism _were_ my instruments for learning. For the first time, I began to see the error in my ways, (and in my manuscripts) and understand why I hadn't gotten published yet.

I struggled with the plot of _A Soul's Journey_ and couldn't find exactly the right message. I lost interest and became discouraged. Because of this, I stopped writing for a while.

I realized when I don't write or allow for a creative outlet, I'm not a very happy person. I guess you could say I fall into a sort of depression. After going through a twelve-step program for people with alcoholics in their lives, I thought I was fixed, but then what was there? Had I truly peaked? Could I even still write if I wanted to?

It wasn't until I had my second son that I realized I hadn't lost anything at all. Another story miraculously emerged, just as it had with my first born. Amidst taking care of an infant, being sleep deprived and working off ninety pounds of baby weight, I wrote an entire science fiction novel in two months. I was multitasking, always somewhere between my fiction world and reality. I didn't need to be all consumed to create, which was incredible. I finally came to peace with my new process. I was still an inspired writer, I had just adapted, shifted and transformed to balance writing with motherhood.

For the first time, I didn't send out manuscript after manuscript in hopes that I would get published immediately. I thought a little more clearly about how and when I wanted to present the precious novel titled _My Beginning_. After all, I had only just begun to outwardly call myself a writer and share my stories with others. I began to open up my heart and listen. Because of this, new opportunities arose that I never would have expected.

Itching to have my new story read, but with no real direction, a friend advised me to apply for an exclusive writing workshop, even though I neither had the financial means or the time to do such a thing. I signed up anyway, with faith that if it were meant to be, it would be.

Miraculously, everything fell into place and I was selected to attend the work-shop. Not only did I get to meet editors in person, but I also got to experience and meet other aspiring writers for the first time. I finally had something to compare my writing to, which was invaluable. Because of this, I discovered I truly am a fine writer with a unique style, all my own.

During those five wonderful days, I gained more insight, knowledge and growth than I ever could have imagined. I networked and made incredible contacts. As an added bonus, a very well known and prestigious editor invited me to send my manuscript to her for review. It was a rare and very much appreciated opportunity. With an entire letter of suggestions and half of my book generously critiqued, I now have even more knowledge and guidance than ever before.

I am excited for what the future holds, but I am learning to take my journey to becoming a published writer slowly. I am a successful writer in my heart, and that is all that matters. Sometimes I have to mentally and physically take a step back and look at my writing from a different perspective because I don't always see it the way someone else might. I get so caught up in my own stories that it is hard to be objective. I have learned that it is important for me to revel in what I have already accomplished, to enjoy and appreciate those moments.

One of my other accomplishments this past year was creating a women's writing group. It has twelve members and we meet every other week to learn from each other's writing experience. Because of it, I have begun to branch out as a writer and am stepping out of my comfort zone. Today, I am writing in more ways than I ever dreamed I could. I am experimenting with short stories, non-fiction and autobiographical material that are helping me to grow. I am a sponge, eager to soak up any bit of knowledge, wisdom, or experience that I possibly can.

After my first few rejection letters, I felt like giving up. Instead, I am doing the opposite - I am pushing forward! If I had given up, I would not have experienced the growth I have – both personally and as a writer. Regardless of the opinions of others, I am following my heart and honoring my creative process. I know without a doubt that I am right where I should be, because I am writing.

Melissa Kline writes in Denver, Colorado where she lives with her husband and two sons. She is a member of the Society of Children's Book Writers and Illustrators and is the leader of a women's writing group. Her preferred genre is young adult but she writes short stories and non-fiction as well. Her calling is to "Reach out to others and give hope through writing." When Melissa is not creating novels, you will most likely find her somewhere out in nature. To contact Melissa, and learn more about her writing group, email her at mdkline@mac.com or read her blog at http://melissakline.blogspot.com

The Yes I Can Essence

Ada Gonzalez

I always loved creating crafty projects, but never considered being creative a career. I did know that whatever career I chose it would lead to having a corner office with a great view. At an early age I believed that a prestigious title brought money and happiness; therefore, in college I aimed to become a caring kick-ass lawyer that would defend the needy - *Ada to the rescue!* However, by junior year in Binghamton University, I realized that I didn't want to become a lawyer after all. The decision gave me peace because I had narrowed down what I didn't want to do. I continued my studies, graduated, and decided to go live with my mom and see what exciting work I could find with a college degree on my Wonder Woman belt. Yes, Wonder Woman was my favorite super hero figure. No, I didn't actually have the belt.

I thought that as a college graduate there would be tons of high paying job opportunities waiting for me. I submitted resume after resume, and 6 months later I was still unemployed. Was I being picky? My mother thought so and declared it on a day I will never forget.

She insisted that I should take action and she gave me her suggestion on what job to take. Her suggestion shocked me. She suggested that I should become a grocery cashier. She went on to say how getting a good paying job was hard these days. My heart sank. And then it happened, with all my might I remember yelling *YES I CAN!* Something in me shifted. My inner guidance was telling me and helping me realize that I was meant for more!

I am grateful to my mom for helping me declare and step up to my desire to achieve more. With my inner shift and declaration, I was quickly hired as an *Assistant Purchasing Manager* in a high-end computer retail store.

The vice president of the company was female, fierce, and feared. She was now my mentor. Within 6 months I was given an awesome raise and within a few years a promotion with a great title. I learned that computer software helped create art. I moved out of my mother's home. I became independent. Then, a shift in the company happened. A CFO was hired. He was obnoxious, racist, and sexist. Soon the VP left the company, and so did I.

I found a position as an *Executive Assistant* to the president of a children's clothing design company. *I thought, design - cool - I am in!* The title of Executive Assistant sounded so prestigious. Little did I know it would be the least respected I would feel. Soon I realized that I was surrounded by a team of employees that were overworked, and underappreciated.

A day came that I had to make coffee and serve it to everyone in a meeting. As I served, I remember a feeling coming over me. I felt invisible. Not one single person looked my way, I felt no appreciation. And the next day I was told that my coffee making skills must improve. I made a decision. I would resign. Was I being vain? I didn't feel angry, nor did I fantasize pouring the coffee onto the president's head, though that would be a funny image. I just felt that I was meant for more. Soon after, I was in the president's office giving my resignation and thanking him for the opportunity. He became angry, declared what a great opportunity I had and how naïve I was. Then he went on to *yell* a question at me – one that, once again, awoke my inner guidance. He asked (quite sarcastically, yet demanding an answer), "Do you actually THINK you can do better than this?"

Without hesitation, with no coffee cup in hand, and with confidence I yelled back, *"YES I CAN! I can and I will."* He seemed shocked. He asked me to get out, and I was escorted by his secretary. I remember her face turning gentle as I said goodbye. It was as if she understood why I had to move on, perhaps even admired my action.

So on to my next job. I spotted an ad for a *Traffic Coordinator* position at a company that *designed* and manufactured cosmetic displays for high-end retail stores. *I thought - design - sounds creative, I am in.* In a very short time I was promoted to *Project Manager* where I enjoyed helping bring design engineering drawings of displays to life and seeing them in stores. I was even sent to a Caribbean island once for a project approval. I stayed at a beautiful resort; however the best part was when I met the vendors for the meeting. I remember being at the head of the conference table, and I felt a sort of outer body experience when I looked around: a joyous smirk kicked in when I realized that I was the ONLY female and the decision maker at the table! I thought, I CAN and I DID!

I was having a blast with work, and going out with friends. Time passed, and the company started shifting, people left, new people came in, and I started feeling that inner shove that something was missing. I was no longer happy at work, I felt irritated. I redecorated my work space replacing an office lamp with a home lamp, and treated myself with fresh flowers at my desk. I created a mini environment that brought me visual peace.

I knew something had to change. I had a job that I liked, but didn't love. Then, one day sitting on the train going home feeling miserable from another work day a question came into my mind. The question was – *What do I want?*

The question took me by surprise, for I had always searched for what was available on the outside; such as, what job positions were open, what major was available in college. NOT, what was inside me – what "I" wanted to do. Without hesitation I received an answer, as if it had been waiting for me to ask. The answer was: I want to bring my own drawings to life to help people in their homes; I want to be an interior decorator. Suddenly the clouds parted from my heart and I illuminated with joy.

Within a few weeks, I gave myself the best birthday present ever. I resigned.

I had 6 month savings and passion in my pocket. I took interior design classes full time and I was in love with my career choice and with my boyfriend. School had given me mocked projects, but I didn't have any real projects as of yet. Then one day, I gave myself homework: to decorate my own living room. I was so excited that I couldn't sleep. The next day I gave my 1st design presentation ever to my boyfriend.

I remember pulling out the design concept boards with the new furniture placement, wall paint color scheme, pictures of the new furniture to incorporate and then I looked at him and my eyes welled up with tears. I felt flushed, I felt excited, I felt happy, I felt I arrived at my destination! Shortly after, we brought my first design to life. And it felt great! The power of changing my home with colors, furniture, accessories that represented me was invigorating.

After graduating, I became the assistant to an interior designer to get hands on experience. The pay was tiny, the experience was priceless. At this point, I was also engaged to my love.

Then one day I got that inner *shove* again. I was running a personal errand for my boss and I realized I didn't mind working for little pay as long as I was learning about the industry, but I wasn't learning anything design-wise doing her personal chores. I made a decision to talk to her about how I felt. I did, she fired me, and I was grateful. It was time to think and act big.

I leaped. I started my own interior decorating company, and started getting wonderful clients. I was an entrepreneur and loved it. Little did I know that my biggest test of endurance was yet to come.

I found out that my biggest supporter, my fiancé, would bring me the biggest heartache I could have ever imagined. Arguments increased. I felt alone as he was having more and more flashbacks of the awful September 11, 2001 attacks that led to the destruction of the WTC Towers in New York and loss of many lives. Memories of him digging trying to find his co-workers and anyone alive haunted him. My fiancé took action and found a couple's counselor for us. After several sessions, it was revealed that he had the disease of alcoholism. I was going to enter a world of darkness that I did not know existed; the darkness drained my passion, my weight, my smile, my business.

In the beginning, I didn't tell my friends or family. I grew up with the mentality that we should not share good things because people would wish us bad, nor share sad things that are occurring because people would gossip about us. The counselor suggested rehab and I convinced him to go. He would go to rehab to be treated and now I could concentrate on my business. I did. My peace of mind once again attracted more clients, and I started shining again seeing their happy faces from the room transformations.

My fiancé came back from rehab and relapsed. I will never forget the image of him being on the corner of the bed, his eyes watery, looking up at me rocking back and forth saying ... *help me, help me. I can't do this.* My heart broke. I knew deep down he wanted to get better. So together we could and would. Or so I thought. He relapsed again.

At this point I had no savings left, no clients, tons of business expenses, and was living with a struggling alcoholic. One day he came home intoxicated, and I heard once again the words that pained and fueled me. He yelled, *"You can't follow your dream, go knock on doors and get a job."* The words stopped me in my tracks. I can't believe the man I love, who had supported me emotionally, now doesn't believe in me. This time I didn't yell "YES I CAN," but I did whisper it to myself. My entrepreneurial passion hadn't died, but it was being suffocated.

He would relapsed right before reaching 90 days of sobriety; a heartbreaking circle of struggle. I went through 3 major stages, and he went to three rehab facilities:

1st stage - after finding out he was an alcoholic, he went to rehab. I educated myself learning about alcoholism so I could help him. He went to AA meetings and I went to Alanon (support group for family and friends of alcoholics).

2nd stage - brought me to my knees literally. He was getting violent punching walls and himself. I was so afraid he would kill himself. He didn't have thoughts of suicide, but I knew alcohol was poison to him. I didn't know what to do besides calling the police. By this time he ended up in the hospital twice: once from a seizure overdose and once from a bloody head trauma. I ended up in the hospital once with an anxiety attack. One day, after more than a decade of not praying, I didn't know where else to turn so I stopped and slowly melted onto my knees. I cried on the shoulder of the universe! I asked for help, guidance, and strength. Then a weird feeling came over me. I felt peace. I felt no longer alone, even though I was the only one in the room. I felt that I could and would endure my current situation. He relapsed again.

3rd stage - I changed *my* life. I again asked myself a question that called for an answer that would change my life. I wanted to help him, but realized that I was drowning staying with him. So I asked myself: Should I give up my life for him? The answer surprisingly came quickly. It seemed harsh, but felt right. The answer was no. I knew in my heart that I had to let go, I could not be his savior. It didn't matter how much I believed in him, or loved him. He had to believe that he 'CAN'. He had to make the inner shift in himself.

He went to rehab again and this time I went to heal myself. We were no longer a couple. I made it clear that until he reached his 90 day sobriety, I didn't want to communicate in any form with him. I went to counseling to help me cope with the statement of: I CAN and WILL go on with my life *no matter what*! This included the worst scenario that he may die. I released the fear of losing. I started healing. I took action steps surrounding myself with love: my mom, my friends, my business, and visual stimulants that made me happy within my home. I now had a #1 client: myself!

I re-decorated my home and the transformation was powerful. I hadn't decorated my apartment since the first interior design implementation of my living room, when I was a student. Now I designed as a professional interior decorator and an entrepreneur. I felt energized with the new wall colors, artwork, furniture, and accessories that I had chosen. My home represented my personality, and ignited my passion to *live happy*. My inside and out were healing. My heart smiled again. My business blossomed, I had more clients, I wrote an interior decorating e-book, and I happily created a national decorating service where I could help people throughout the USA decorate their homes.

So what happened to my ex-fiancé? I went to his 2 year sobriety birthday celebration. He is healthy and sober, he is helping others with his story, he is now my husband. We had a spiritual wedding on a beach in Hawaii, honeymooned in Tahiti and Bora Bora (my dream destinations), and purchased a beautiful home. I now have my corner office with a great view, and I also manifested my dream car, a convertible BMW. I write manifested, because I did. When we surround ourselves with happiness, including visual stimulants and faith, energetic vibrations brings us more happiness. I listened to my inner guide to follow happiness, which led me to change, and which continues to lead me to new found joy beyond my dreams.

What have I learned? That sometimes our inner guidance gives us a gentle tap on our shoulder, and sometimes it is a punch in the gut that brings us to our knees telling us it's time to move on. Either way, when we follow our passion with an *I can attitude*, let go of all fears, and surround ourselves with visual and inner beauty, miracles happen. A prestigious title does not make us happy, our choices to follow our passion does.

Every day I wake up and choose to be happy. I love my career in helping people live and feel better within their homes and heart. Hmm, maybe I am a bit like the Wonder Woman superhero after all - *Ada to the rescue decorating homes that make an impact on the heart!*

I believe that every situation we encounter, we either get what we want or we learn from it. Every job and situation that I have gone through has been a preparation for where I am now. I am happy. My assistants don't make coffee for me; I make it for them with love and gratitude.

I know I can. You can too.

Ada Gonzalez is the go-to-designer for entrepreneurs and is nationally known as the 'Interior Decorator for the Star in You' because her designs focus on illuminating her clients' personality, passion, & style throughout their homes. She offers full design concept-to-implementation service and consultations in New York; for clients throughout the USA she offers her Dream Design Kits tm where she designs their rooms and mails the designs with all the buying resources. Ada has been featured on the radio, newspaper and magazines. She loves puppies, mint chocolate chip ice cream, being married, & seeing her clients' happy expressions. To learn more about Ada and grab your free copy of her interior decorating e-book called Delicious Decorating for the Star in You go to www.adasdecoratingsolutions.com.

Finding Life's Purpose

Heather Baruch

For as long as I can remember, I have always enjoyed helping others. I love connecting with people and always feel a sense of joy when discovering a connection with someone. When I was a little girl, I spent a week at my grandparents' house in Iowa every summer. My grandparents volunteered for a service called "Meals on Wheels," where they delivered meals to elderly people who were unable to cook for themselves. While visiting during the summer, I helped them deliver the meals. It was so much fun; I loved to see the delight on the recipient's face when they opened the door and I handed them their meal. Doing good things for others always sparks a happy feeling in my soul. I believe helping my grandparents with "Meals on Wheels" allowed me to tune into my passion to help others when I was a little girl. I will always be grateful to them for helping me discover my passion.

Teaching the simple value of loving and giving is such an important life lesson. My parents encouraged me to continually ignite those happy feelings by providing me with opportunities and encouraging me to give back to our community, such as baking cupcakes for the residents of a local nursing home, raking leaves for the elderly and participating in various volunteer activities.

As I got older and began thinking about what career to pursue, I decided I wanted to be a registered nurse. I was accepted into the nursing program at South Dakota State University and graduated with my BSN (Bachelor of Science in Nursing), in 2000 and knew that I was ready for a change and the challenge of a new location.

I had never been to Colorado, but had seen pictures and heard it was a great place to live. I researched the hospitals in the Denver area, applied and scheduled some interviews. My sister and I took a road trip to Colorado for the interviews and to see if this was the place where I wanted to live and start my new career. As soon as we drove through Colorado and I saw the beautiful mountains, my whole being lit up. I knew this was the where I was supposed to be. I was offered a job and relocated to Colorado at the end of July in 2000.

Working as a new graduate RN on a Surgical Cardiac unit in a large hospital was exciting, intense, intimidating and overwhelming. I enjoyed the challenge, yet I was frustrated by the amount of time I had to spend charting. I wished for more time with my patients.

My favorite part about working as an RN was the connection that I developed with some of the patients and/or family members in my care. I loved being able to help them understand what was going on with their plan of care. It's an incredible feeling of fulfillment to receive appreciation from people, and to know that you have made a difference in their day or in their life. Unfortunately, the hospital is a stressful place. People are sick, family members are worried and scared; it's fast paced and busy. That stress can be overwhelming, making it more difficult to focus on the positive elements of the work.

There were many stressful days working in the hospital environment. After several years of working as an RN full time, I started to feel burned out. More and more my career direction was not fulfilling my individual needs. Trying to be positive and upbeat was exacting a personal toll. I remember telling myself when I was doing clinical rotations in nursing school that if I got to a point where I was burned out and unhappy that I would do something different. I was unhappy and wasn't being true to myself. I knew I needed to make a change.

I found myself looking for another way to serve people by starting a home business. I sold nutritional supplements and recruited people to join the company. I worked twelve hour night shifts at the hospital and would come home in the morning and make business calls. I got very little sleep and was exhausted.

I loved learning about the nutritional supplements and enjoyed that aspect of the business, but the schedule was overwhelming. I was interested in something that allowed more independence. A few months after I started, I was presented with an opportunity to warehouse and ship product for other distributors within the same company. I decided to shift my focus to distribution and discontinue the recruiting side of the business. Although it wasn't my dream job, I was grateful to be able to work from home doing a simple business helping other distributors keep their business running effectively. Fortunately, this allowed me to complete my last nursing contract and to focus on my warehousing and shipping business.

Working with nutritional supplements invoked an interest in learning more about herbs and nutrition. I remember watching the movie "The Secret". After watching it, I wrote down what I wanted in life and one of the things I wrote was that I wanted to be an Herbalist.

Shortly after writing down that I wanted to be an Herbalist, I saw an ad about an Herbalist in a local magazine, contacted her and scheduled an appointment for a consultation. I remember being so excited for my consultation to learn what might be causing my ears to be plugged. I had problems with my ears being plugged on and off for over three years. I had several doctors and ENT (Ear, Nose and Throat) doctors look in my ears and had multiple medications prescribed, allergy testing and an evaluation for temporomandibular joint problems. None of the doctors could come up with a diagnosis; the medications didn't work. After trying multiple allergy meds without any results, my doctor decided to try a trial run of a steroid called Prednisone as a last resort thinking that it would decrease inflammation which may have been a cause of my ears being plugged.

Prednisone is a very potent medication that has several unwanted side effects. I took Prednisone for two weeks and there was no improvement-my ears were still plugged. I couldn't believe that such a potent medication hadn't help at all. I was very frustrated that I couldn't find out what was causing the problem and felt defeated.

After my consultation with my Herbalist, she told me that she thought I had issues with Candida and recommended changes in my diet and some nutritional/herbal supplements. I was thrilled, and I implemented all her recommendations right away. Some of the nutritional changes were a difficult adjustment, but I was feeling great. I lost weight (which had been a lifelong struggle for me), had more energy, felt great, and I haven't had any problems with my ears since. I was amazed at how simple it was and was intrigued to learn more.

She taught an Herbalist and Master Herbalist Certification program. This was the first time that I had spoken to the universe and received what I had asked for and my soul sang to me! I knew at that moment that my life would be changed forever.

I started the Master Herbalist courses and loved every minute of it. Every class I left, I was inspired and amazed at what I was learning and how simple it was. The power of nutrition and herbs are incredible. My plan was to start a business doing consultations with clients to help them achieve their health goals, prevent illness and disease and overcome their health issues naturally. I couldn't wait to get started. If I could serve by educating people about herbs and natural healing and open the door to the excitement I felt when I discovered herbs that would be the best job I could imagine!

After getting married, and having two children, my business plans were delayed, which I now believe was meant to be. I had originally planned to do consultations with people and never had any intention of making products. Since I waited to fully launch my business plan until my daughter was older, I discovered my desire to make products in addition to doing consultations. I became interested in making my own products during my Herbal Preparations and Aromatherapy classes and from having difficulty finding products that are truly natural in the stores. I have found pure joy in making natural products out of creations from the earth.

I am very thankful for all that I learned and for the experiences that I had while I worked as an RN in the hospital setting and realize that was a stepping stone to where I am now. I believe my training and experience in nursing, coupled with my Master Herbalist Certification courses gives me a unique opportunity to provide my clients with integrated health care solutions. I am dedicated to continue learning about natural health and healing in order to provide my family and clients with the best possible care and to make and create the highest quality natural products I can provide.

I truly believe that everything happens for a reason and even though we may not always know what that reason is at the time it's a true stepping stone to reveal your life's purpose. I have found my purpose and passion in life and it's one of the greatest feelings in the world. I love looking back to when I was a child when my purpose was beginning to surface by realizing I had a passion for helping people and see how it's playing out in my adult life.

Life will pose it challenges and every moment may not be happy, but I believe we learn something from all of our experiences that helps us in some aspect of our lives. The universe is an amazing thing and I can't wait to see what it has in store for me, my family and my business in the future. It's a beautiful thing when things, people and events start to fall into place and help you build the life of your dreams.

Heather is the founder of Taspen's Natural Healing. She makes organic herbal creations for pregnancy, post partum and baby products, along with products for all other stages of life. She makes herbal tea and bath blends, herbal salves, skin care products, herbal syrups, extracts and tinctures and aromatherapy blends. Heather loves working with herbs, making products, educating and helping people learn how to feed and nourish their bodies so that their body can heal itself. She utilizes tools including a computerized body analysis scan, iridology, kinesiology/muscle testing, pH balancing, nutritional modifications, aromatherapy, and nutritional supplements. She collaborates with a variety of alternative health practitioners and refers clients to them when appropriate. In her personal life, Heather loves to play with her kids, spend time with her family and friends, hiking, biking, camping, snowboarding, snowshoeing, music festivals and shows, traveling, scuba diving, reading, spirituality and beautiful sunsets. Website: http://www.taspensnaturalhealing.com Email: taspensnaturalhealing@yahoo.com Phone: 303-838-5946

Getting a Glimpse of the Peak:
One Woman's Discovery on the Summit

Deb Roffe

Love and appreciation for the mountains has been passed down from generation to generation in my family. I've always said it's in our blood. Being a part of my family requires strength, determination, and a love for the outdoors. There's even a family song that my Great Grandpa Pratt wrote in the 1800s. This song has carried us over miles and miles of mountain trails. I come from a family that has always been drawn to the mountains, by their splendor and brilliance.

When my father was a child, his mother drove them from Buffalo, New York to the woods of Allegheny State Park every summer to camp for months at a time. This was in the 1920s and 30s when specialized camping equipment was not available. They set up tents, cooked over open fires, swam in the creeks, and just enjoyed being in nature. Not surprisingly, my father carried on the tradition years later with my brothers and me.

I grew up in Shaker Heights, Ohio where my family was known for being adventurous, daring, and risky. We frequently went back country skiing, drove across the country, and camped for weeks. The sky was the limit. Just as my Grandma Dohn drove my father to the woods, my own mother would load up the station wagon full of kids, skiing and camping equipment, and drive us over twenty-four hours to Colorado. My father was a renowned neurosurgeon with limited time off, but he would always make the effort to show us the ins and outs of backpacking, camping, and hiking. If he couldn't drive with us to Colorado, he would fly out and meet us on the mountain. We were very unique in this way, and the adventurous spirit of the Dohn family was engrained in me at an early age. In turn, I had an attraction, a strong desire, a longing to be in the mountains. In nature I felt alive, inspired, and ready to create.

This admiration and understanding of the mountains grew even deeper during the summer of 1971. It was several months after my eighteenth birthday when my family set out to hike to the top of a mountain. As a teenager, I was spirited, strong, and energetic. Being the only girl in the family, I learned how to keep up with my two brothers. Any type of physical activity they could do, I could do. I was determined, never complained, and nothing could hold me back, not even a 14,000 foot mountain. After backpacking in the Gore Range, outside of Vail, Colorado for an entire week, we were going to conclude our trip by climbing Mount of the Holy Cross. This wasn't just any old mountain. Not only was it 14,005 feet high, but Holy Cross was a legendary peak in the Rocky Mountains and in the Dohn family.

The hiking party included my dad Don Dohn, my two brothers David and Doug, a family friend, my cousins, the Pratts, and me. The night before, we had hiked over Half Moon Pass and set up a base camp. Back then we didn't have the type of gear and equipment that is available now. We wore jeans, leather boots, thick wool socks, and we carried heavy tents in heavy packs with heavy metal frames. The grueling climb over and into the pass took a toll on our bodies, especially because we were flatlanders from Ohio.

Tired and sore, we arose early the next morning to start our ascent to Holy Cross. I had heard all about this mountain and its legendary history of the people who made the trek up its peak and down to the Bowl of Tears to dip their prayer cloths into its holy water in the 1800s. My parents had an old leather bound book about Holy Cross that was filled with black and white pictures of the courageous men and women completing their pilgrimage across the ridge in suspenders, wool coats, dresses, bonnets, and laced up leather shoes. The pages explained how the mountain received its name from the snow left each year in a large crevice on the mountain, forming a giant cross. It was believed to be a mountain of healing, one with a strong spiritual essence. As I stood before the mountain, it was an astounding sight to see the photographs etched in my memory come to life right before me. I was in awe.

We started up the mountain and quickly got into a rhythm, my dad leading the way. I remember walking behind him, following in his footsteps and taking in the breathtaking view. Even at eighteen I felt something magical in the spirit of the mountain, although it would take me years to recognize it to the extent I do now.

The trail switch-backed through the trees and we slowly zigzagged our way along. I welcomed the cool shade and enjoyed the tranquil feeling of being surrounded by forest trees. As we hiked, the trees grew sparse until there weren't any at all. We passed through the open fields of alpine tundra filled with tiny grasses and flowers. I was surrounded by beauty. The ground gradually became rockier until there was nothing but large boulders. I could already see the tips of surrounding peaks and we had gained a significant amount of altitude.

After climbing through an endless field of boulders, the path marked only by cairns every twenty or so feet, we were nearing the top. The 5,400 feet elevation gain and hours of exertion had left my legs feeling weak and my head feeling dizzy. Rows of mountain peaks began to come into view as we ascended higher and higher. It was as if I could reach out and touch the clouds overhead. I paused for a moment looking over the range of mountains and breathed in its magnificence. We were so incredibly high!

As we took the final steps towards the summit, I had no idea how life changing this climb would be. When I reached the top, something miraculous happened. For the first time I realized that I could accomplish whatever I wanted to in life. If I could climb this mountain, I really could do anything! In this moment I discovered something bigger than myself. Something or someone had to exist. The beauty and glory of this place simply could not be present without the work of some divine entity. There were mountains and mountains, as far as my eyes could see. To the east, to the west, the north, and the south. It was as if I had an audience and they were all applauding my accomplishment. It was an absolutely breathtaking sight! My heart leapt as I spun around and took in the view. I spread my arms wide and welcomed this feeling. I was standing on top of the world!

It was then that I began to dream. I dreamt about other mountains I could climb. I dreamt about my future. I dreamt about accomplishing the unthinkable. I didn't know at the time where those dreams would take me, but I was dreaming nonetheless.

Over the years, the amazing dreams I envisioned on Holy Cross that day in 1971 slowly started to fade. During the course of the next thirty-four years, my love for nature remained, but backpacking gradually slipped away as children, work, and other commitments became high priorities. Life had gotten complicated, messy, and busy. There were too many distractions, I was too out of shape, I didn't have the time…any excuse worked really. Life had just gotten in the way.

It was August of 2005 and my dad, now known as Grandpa Dohn, was turning eighty. To honor his wisdom of the outdoors and his eightieth birthday, we all decided to return to the mountain we had often talked about, dreamt about, and shared stories about with our children. We were going to hike Holy Cross. Dad was going to stand on its peak just one last time.

After months of planning, training, borrowing, and buying equipment, our large family took off on our adventure. We backpacked over Half Moon Pass to our base camp. The next morning some of us were up before daylight to start the ascent of the mountain. The group consisted of my husband Kirby, my oldest son Greg, his fiancée Stefanie, my youngest son Matt, my dad, and me. There was a lot of excitement, anticipation, and nervousness because this was the first fourteener for everyone except for Dad and me.

The hike started off and we quickly fell into our line of order, with my dad leading the way as he always did. He set the perfect pace for the group and as we ventured through the forest we reminisced about old times, memories with family and friends, and classic Dohn stories. I was excited to be back in this place with my father and to take part in such a meaningful journey with him to the summit.

But about two thirds of the way up, my dad turned to me and said, "Deb, I can't go any farther." I was shocked. I'd never heard my dad speak those words ever in my life. We all stood in silence while we caught our breath. He was the leader, the pathfinder, the person we leaned on. He was the one who had always given us words of encouragement, such as, "It's just around the corner. Don't give up. Put one foot in front of the other. Let's sing a song. " At first I tried to convince him to keep going, to make it to the top this one last time. He said again, "No, Deb. It's okay. I'll be okay. You guys keep going." In that moment I knew what my dad was saying to me. *Now it's your turn Deb. You show the next generation of this family what the mountains mean. You pass on the mountain's gifts, their lessons; the power, inspirations, and glory.* He was handing the baton to me. It was my turn to lead, to pass it on to the next generation. In that instant everything held still. It will always be burned into my memory: the steepness of the trail, the beautiful tiny tundra flowers, the beginning of the boulders, and the vastness of the deep blue sky. We all had tears in our eyes as we watched my dad go back down the trail by himself.

After I had caught my breath and wiped away the tears, I knew I had to keep going. I had to be that strong eighteen-year old again, the girl who was driven and full of dreams. Dad's silhouette disappeared back into the trees and we all started up the boulder field. It was strange how this mountain, which is one of the more difficult fourteeners to climb, was so easy to summit that day. Dad's dream had begun to spread to each one of us. His presence combined with the spiritual energy of the mountain compelled us over the incredible boulder fields, through the snowflakes, to the summit. It was truly an amazing experience. On the trail, I fell into last place, at the back of the line, so I could push Matt, Greg, and Stefanie the rest of the way. Again the excitement built as we got closer and closer to the top.

Once we were standing on the summit, my oldest son Greg, turned to me and said, "Mom, I have been hearing about this mountain all my life. And I'm finally here." Stef was smiling through teary-eyes, taking in the panoramic view. Matt and Kirby were celebrating. And right away I knew their lives would be changed forever because of the experience of summiting this incredible mountain. Yes, I thought to myself, the next generation understands, it's in their blood!

Feeling the power of the mountain, I looked out and again soaked it all in. It was a bittersweet moment, standing there with my children, but knowing that I would never stand on another peak with my father. It was now my responsibility to carry on the tradition, to keep the mountains a part of our family. This time on Holy Cross I felt different. The dreams I once had here came rushing back to me. This time I was going to make them come true.

When I returned home, I continued dreaming about how my life could be different. I had been doing the same job for the last thirty years. I was a nurse in a gastrointestinal lab and I performed the same procedures day in and day out. I worked in an enclosed room with no windows, and with patients who were unconscious. There were no opportunities for me to interact, be creative, or grow. My job was mindless, boring, and unfulfilling. I had often wondered what my life would be like had I chosen a different profession. I had wished I had been a counselor, a therapist, maybe even a teacher—something better than this. But I always told myself it was too late, too expensive, and too risky to change my career at this point. I expected to live and die in that G.I. lab, even though the thought of staying much longer was agonizing.

The day I climbed Holy Cross, I finally could imagine doing something else. I could now see the possibilities of making a career change, even at the age of 50. I started looking into life coach trainings and programs. That summer I signed up for classes to become a certified life coach. By the following year, I had finished my training and created two businesses, Summit Life Coaching and The Nurse Coach. My clientele continued growing and I started doing workshops and retreats. In December 2008, I quit my job as a nurse and I started coaching full time. My dream had finally come true!

Many times we go through the motions of life. We get caught up in the daily tasks of our jobs and families and our own desires become distant whispers and faded memories. We get comfortable in our lives, as I did as a G.I. nurse. We tell ourselves it will be too much work, too scary, or even too selfish to make our personal dreams come true. Sometimes we don't even realize we have these dreams or desires in the first place.

It is all too easy to constantly focus on what life expects from us, forgetting what we really expect out of life. Once I realized this and took the plunge, my dreams starting becoming realities. I finally can say that I love what I do every day. And the dreaming is not over. I am working on publishing my first self-help book. Who knows what I could accomplish next?

Now is the time to discover your dream and find out what *you* want for your life. Getting a glimpse of what is possible and seeing your full potential is the first step to discovering your dreams. Even before I choose which mountain I am going to climb in Colorado, I see myself reaching the top. In the same way you must start believing that you can reach your life's "peak." Envision yourself accomplishing your wildest dreams. What would those be? How do you see yourself or what do you see yourself doing if you had no constraints holding you back? For a moment put aside your role as a wife or husband, as a parent, an employee, or a boss and allow yourself to dream…

It is *my* dream to now share the gifts I have received and the lessons I have learned from climbing mountains. The mountains are a metaphor for life. Making it to the top involves dreaming, planning, preparation, and determination. But once you are on the summit, you feel as though you are standing on top of the world! You have the power to create the vision of what you really want in life and to achieve it. Climbing a mountain is no small task, but it is not impossible. You too, can climb mountains. Whatever it is you have been dreaming of, wanting to change, or wishing to accomplish—you can do it! Start right now. Take the journey from the trailhead, through the trees, over boulder fields, and up to the summit!

"You see things; and you say, 'Why?' But I dream things that never were; and I say, 'Why not?'" ~ George Bernard Shaw

Deb Roffe is a Certified Life Coach and founder of Summit Life Coaching. Deb brings a wealth of experience to her role as a life coach, as a nurse, an artist, independent business owner, mother of three, and outdoor enthusiast. Deb has a natural gift to communicate with people, and her creativity and caring for her clients have helped many to not only create and believe their vision, but to manifest their professional and personal goals. Deb conducts individual and group coaching sessions, along with facilitating various empowering workshops and outdoor adventure women's retreats. She is currently working on Reach Your Summit and Beyond: Inspirational Lessons From the Mountains, a self-help book presenting the mountains as a metaphor for life. Her independent business, Summit Life Coaching, is the result of Deb's journey to achieve her vision of helping others see the life they've dreamed of become a reality. Visit her websites at: www.summitlifecoaching.net and www.thenursecoach.com.

ABOUT US

Lisa Shultz has always had a deep desire to help others. As a former physical therapist she helped her patients overcome pain and physical challenges, but found her heart's work through connecting and empowering women with her networking organization Women, Wine, and Wellness, www.WomenWineAndWellness.com. A public speaker, author, and networking expert Lisa now inspires other women to create the life of their dreams. Her previous books include a series beginning with *8 Strategies for Creating an Extraordinary Life*. In just a few years Lisa has touched thousands of women and is passionate about expanding her vision. She's excited about supporting women in speaking their truth and sharing their personal stories. She can be reached at www.LisaJShultz.com or by email at info@lisajshultz.com.

Andrea Costantine was born with an entrepreneurial spirit and is passionate about service, contribution, and making a difference. After spending ten years in the mortgage and real estate industry, Andrea found herself on a quest to find more meaning in her work. She returned to school and obtained her master's degree in counseling and through her studies found a love for writing, speaking, and coaching. She enjoys inspiring others to shift their perspective, adopt new ways of living and being, and allowing others the space to fully create, be self-expressed, and feel a sense of freedom in their life and work. She can be reached at www.andreacostantine.com or by email at info@andreacostantine.com.

ABOUT THE ARTIST

Janice Earhart, the illustrator for the book, is delighted to be a part of this wonderful collaboration of women telling their courageous stories.

iZoar is her primary art business and the Village of iZoar is where her whimsical and inspiring characters live. As an artist, writer and the creator of iZoar you will find her witty, profound, funny, insightful and her characters speak volumes. With a succinct writing style she is able to capture big emotions in a simple sentence. This signature style of whimsical characters and simple clear messages makes her work appeal to women in all walks of life. Her prints, cards and gifts are sold all over the world in boutiques, galleries and gift stores.

Janice's background is as diverse as her characters. Confessing to be a serial entrepreneur she has enjoyed owning a variety of businesses. She has designed sets, jewelry, gift packaging and interiors and has enjoyed being a teacher, florist, photographer, fund-raiser, business coach, corporate trainer and artist.

Her life is her story. iZoar teaches what she has learned. They deliver the messages she uses to make her life remarkable. Her wish is that you receive inspiration from them and her prayer is that you become all that you can be.

When she is not in the world of iZoar, Janice enjoys hiking the mountains of Colorado with her husband and their Golden Retriever. Chronically curious, she finds the world incredibly interesting. Thus, she keeps her life as fascinating as her characters.

Janice Earhart
Artist/Creator
iZoar
Visit her on-line
www.iZoar.com

WANT TO SPEAK YOUR TRUTH?

If sharing our stories has inspired, moved, or empowered you, we would love to hear from you.

All of the stories you have read in this book were submitted by readers just like you who have a personal story to tell and who wanted to help inspire and empower other women.

We expect to publish future volumes of Speaking Your Truth and perhaps your story could help to inspire and empower other women on their journeys.

If you would like to become a part of the Speaking Your Truth book project we invite you to submit a chapter for consideration to a future volume.

There's no need to be concerned with being a professional writer, simply get your story to us and we can help with the editing. The main thing is to speak your truth. You can simply let others know where you've been, what you've achieved, and help lift and inspire others who have or are now experiencing something similar.

You may submit an original piece that describes your experiences, life story, and/or something you have overcome or succeeded in.

To obtain a copy of our submission guidelines please write to us at:

Lisa Shultz – info@lisajshultz.com

Andrea Costantine – info@andreacostantine.com

Be sure to include "Speaking Your Truth Submission Request" in the subject line. You will be credited for your submission at the end of your story.

For information about speaking engagements, others books, workshops, and training programs, please contact us directly. We look forward to hearing from you.

Sincerely,
Lisa Shultz & Andrea Costantine

Come visit our blog and share your experiences with our growing Speaking Your Truth community http://speakingyourtruth.wordpress.com

Are you interested in buying multiple copies of *Speaking Your Truth* for your business, network, community, or clients? You can receive special discounted pricing, great service, direct shipping, and more.

Contact us directly at info@lisajshultz.com or info@andreacostantine.com for more information or visit our website: www.speakingyourtruthbook.com.

Made in the USA
Lexington, KY
27 August 2010